Migration Law in Portugal

Migration Law in Portugal

Ana Rita Gil
Maria Helena Varela

This book was originally published as a monograph in the International Encyclopaedia of Laws/Migration Law.

Founding Editor: Roger Blanpain
General Editor: Frank Hendrickx
Volume Editor: Helen Oosterom-Staples

Wolters Kluwer

Published by:
Kluwer Law International B.V.
PO Box 316
2400 AH Alphen aan den Rijn
The Netherlands
E-mail: lrs-sales@wolterskluwer.com
Website: www.wolterskluwer.com/en/solutions/kluwerlawinternational

Sold and distributed by:
Wolters Kluwer Legal & Regulatory U.S.
920 Links Avenue
Landisville, PA 17538
United States of America
E-mail: customer.service@wolterskluwer.com

ISBN 978-94-035-0007-2

e-Book: ISBN 978-94-035-0017-1
web-PDF: ISBN 978-94-035-0027-0

This title is available on www.kluwerlawonline.com

The Authors

Ana Rita Gil holds a PhD in Public Law (with thesis on human rights of immigrants) and is Professor at the Faculty of Law, University of Lisbon and Researcher at the Lisbon Public Law Center – Centro de Investigação em Direito Público. She worked as a legal advisor for the Portuguese Constitutional Court and as an advisor to the Portuguese Ombudsman. She was also a member of the National Preventive Mechanism until 2020. Her main areas of expertise include immigration and asylum law and policy. She has more than fifty publications in these areas and has participated as a speaker in more than hundred conferences, short courses, master's and post-graduation courses organized by several national and international entities. Dr Gil is also a national expert at the Global Citizenship Observatory (GLOBALCIT), coordinated by the European University Institute and the Robert Schumann Centre for Advance Studies.

Maria Helena Varela graduated in Law from the Law School of the University of Coimbra and holds a Master's in Business Law (specialization in labour law) from the University Institute of Lisbon (ISCTE).

She is currently doing her PhD on the human rights of undocumented migrant workers at the NOVA School of Law. She is also a researcher at the Centre for Research and Development on Law and Society (CEDIS), a citizenship expert at Global Citizenship Observatory (GLOBALCIT) and team leader of a research group on migration, labour and social solidarity at the NOVA Refugee Clinic-Legal Clinic.

The Authors

Table of Contents

Table of Contents

List of Abbreviations

AL	Asylum Law
Art.	Article
CC	Criminal Code
Cit.	cited
CIDOB	Confederación de Pueblos Indígenas de Bolivia
CJEU	Court of Justice of the European Union
CPLP	Community of Portuguese-Speaking Countries
CPR	Portuguese Refugee Council
ECHR	European Convention on Human Rights
ECtHR	European Court of Human Rights
EEA	European Economic Area
EU	European Union
EUR	European Dollars
FMD	Free Movement Directive
FML	Free Movement Law
GAOC	General Administrative Offence Code
GAOS	Gemini Adaptive Optics System
HCM	High Commissioner for Migration
IAPMEI	Agency for Competitiveness and Innovation
IAS	Indexing Value of Social Support
Ib.	*ibidem* – in the same place
ICESCR	International Covenant on Economic, Social and Cultural Rights
ICCPR	International Convention on Civil and Political Rights
ICT	Intra-corporate Transfer
IL	Immigration Law
ILO	International Labour Organization
IR	Immigration Regulation
LC	Labour Code
LFM	Law on Free Movement

List of Abbreviations

LPCYD	Law on Protection of Children and Youngsters in Danger
LTD	Long-Term Residents Directive
NGO	Non-governmental Organization
NPM	National Prevention Mechanism
MIPEX	Migration Integration Policy Index
RGCO	General Regime of Administrative Offences
SBC	Schengen Borders Code
SEF	Foreigners and Borders Service (*Serviço de Estrangeiros e Fronteiras*)
SIS	Schengen Information System
SOS	Save our Ship
TCAS	Central Administrative Court of the South
TFEU	Treaty on the Functioning of the European Union
TPL	Temporary Protection Law
UDHR	The Universal Declaration of Human Rights
UN	United Nations
UNHCR	United Nations High Commissioner for Refugees
UNESCO	The United Nations Educational, Scientific and Cultural Organization
UNICEF	United Nations International Children's Emergency Fund
VC	Visa Code
VIS	Visa Information System

Preface

Portugal was, historically, a 'country of emigration'. With the decolonization period at the end of the 1970s, the country witnessed the first significant movement of persons entering the territory. It was confronted with an average of half a million of persons returning from overseas. Although most of these persons were Portuguese nationals, some of them only held the nationality of the former Portuguese colonies.

The first big wave of immigration movements happened in the late 1990s, when Portugal, as the other Member States of the European Union (EU), became a country of destination for many nationals of Eastern European countries. This era marked the first wave of immigration in the territory in the contemporary age, and national laws and institutions had to adapt to this new reality.

To that effect, the Portuguese Government created a new institution aimed at promoting a successful integration of migrants into the territory, which became the main characteristic of the Portuguese reception system – the High Commissioner on Immigration and Ethnic Minorities, which is now the 'High Commissioner for Migrations' (hereinafter 'HCM'). This institution's activity is one of the reasons why Portugal is internationally seen as having one of the best practices as regards immigrants' integration policies. Indeed, integration and inclusion of migrants and new cultures in the Portuguese society have been distinguishing the Portuguese immigration and asylum policy. In this context, besides the mentioned institutional framework, the Government has been adopting successive multiannual plans on integration of migrants, where several measures are foreseen to be adopted by different governmental departments, according to a policy of a whole-governmental approach. Some concerns have been mentioned in all plans, such as the integration of immigrants coming from countries with which Portugal does not have historical and cultural ties, the intercultural training of teachers and other professionals, as well as relating to the advocacy of intercultural principles through the media and to the general public.[1] The fight against territorial segregation has also been referred to in these instruments.[2] Fighting against racism and xenophobia are equally seen as pivotal. For that purpose, the Government has also created, under the HCM's supervision, an independent commission aimed at promoting equality and fighting

1. Measure 23 of the II National Plan for the Integration of Immigrants.
2. Measure 65 of the II National Plan for the Integration of Immigrants.

against racial discrimination, which is entrusted with the competence to receive complaints and forward them to the competent authorities.[3]

The last plan – the Strategic Plan for Migrations/2015–2020 – identifies five major challenges for Portugal in the field of immigration. One of the first concerns is the demographic deficit. Portugal has been referred to as one of the countries of the European Union with one of the most aged populations.[4] In this realm, immigration is seen as a solution to invert the demographic trend, to balance the labour economy and ensure the sustainability of the Welfare State. The so-called circular immigration has in particular been mentioned in the last governmental acts as a way to streamline the Portuguese economy while at the same time ethically preventing the 'brain drain' effect on the countries of origin.[5]

Second, the Plan calls for broadening the integration of migrants, aligning it with the paramount values of tolerance and of fostering cultural, ethnic, and religious diversity. In this respect, until very recently, Portugal hosted a majority of Portuguese-speaking (Lusophone) countries' citizens. In the last decade, however, the origin of those who came to reside in the country has changed significantly. Currently, the majority of migrants entering into the country come from different cultures with which Portugal did not have historic ties of affinity bonds. Public entities are aware of the heterogeneity of these new migration flows and thus are interested in preventing the rise of intolerance.

The Plan has also identified the inclusion of the 'new Portuguese citizens' in the community as a major concern. In this part, the Plan refers to those who have acquired the Portuguese citizenship through naturalization after the 2006 amendments to the Nationality Act.[6]

Finally, and equally important, the Plan also mentions the need to attract qualified workers to the Portuguese labour market. This purpose is not without link to the emigration flows that have affected Portugal in recent years. From 2011 to 2016, an economic crisis deeply affected the country, as well as other EU Member States. Among other negative consequences, the country experienced a new era of negative immigration rates. Immigration numbers have dropped, while the number of young qualified emigrants rose significantly, as many Portuguese citizens chose to abandon the country to seek better living conditions and job opportunities abroad. These

3. This Commission aims at enforcing several legal acts that forbid racial discrimination. That is the case of Law n. 93/2017, of 23 August that has transposed the Council Directive 2000/43/EC of 29 Jun. 2000 implementing the principle of equal treatment between persons irrespective of racial or ethnic origin, http://www.acidi.gov.pt/_cfn/528cd98b76aca/live/Lei+n%C2%BA+18%2F2004%2C+de+11+de+Maio+%E2%80%93+Transp%C3%B5e+a+Directiva+Ra%C3%A7 and Law n. 134/99 of 28 August that forbids any discrimination on the grounds of race, colour, nationality and ethnic origin regarding the exercise of rights. *See* the website of the Commission at https://www.cicdr.pt/.
4. Preamble of Decree-Law n. 31/2014 of 27 February.
5. Preamble of Decree-Law n. 31/2014 of 27 February. *See also* measure 73 of the II National Plan for the Integration of Immigrants, approved by Resolution n. 74/2010 of the Council of Ministries.
6. These amendments changed the very nature of naturalization, which ceased to be a discretionary power of the Government. Naturalization became a subjective right of those who fulfil the criteria foreseen in the Nationality Law. These criteria were, on their turn, facilitated and acquisition at birth was also expanded. As a result, the numbers of Portuguese nationality acquisitions have risen at about 700 percent. The Nationality Act corresponds to Law n. 37/81, of 3 October, as last amended by Organic Law n. 2/2020, of 10 November.

new emigrants were quite different from the Portuguese emigrants in the 1970s and 1980s, who were mainly non-qualified workers. In the second decade of 2000s, Portuguese expatriates were mainly highly qualified young professionals, seeking competitive career opportunities in top professions, such as medicine, technology, science, and research. Due to the lack of investment and job opportunities, Portugal experienced a 'brain drain' phenomenon. Besides the objective to attract qualified immigrants to Portugal, the Plan also stresses the importance of adopting strategies aimed at convincing Portuguese youngsters to remain and return to Portugal.

Due to its several strategic plans and the HCM's permanent activity, Portugal has been qualified as the most generous country regarding integration of immigrants by the 2009 Human Development Report of the United Nations.[7] In 2015, Portugal was voted, together with Sweden, the best country for integrating migrants by the Migration Integration Policy Index (MIPEX) report.[8] The report describes the Portuguese activity in this field as follows: 'Despite the crisis and austerity, PT maintained its investment in integration and even worked to increase its reach and effectiveness. PT continues to climb ahead on MIPEX: +1 point from 2007 to 2010 during the start of the crisis; immigrants benefited from more realistic family reunion requirements and more targeted support to pursue jobs, training and recognition procedures. PT rose another +1 point from 2010 to 2014; more immigrants can access protections against domestic violence and expanded targeted employment programmes, e.g. Mentoring for Immigrants Programme. Moreover, PT's integration policies have been given a new overall focus after the crisis. The new mobility and social realities reconfirmed that PT is a country of emigration (both for PT and non-EU citizens now working abroad) and a country of integration (both for non-EU families settling long-term and PT citizens living in a more diverse society).'

While some EU Member States have tightened their migration laws after the Charlie Hebdo terrorist attacks,[9] Portugal has *grosso modo* maintained its legal regime. Although it is true that the Immigration Law (IL) was amended in 2015, incorporating several clauses aimed at protecting the community against threats to the public security following other EU countries, since then, all other amendments aimed at strengthening the protection of migrants' rights and opening the access to the Portuguese society.

Portugal has also been adopting important measures aimed at transposing some of the most recent initiatives adopted internationally. That is the case of a national

7. United Nations Development Programme, *Human Development Report*, 2009.
8. Thomas Huddleston, Özge Bilgili, Anne-Linde Joki & Zvezda Vankova, *Migrant Integration Policy Index 2015,* Confederación de Pueblos Indígenas de Bolivia (CIDOB) and MPG, Barcelona, Brussels, 2015, p. 177, available in: https://www.mipex.eu/sites/default/files/downloads/files/mipex-2015-book-a5.pdf.
9. Austria and France were some of the EU Member States that amended their laws following these attacks that took place on 7 Jan. 2015. The attacks were performed by two French Muslim terrorists and brothers, Saïd and Chérif Kouachi, who forced their way into the offices of the French satirical weekly newspaper *Charlie Hebdo* in Paris. Armed with rifles and other weapons, they murdered twelve people and injured eleven others. The gunmen identified themselves as belonging to the Islamic terrorist group al-Qaeda in the Arabian Peninsula, which took responsibility for the attack.

plan aimed at implementing the Global Compact for Safe, Orderly and Regular Migration, adopted in Marrakech in 2018; it was the first plan to be adopted, as soon as in 2019.[10]

Despite the willingness to speedily implement the Global Pact, Portugal has, nonetheless, adopted a conservative approach as regards other international initiatives. That is the case of the 1990 United Nations Convention on the Protection of the Rights of All Migrant Workers and Members of their Families. Like all other EU Member States, Portugal has decided not to ratify this Convention. From time to time, there are some initiatives by institutions (such as the High Commissioner for Migrations), Non-governmental Organizations (NGOs) or political (mostly left-wing) parties, who advocate the ratification of this Convention.[11] However, so far, none of the Portuguese Governments made efforts to start such procedure. This lack of political willingness may be due to the fact that no other EU Member State is a party to the Convention.

10. The Plan was adopted by the Council of Ministries' Resolution dates of 1st Aug. 2019. For an analysis of the Global Compact, *see The relevance of migration for the 2030 Agenda for Sustainable Development: The Global Compact for Safe, Orderly and Regular Migration*, Constança Urbano de Sousa (org.), 2019.

11. *See* Resolution Project n. 153/X of the Communist Party, of September 2006.

General Introduction

§1. Immigration History and Statistical Information

I. Immigration History

1. There are few studies on the history of Portuguese immigration. Portugal is historically a country where the number of emigrants always exceeded the number of immigrants, even though, during the 1960s and the Salazar's dictatorship, emigration was not constitutionally protected and those who wanted to emigrate needed to ask for an emigration passport. Nevertheless, there was already some irregular emigration from the country.

2. One of the first legislative statutes dealing with immigration was Decree n. 18415 of 3 June 1930. One of its aims was the fight against the unemployment crisis. The Act recognized that there was a collision between national interests, 'which was sacred above every other interest' and other public goods, which were considered 'extraneous' to the public interest, despite being also 'respectable'. Thus, it determined that every Portuguese commercial and industrial company could employ Portuguese workers only, at least when there were still records of unemployed Portuguese workers. The only exceptions concerned Brasilian national citizens and the companies that already employed foreign citizens. The rights conferred to foreign citizens by international conventions duly ratified by the Portuguese State were also excepted. All other companies could only employ foreign citizens with a special authorization given by the Ministry of the Interior. Restriction on immigration was thus a way of fighting against unemployment.

3. The process of decolonization led to the creation of five new African countries: Cape Verde, Guinea-Bissau, São Tomé e Principe, Angola and Mozambique. The decolonization procedures led to the largest population movement in recent Portuguese history.[12] Many Portuguese citizens who were born abroad returned to the metropolis and came to live in the country of their nationality. Moreover, Portugal became a destination for a large number of nationals of Portuguese-speaking African countries. The common language and history shared among Lusophone countries were the determining factors.

12. Rui Pena Pires, *Migrações e Integração. Teoria e aplicações à sociedade portuguesa*, Celta Editora, 2003.

4. On 25 April 1974, the authoritarian *Estado Novo* regime was overthrown, and the path to a new democratic regime began. As a consequence, a new Constitution was drafted in 1976, which is still in force today, despite several constitutional amendments. This democratic Constitution established provisions aimed at maintaining and developing mutually privileged ties with the countries that had emerged from the decolonization war. Those ties became a fundamental principle in Portuguese Foreign Policy (Article 7(3) of the Constitution). Article 15(3) of the Constitution gave citizens of Lusophone countries, through international agreement and reciprocity, rights that other foreigners did not have, with the only exception being access to higher positions in the Government of the country.

5. As an answer to this massive increase of immigration into Portugal, several legal acts were adopted. First, Decree-Law n. 189-B/76, of 15 March 1976, established measures on expulsion of foreigners. According to this statute, several categories of foreigners could be expelled from the country, such as those who have entered irregularly into the territory, those who constituted a threat to the national security, to the public order or to the 'public morality', those who participated actively in political activities without being duly authorised to or those who did not respect the necessary conditions for their stay in the Portuguese territory. The adoption of this statute was justified with the concern of 'creating a minimum of guarantees to foreigners, in order to avoid the arbitrariness that characterised the previous legal regime'.[13] Second, the Government adopted Decree-Law n. 97/77, of 17 March 1977. This Act foresaw several provisions regulating the foreigners' access to labour in the Portuguese territory. For example, it established quotas for the number of foreign workers that were admitted to be employed by Portuguese companies. A national registry was implemented for that purpose, and immigrant workers had to prove their legal status in order to be employed. Thus, as we can see, the first significant migratory movement for Portugal was already accompanied by some protectionist measures as regards the national labour market.

6. In 1981, the Government enacted Decree-Law n. 264-B/81, of 3 September 1981, on entry, stay and expulsion of immigrants. This Act is considered to be the first legislative act aimed at regulating, in a systematic and comprehensive way, the State's powers on immigration matters. It encompassed rules on the conditions for entry and stay in the Portuguese territory, such as the required travel documents, visas, residence permits, as well as the expulsion cases and procedures. This statute was followed by Decree-Law n. 312/86, of 24 September 1986, which was aimed at preventing the entry into the territory of immigrants who did not have sufficient economic means.

7. During the XI Constitutional Government (1987–1991), the Portuguese Government recognized its transformation into a 'country of immigration'. Indeed, in the 1990s, the immigration movements experienced a major shift, which can be explained both by the increase of *push factors* in the countries of origin and by the increase of *pull factors* in Portugal. As for the first, in that time, several countries

13. Decree-Law n. 189-B/76, of 15 Mar. 1976, Preamble.

experienced an escalation of the poor quality of living, armed conflicts, systematic violations of human rights, ethnic rivalries, among other forms of violence, some of them resulting from poor decolonization processes and difficult transitions to democracy. However, Portugal was experiencing economic growth due to its joining to the European Economic Community and the Schengen agreements. Portugal became a new immigration destination for the citizens of some European countries and of the new countries that belonged to the former Soviet Republics. In 1981, there were 54.414 foreign residents living in Portugal. Ten years later, that number had increased to 107.767 individuals.[14]

8. This new reality led the Portuguese Government to undertake several legal reforms on immigration. The 1990s were, then, proficuous on legislative production regarding immigration. Law n. 59/93 and Law n. 60/93, both of 3 March 1993, transposed several rules aimed at the implementation of the Schengen agreements at the Portuguese borders. The European Union had started, by then, to develop a common immigration policy. However, the Portuguese regulations on immigration were not sufficient to correspond to the European legal developments. In fact, Portugal did not have, strictly speaking, a coherent system of 'immigration policy'. During the XII Constitutional Government (1991–1995), several measures were adopted in order to reorganize border control and the internal security system. These measures were aimed at adapting the Portuguese immigration control system to the new EU and Schengen rules.

9. For some immigrants, the developments on Immigration Law during the 1990s led to restrictions that they had not experienced before. That was the case of the citizens from the African Portuguese-speaking countries, who had almost free access to the Portuguese territory. These citizens had, from then on, to comply with the rules applicable to all EU's third-country nationals. Nevertheless, the Brasilian citizens could maintain their privileged relation with Portugal due to a Treaty for the Suppression of Visas, signed in 1960. This Treaty allowed Brasilian citizens to enter and remain in the Portuguese territory, without visa, for a maximum period of six months.

10. In fact, Portuguese Governments struggled to maintain a balance between the commitments that arose from the common immigration policy of the European Union and its privileged relations with the Portuguese-speaking countries.[15] In this context, one of the first debates regarding regularization of immigrants took place in 1992, in order to eradicate the high number of irregularly staying immigrants coming from the African Portuguese-speaking countries (a number that amounted to 100,000 immigrants). Trying to respond to these concerns, the Government decided to promote an extraordinary regularization procedure in 1996, through Law n. 17/96 of 24 May.

14. SEF, Relatório de Imigração, Fronteiras e Asilo 2012, Serviço de Estrangeiros e Fronteiras, Lisboa, 2013.
15. Vanda Santos, *supra* p. 148.

11. It was also in the mid-1990s that Portugal created the so-called – at the time – High Commissioner for the Immigration and Ethnic Minorities. Trying to respond to the new reality of Portugal as an immigration country, this body would be responsible for promoting the integration of immigrants into the Portuguese community. It had to promote a dialogue between the foreigners and the border police or other governmental bodies. As already mentioned, this body has successfully developed several integration policies and, despite several reforms, its importance has been increasing throughout the years. In 1998, a council for discussing integration issues was created – the Consulting Council for immigration issues. It is composed of members of the High Commissioner, members of other governmental bodies, as well as representatives of immigrant associations.

12. During the XIII Constitutional Government (1995–1999), in order to transpose some of the EU Directives and the Schengen agreements, a new statutory Act on immigration was adopted – Decree-Law n. 244/98 of 8 August 1998. For several scholars, this Act represented the first structural immigration policy statute.[16] The objectives were mainly three: integration of resident immigrants, restrictions to immigration – with the exception of the citizens of the Portuguese-speaking countries – and regulation of immigration coming from the Portuguese-speaking countries. These new measures were highly criticized by some associations, trade unions and the Catholic Church, who claimed that they were too restrictive.[17] In fact, the Act treated the problem of irregular immigration as a paramount priority and, thus, the trafficking of immigrants became more harshly punished under Portuguese criminal law. Detention and administrative expulsions of irregularly staying immigrants were also foreseen by the new law. One can say that these typical 'criminal' concepts entered, for the first time, into the immigration's lexicon.

13. However, the foreign population in Portugal did not cease to increase. In 2000, there were 207,607 foreigners residing in Portugal; in 2001, that number amounted to 350,503.[18] According to the official statistics, these immigrants continued to come mainly from the Portuguese-speaking countries, the majority of whom were from Angola, Cape Verde and Brazil.[19]

14. In response to several demands made by Brasilian citizens – who represented a significant share of foreign residents in Portugal – a treaty of friendship and equal rights was signed in 2000 between Portugal and Brazil, strengthening the Luso-Brasilian citizenship status created by a 1971 Convention. Furthermore, the 2001 constitutional review reworded Article 15, n. 3 allowing the law to confer to citizens of Lusophone states with permanent residence in Portugal broad citizenship rights which are not conferred to other foreigners, as long as reciprocity conditions are met. The only exceptions are access to positions of President of the Republic, Speaker of the Portuguese National Parliament, Prime Minister, President of the

16. Vanda Santos, *supra* p. 109.
17. Vanda Santos, *supra* p. 147.
18. Vanda Santos, *supra* p. 108.
19. Vanda Santos, *supra* p. 109.

Supreme Courts as well as service in the Armed Forces and in Diplomatic Corps. This constitutional provision was a decisive step in creating the 'citizenship of the Community of Portuguese-speaking Countries'. This so-called *citizenship of the Community of the Portuguese-speaking Countries* is different from European Union citizenship. First, it allows for various political rights to be exercised, not only at a local but also at a national level, and provides access to public offices which are not predominantly of a technical nature. Second, and contrary to European Union citizenship, Lusophone citizenship does not provide any right to entry and (permanent) residence in Portuguese territory nor to diplomatic protection in another country.

15. In 2001, a new legal statute for the regulation of entry, stay and expulsion of foreigners was adopted (Decree-Law n. 4/2001 of 10 January).[20] First, it aimed at fostering the integration of legally staying migrants in the territory and at simplifying procedures for legal residence. In this context, family reunification was one of the measures that were most promoted. Second, it aimed at reinforcing the fight against exploitation and illegal employment. Moreover, a regularization procedure was again decreed, through the creation of a special residence permit, called 'authorisation of stay', which could be granted in cases where the migrant had a labour contract. With these three measures explained above, the total number of granted authorizations was 131,000.[21]

16. However, and perhaps quite contradictorily with the goal of facilitating channels to legal migration, during this decade, the Government also began to determine an annual quota of maximum entries of third-country nationals for work purposes. The XV Government (xxx – year x) decided to be stricter regarding control of immigration, to fight against irregular immigration and to end the extraordinary regularizations. In parallel with the European common immigration policy, the Government was also concerned with cooperating with the countries of origin to fight against irregular immigration and to negotiate the concession of visas. In order to design a whole new regime, and repeal the previous Immigration Law, the Government enacted Decree-Law n. 34/2003 of 25 February, which revoked the 'authorisations of stay', due to the increasing number of irregularly staying migrants. The new legal framework favoured the award of residence permits through the regular procedure, from the country of origin, upon submission of a labour contract in Portugal. The number of entries was limited according to a report on the needs of manpower. The new statute also harshened the measures for fighting against the employment of irregularly staying immigrants, and the first measures aimed at expelling large numbers of irregularly staying immigrants were also adopted.[22]

17. Bearing in mind the new and different immigration patterns, the Government decided to increase the budget for the integration of immigrants with 331%, from 2002 to 2003. The new migration movements encompassed migrants who

---

20. This Decree-Law was regulated by Regulamentary Decree n. 9/2001.
21. Vanda Santos, *supra* p. 120.
22. During 2013, eighty irregularly staying immigrants were expelled during the month of March. Vanda Santos, *supra* p. 128.

came from countries with no historical or cultural ties with Portugal. Their integration required different tools, such as the promotion of Portuguese language courses, support to immigrants' associations, and awareness-raising of their fundamental rights and duties and basic notions of Portuguese culture. The suggested measures were not without criticism, as some authors claimed that these policies' major concern was the integration into the Portuguese culture and not the promotion of an intercultural inclusion.[23]

18. In 2007, a new immigration law was enacted (Law n. 23/2007 of 4 July), which is still in force. This law was aimed at transposing several EU Directives and several developments in the field of human rights of immigrants, advanced both by the Portuguese Constitutional Court and by the European Court of Human Rights (ECtHR). It was amended several times, for instance, in 2012 (Law 29/2012 of 9 August), in order to transpose new EU instruments. This amendment is the mirror of the concerns of the 'European agenda' on immigration. Thus, several provisions were adopted that were mainly restrictive (that is the case, e.g., of the reinforcement of the fight against irregular immigration, illegal employment, terrorism and sham marriages); others were aimed at attracting skilled labour (that is the case of the transposition of the measures of the 'blue card' Directive)[24]. Moreover, the restriction of immigration on the grounds of national 'public order' was strengthened.

19. In 2006, the current Nationality Act was enacted. This was a pivotal normative change, which had the objective to keep and increase the links between Portugal and its expatriates, and to respond to the reality of Portugal as an immigration country and, therefore, to be inclusive regarding those who had chosen the country as a place to live. Portugal had a long tradition of favouring *ius soli* which dates back to the seventeenth century. The 1981 Act, approved in the context of a large Portuguese emigration, ended this tradition and introduced the prevalence of the *ius sanguinis* principle. In 2006, this Act was profoundly amended by a reform which broadened the modes for the acquisition of Portuguese citizenship. The reform maintained and, in some respects, even reinforced the *ius sanguinis* principle, taking into consideration the large community of Portuguese descendants who reside abroad. At the same time, it also created new ways to acquire citizenship through *ius soli*, taking into consideration the inclusion of immigrants of the second and third generations. The inclusion objective is favoured by the complete acceptance of dual citizenship, which has been in force since 1981. But, perhaps more significantly, it has created a *subjective right to naturalization*, which could be considered the ultimate way to promote immigrants' full integration in Portuguese society.

20. The Immigration Law was further amended in 2015[25] with a restrictive purpose, following the Charlie Hebdo terrorist attacks. As in many other EU countries,

23. Vanda Santos, *supra* p. 132.
24. Council Directive 2009/50/EC of 25 May. 2009 on the conditions of entry and residence of third-country nationals for the purposes of highly qualified employment.
25. Law n. 56/2015, of 23/06 and Law n. 63/2015, of 30/06.

Portugal also introduced several clauses in its immigration, asylum and nationality laws for the protection of public order, national security and prevention of terrorism. The law was again amended in 2017[26], and the requirements for residence permits for investment and for studies and research purposes were changed. The greatest change, however, concerned the creation of a subjective right to regularization of irregularly staying migrants who were working or developing an independent professional activity, provided that these foreigners would fulfil some requirements, such as holding a valid work contract or a binding work proposal, contributing to the social security and having entered legally in the territory. This right was further expanded in 2019,[27] by introducing a clause that would allow those who had entered irregularly in the territory but who had, nonetheless, worked and paid social security contributions in the previous year to be also eligible for regularization. Although these amendments aimed at responding to the humanitarian needs of a large number of persons who, residing in the country, working and contributing financially to the community, were deprived, due to their legal status, of several rights, this legislative change was not accompanied by a reinforcement of the Foreigners and Borders Service's personnel. This led to a severe crisis in the immigration system, as there were neither material nor human capacities to respond to the high levels of requests that followed these amendments. Moreover, these difficulties also affected other administrative decisions, delaying attributions and renovations of other residence permits, including regarding family reunification.[28]

21. Also worthy of note is the amendment that took place in 2018,[29] which aimed at protecting unaccompanied children that would arrive in the Portuguese territory, who would also benefit from a right to regularization.

22. Portuguese legislation throughout the years had, thus, been characterized by two apparently contradictory tendencies: fighting against irregular immigration, on the one hand, and, at the same time, keeping some schemes to respond to the numbers of irregular migrants living in Portugal, on the other. If the former has been promoted by the EU in the context of the development of a common immigration policy, the latter have been exclusively national measures – which the majority of the other EU Member States have not followed.

23. The law was amended once again in August 2022.[30] This amendment had a double purpose. On the one hand, it aimed at implementing the Agreement on Mobility between Member States of the Community of Portuguese-speaking Countries, signed in Luanda, on 17 July 2021. This agreement creates ways to enhance mobility between citizens of the several State Parties. With this change, Portugal reoriented its immigration policy to strengthening of ties with other Lusophone

26. Law n. 59/2017, of 31/07 and Law n. 02/2017, of 28/08.
27. Law n. 28/2019, of 29/03.
28. On this topic, Ana Rita Gil, 'Regularizações do estatuto do estrangeiro – de alteração em alteração, um direito em expansão', Vida Judiciária, novembro de 2019.
29. Law n. 26/2018, of 05/07.
30. Law n. 18/2022 of 25/08.

countries. On the other hand, the 2022 amendments created mechanisms to facilitate economic migration, especially migration for work purposes. They introduced a new and very important channel of legal migration: the *visa for the purpose of job search*, which is a breakthrough in the context of the European immigration system. The new version of the IL also facilitated the acquisition of a visa for work purposes and access to the labour market by different categories of residents, and eliminated some protectionist clauses. With these solutions, Portugal stands out as a country that is creating new paths for legal migration to Europe.

II. Statistical Information

24. The Foreigners and Borders Service publishes annually statistic studies on the number and countries of origin of the foreign population residing in Portugal. Annual reports also illustrate the geographic distribution of migrants in the national territory. The following figure shows the evolution of the total number of foreign residents in Portugal over the years:

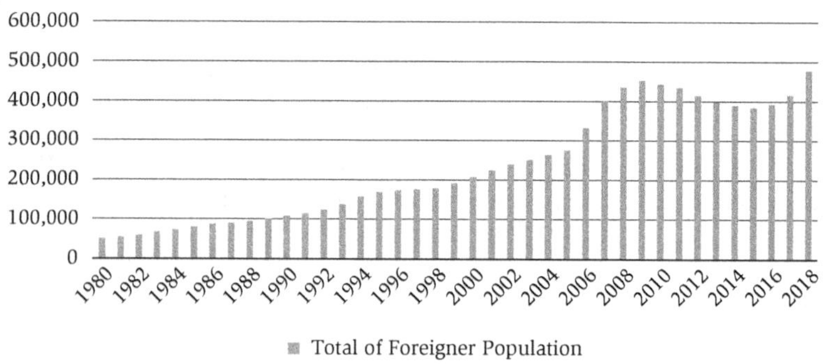

Source: Foreigners and Borders Service – http://sefstat.sef.pt/evolucao.aspx.

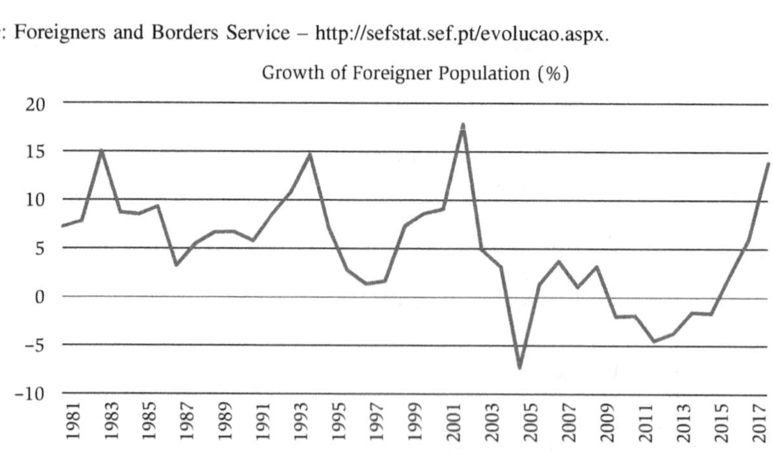

Source: Foreigners and Borders Service – http://sefstat.sef.pt/evolucao.aspx.

25. The portrayal of Portugal in the context of migration has deeply changed in the last decades. As already pointed out, Portugal was traditionally a country of emigration, but it started to be chosen as country of destination, mainly after the 1990s. This change of profile has several explanations: the improvement of economic conditions, which led to greater attractiveness for workers from other States; extensive public works and infrastructure construction programmes, which enabled the absorption capacity of many workers in these sectors, mostly in low-qualified positions; and finally the political and social instability in countries with which Portugal has historical cultural relations and linguistic affinities, which justified the demand of these workers for better living conditions in Portugal.[31] The type of migratory titles has also changed in the last decade. In 2008, most migrants entered the Portuguese territory with labour or family reunification residence permits. However, in 2012, the share of these titles had decreased, and the number of residence permits for the purpose of study, namely in high education institutions, rose significantly.[32] The new Portuguese immigration pattern has been composed of more complex migratory flows, which are no longer exclusively labour-based.[33]

26. Due to the economic crisis, which has deeply affected the country from 2010, Portugal witnessed a new era of emigration. At the same time, the country ceased to be attractive to economic migrants, due to the high unemployment rates and, consequently, the immigration rate became negative – a phenomenon that had not happened since the nineties. After the economic recovery in 2016, the migration rate began to recover at a fast pace. Nowadays, Portugal can be characterized as both an emigration and an immigration country.

27. According to the Foreigners and Borders Service, in 2022, the number of foreign residents in Portugal was the highest ever. The foreign population represents about 5.4% of the resident population in Portugal, and about 8% of the working population.

28. According to the most recent statistics of the Foreigners and Borders Service, in 2021, the foreigner population in Portugal had the following national origins: Brazil (29.3%), United Kingdom (6%), Cape Verde (4.9%), India (4.3%), Romania (4.1%) and Ukraine (3.9%).[34] Although nationalities are diverse, what is still visible is the influence of the historical, cultural and linguistic ties with the communities from the Portuguese-speaking countries.

31. Alto Comissariado para as Migações, *Plano Estratégico para as Migrações 2015-2020*, p. 1.
32. Alto Comissariado para as Migações, *Plano Estratégico para as Migrações 2015-2020*, p. 2.
33. Decree-Law n. 31/2014, of 27 February.
34. SEF, Relatório de Imigração, Fronteiras e Asilo 2021 Serviço de Estrangeiros e Fronteiras, Lisboa, 2022. Accessible in https://www.sef.pt/pt/Documents/RIFA2021%20vfin2.pdf, p. 32.

§2. Overview of National Legal Instruments

I. Portuguese Constitution

29. The Portuguese legal system must respect the Portuguese Constitution and the international legal instruments to which Portugal is part, which are directly applicable in Portugal, upon their regular ratification (Article 8 of the Constitution), and prevail over the legal instruments.

30. The Portuguese Constitution is deeply grounded in the principle of human dignity and the universality of human rights – both of which have deep consequences for the enjoyment of fundamental rights by foreign citizens. Article 1 sets forth that the Portuguese Republic is based on the principle of human dignity, which imposes that *every human being has the same dignity*. Portugal has, then, agreed to respect, guarantee, and promote the same dignity for national citizens and foreigners alike. For some authors, this principle reflects the overcoming of an exclusive or primary conception of citizen-based fundamental rights, to the benefit of a universalist reading, which links fundamental rights to the mere concept of person.[35] This is not a mere philosophic assertion, as the Constitutional Court has already shown the important practical implications of this principle. In ruling n. 296/2015, the Court considered that the social minimum income, which aims to guarantee that all persons residing in Portugal must be granted with minimum living conditions, was intended to guarantee a 'right to a minimum dignified existence', which was a direct imposition of respect for human dignity. The Court considered that excluding this benefit from foreigners who did not reside for the past three years in the territory would be unconstitutional due to the disrespect of the principle of human dignity.[36]

31. Article 12, on its turn, enshrines the principle of universality, according to which everybody enjoys the same rights and is subject to the same duties enshrined in the Portuguese Constitution. But the most important principle regarding the enjoyment of fundamental rights by foreign citizens is undoubtedly the principle of equivalence. Such principle is enshrined in Article 15, which reads as follows: 'Foreigners and stateless persons who are staying or who reside in Portugal enjoy the same rights and are subject to the same duties as Portuguese citizens.' In all cases that concern the fundamental rights of foreigners, the Constitutional Court resorts, primarily, to Article 15. This provision was inserted in the constitutional original text, in 1976, and marked a different perspective compared to the previous Constitution, which only recognized some fundamental rights to foreigners – only those which would not represent a 'burden' to the State.

32. The principle of equivalence is a general clause, so it applies where no exclusions or restrictions are expressly foreseen. This means that, unless prescribed otherwise, foreigners shall enjoy the same rights as national citizens. This assertion

---

35. Anabela Costa Leão, 'Ac. TC n. 232/04 (expulsão de estrangeiros com filhos menores a cargo)', *Jurisprudência Constitucional*, n. 3, 2004, p. 38.
36. Constitutional Court, ruling n. 296/2015, of 25 May 2015.

encompasses all fundamental rights, including social and economic rights.[37] This interpretation was confirmed in the above-mentioned ruling n. 296/2015, which declared the unconstitutionality of the provision that required a minimum period of three years of residence in the national territory for foreigners to benefit from the social inclusion income.

33. Nevertheless, some exceptions are indeed foreseen – either in Article 15 itself or in legal acts. First, Article 15 reserves the enjoyment of political rights and of public functions without predominant technical nature to Portuguese citizens. Moreover, it sets forth that other constitutional provisions may foresee other exceptions. That is the case of Article 44, which guarantees the fundamental right to return to the country and which is exclusively pertaining to national citizens. Finally, Article 15 allows the law to foresee other exceptions. However, these exceptions must be understood as restrictions to fundamental rights and, thus, must respect the constitutional principles on this matter.[38] Hence, the exclusion of a foreigner from the enjoyment of a fundamental right must be justified with the need to safeguard a prevalent constitutional value or other right and must respect the principle of proportionality.

34. There are some specific thorny questions worthy of note. The first would be the principle of reciprocity, which has been highly debated by Portuguese scholars. This principle is enshrined in some statutes, as Article 14(2) of the Portuguese Civil Code. According to this principle, some rights are only recognized to foreigners as far as the same right is recognized to Portuguese citizens by the State of origin of the former. Several scholars claim that these provisions are unconstitutional for disrespecting the principle of assimilation.[39] These provisions do represent a challenge to the respect of several constitutional principles: not only the principle of equivalence but also the principle of equality, which forbids any discrimination based on the country of origin (Article 13). Moreover, these reciprocity clauses are based on outdated conceptions of international law, relating to the traditional concept of collective responsibility of the people for belonging to a certain State. That is why some scholars claim that, more than reciprocity clauses, these provisions establish true retaliation clauses.[40]

---

37. Carlos Pamplona de Oliveira, *A Jurisprudência Constitucional sobre Cidadãos Estrangeiros,* Relatório apresentado no encontro trianual dos Tribunais Constitucionais de Portugal, Espanha e Itália, em Madrid, 26 e 27 de setembro de 2008, p. 5, Jorge Pereira da Silva, 'Artigo 15.º – Princípio da Equiparação', in Jorge Miranda, & Rui Medeiros, *Constituição da República Portuguesa Anotada*, Tomo I, 2ª Edição, Coimbra Editora, 2010, p. 276, Ana Rita Gil & Lino Ribeiro, *Prestações Sociais e Cidadania,* Relatório do Tribunal Constitucional Português apresentado à XVII Conferência Trilateral dos Tribunais Constitucionais de Espanha, Itália e Portugal, 2016.
38. Ruling n. 124/87, dated 10 Feb. 1987.
39. Jorge Pereira da Silva, *Direitos de Cidadania e Direito à Cidadania*, Alto Comissariado para a Imigração e Minorias Étnicas, 2004, p. 145, Carla Amado Gomes & Anabela Costa Leão, *A Condição de Imigrante – Uma análise de Direito Constitucional e de Direito Administrativo*, Almedina, 2010, p. 39.
40. Mário Torres, 'Os Direitos dos Imigrantes na Legislação Portuguesa', in AA.VV., *A Política Europeia de Imigração,* Actas do Seminário de Lisboa de 9 de Outubro de 2001, Serviço das Publicações Oficiais das Comunidades Europeias, Luxemburgo, 2002, p. 62.

35. Finally, and still in the context of the principle of equivalence, there is even now an ongoing debate on whether it shall be applicable to migrants with irregular status. Article 15 refers *to all foreigners who are present in* or reside in the Portuguese territory, not mentioning any requirement concerning 'legal residence'. In this context, we must stress that the Constitutional Court has repeatedly underlined that foreigners who are in Portugal for any reason, even if they do not reside there, enjoy the rights and duties inherent in Portuguese citizens, pursuant to Article 15 of the Constitution.[41] In our opinion, non-legal resident foreigners are encompassed by this provision.[42] That does not mean that any exceptions to the rule are forbidden. The law may indeed exclude irregular migrants from enjoying certain rights, guaranteeing these rights only to those who are in a legal position. Thus, the question is not related to the *subjective scope of the principle of equivalence*, but to the admissible restrictions to fundamental rights.[43]

36. Besides these general and paramount principles, there are also some constitutional provisions expressly destined for foreign citizens. First, the Portuguese Basic Law sets forth some guarantees for the expulsion of legally staying migrants. Article 33(2) foresees that deportation of a foreigner 'who has properly entered or is properly present in Portuguese territory, who has been granted a residence permit, or has submitted a request for asylum that has not been refused, may only be ordered by a judicial authority'. Article 33(8), on its turn, specifies that 'the right of asylum shall be guaranteed to foreigners and stateless persons who are the object, or are under grave threat, of persecution as a result of their activities in favour of democracy, social and national liberation, peace among peoples, freedom or rights of the human person'. According to Article 33(9), the status of political refugee shall be defined by the law. Asylum is, thus, a fundamental right enshrined in the Portuguese *Grundnormen* – as well as an institutional guarantee.

37. Some rulings of the Portuguese Constitutional Court are especially worthy of note, especially those that have affirmed principles now enshrined in the Immigration Law. That is the case of the decision that has declared the unconstitutionality of some legal provisions that would apply an expulsion punishment to foreign nationals who were parents of Portuguese children.[44] The Court considered that such an expulsion would amount to a violation of the principle of family unity, especially the prohibition of separation of children from their parents, protected under

41. *See*, among others, ruling n. 407/95, dated 28/06/1995.
42. Against, Jorge Pereira da Silva, 'Artigo 15.º … ', p. 266. In favour, Assim, também, José Leitão, & Luís Nunes de Almeida, 'Les Droits et Libertés des Étrangers en Situation Irrégulière – Portugal', *Annuaire International de Justice Constitutionnelle*, Presses Universitaires d'Aix-Marseille, Economica, 1998, p. 299, Mário Torres, *supra* p. 58, Carlota Pizarro de Almeida, 'Exclusões Formais, Exclusões Materiais – o Lugar do Outro; Discriminação contra Imigrantes', *Revista da Faculdade de Direito da Universidade de Lisboa*, vol.XLV, ns. 1 & 2, 2004, p. 42, Duarte Miranda Mendes, 'Estrangeiro', AA.VV., *Enciclopédia da Constituição Portuguesa*, Jorge Bacelar Gouveia & Francisco Pereira Coutinho (coord.), Quid Juris, 2013, p. 146, Gonçalo Saraiva Matias, *Migrações e Cidadania, Fundação Francisco Manuel dos Santos,* 2014, p. 34.
43. *See* Ana Rita Gil, *Imigração e Direitos Humanos*, Petrony, 2017, p. 270.
44. Ruling n. 181/97, dated 5 Mar. 1997.

Article 36, n. 6 of the Portuguese Constitution and in Article 8 of the European Convention on Human Rights (ECHR). In order to guarantee the maintenance of family unity, children would have to follow the expelled immigrant to their country of origin, which, on its turn, would amount to a violation of the constitutional prohibition of expulsion of nationals, enshrined in Article 33.[45] As a result, the current Portuguese Immigration Act expressly prohibits the expulsion of migrants who are parents to Portuguese citizen children as long as they provide for their livelihood.

38. Regarding the right to immigration, the Constitutional Court has affirmed that it is not guaranteed by the Portuguese Constitution as such. It has stressed several times, for example, that expulsion did not deprive a foreigner of the right to remain in Portugal or to establish residence therein, or the right to enter into the Portuguese territory, for the simple reason that a foreigner does not hold such rights.[46] One must stress, however, that the Constitution sets forth some limits to the application of the expulsion measure. First, as said, those who have entered or remain legally in the national territory, or who have lodged an asylum application, can only be expelled after a decision made by a judicial authority.[47] Moreover, the Constitutional Court has decided several times that an expulsion penalty for the conviction of certain crimes was unconstitutional, when applied *automatically*, as such measure disrespects Article 30(4) of the Constitution, which sets forth that no judicial decision shall automatically involve the loss of any civil, professional, or political rights. The Court considered that the right to reside in any part of the country is a civil right enjoyed by migrants who are legally staying in Portugal – thus, could not be automatically removed because of a criminal punishment.[48]

39. The Constitutional Court has also decided several cases regarding access to free legal aid by immigrants. First, it affirmed that irregularly staying foreigners had the right to free legal aid for asylum claim proceedings.[49] After several rulings, the Constitutional Court declared the unconstitutionality of the legal provisions that denied legal aid to foreign nationals who intend to challenge the administrative decisions on asylum requests.[50] This case law was then adapted to the protection of irregularly staying foreigners in criminal procedures[51] and labour law procedures.[52]

45. For further developments, *see* Ana Rita Gil, 'Um Caso de Europeização do Direito Constitucional Português – A Afirmação de um Direito Fundamental ao Reagrupamento Familiar', *Revista de Direito Público*, ano I, 2009, n. 2, p. 9-62.
46. Ruling n. 442/93, dated 19 Jan. 1994, ruling n. 288/94, dated 17 Jun. 1994.
47. Article 33(2) of the Portuguese Constitution.
48. *See*, among others, ruling n. 434/93, dated 19 Jan. 1994, ruling n. 442/93, dated 14 Jul. 1993, ruling n. 288/94, dated 17 Jun. 1994, ruling n. 41/95, dated 26 Apr. 1995. For further developments, *see* Ana Luísa Pinto, *A pena acessória de expulsão de estrangeiros do território nacional*, Coimbra Editora, 2005.
49. *See*, among many others, ruling n. 340/95, dated 22 Jun. 1995, ruling n. 240/96, dated 29 Feb. 1996.
50. Ruling n. 962/96, dated 11 Jul. 1996. Constitutional decisions having general mandatory effects amount to an eradication of the unconstitutional legal provision from the Portuguese legal order.
51. Ruling n. 433/2003, dated 29 Sep. 2003.
52. Ruling n. 208/2004, dated 24 Mar. 2004.

II. Current Applicable Legislation

40. The current Immigration Law – Law n. 23/2007 of 4 July as last amended by Law n. 18/22 of 25 August, sets forth the conditions and procedures on the entry, stay, exit and removal of foreign citizens from Portuguese territory, as well as the long-term resident status. It is the main legal text on the matter, and we will name it hereinafter as 'IL'. It is implemented by Regulamentary Decree n. 84/2007 of 5 November, as last amended by the Regulamentary Decree n. 04/2022 of 30 September (hereinafter 'IR'), as well as by several governmental ordinances and orders on specific points (bulletin of accommodation, fees, etc.).

41. According to Article 4 IL ('Scope'), its provisions shall apply to foreign and stateless persons, but not to: (i) nationals of EU Member States and their family members, (ii) nationals of the States Parties to the European Economic Area and their family members, (iii) family members of Portuguese citizens. The law governing the entry, stay and residence of these latter categories of persons is the law on the right to free movement of citizens of the European Union in the Portuguese territory – Law n. 37/2006, of 9 August, which transposed Directive 2004/38/CE of 29 April. The EU citizen registration certificate and residence document are regulated by Portarias 1334-D/2010 of 31 December and 164/2017 of 18 May.

42. The IL shall not be applied either to third-country nationals: (i) who reside in the Portuguese territory as refugees or beneficiaries of subsidiary protection under the provisions on asylum, or as beneficiaries of temporary protection and (ii) who are family members of a foreign citizen covered by the aforementioned situation. Conditions and procedures for granting asylum or subsidiary protection and the statuses of asylum seeker, refugee and subsidiary protection are regulated by Law n. 27/2008 of 30 June, as amended by Law 26/2014 of 5 May, which transposed the several pertinent EU Directives into Portuguese Law.

43. Finally, all matters pertaining to acquisition, loss and reacquisition of nationality are dealt with by the Portuguese Nationality Act.

44. With the exception of the Law on Free Movement of Persons, all abovementioned acts have suffered several amendments since their entry into force. These amendments had several purposes: to transpose legal acts of the European Union, to accommodate the case law of both the Constitutional Court and the European Courts and to accompany changes in national policy. We will refer to these amendments when relevant.

45. Finally, there are other instruments that regulate certain aspects of the Immigration Regulation (IR), such as Law n. 34/94 of 14 September, on the legal regime of foreigners' temporary accommodation centres. Portaria n. 1563/2007 of 11 December is also an important instrument, as it sets forth the amounts of the means of subsistence that foreign citizens must have at their disposal for entry and stay in the national territory.

46. Other instruments foresee important rights for some categories of migrants. That is the case of Decree-Law n. 67/2004 of 25 March, which creates a national register of foreign minors who are in an irregular situation in the national territory, for the purposes of guaranteeing a right to access schools and medical care.

47. Finally, Decree-Law 154/2003 of 15 July, on attribution and registration of equality status to Brasilian citizens, must be of reference when regulating the rights of Brasilian citizens. This Act regulates Treaty of Porto Seguro, celebrated between Portugal and Brazil in 2000. According to this Treaty, Brasilian citizens who acquire this status may benefit from some important civil and political rights in Portugal.

§3. ADMINISTRATIVE AND JUDICIAL AUTHORITIES

I. Administrative Authorities

48. The competent national authority in matters of migration and residence, including international protection, is the National Director of the Foreigners and Borders Service (*Serviço de Estrangeiros e Fronteiras* – hereinafter 'SEF'), personally or by delegation of powers. However, there are some decisions – expressly mentioned in the law – where the competent authority is the member of government responsible for internal affairs – the Ministry of Internal Affairs or of the Interior. That is the case of matters that require a certain degree of political assessment (for instance, the exceptional granting of a residence permit to a foreign citizen who does not meet the legal requirements, for humanitarian reasons or for reasons of national or public interest). Apart from that, it is up to the SEF to make all decisions on migration matters. This includes a very wide scope involving decisions not only on the refusal of entry due to threat to public order, decisions on administrative expulsion, but also on fundamental rights, such as the case of family reunification and asylum. It is somehow controversial that the same authority has the competence to both exercise police tasks and to decide on international protection. Although these competences fall under different departments, it nonetheless raises the issue of making it more difficult to decide on both matters in an independent way.

49. The High Commissioner for Migration is another important entity, as already mentioned above. It functions under the supervision of the Council of Ministries, and its main tasks are to provide assistance to migrants' integration in the country, namely by helping them to benefit from the rights that are guaranteed to them under the Constitution, such as enrolling children in schools, providing support to access to health and medical care, housing, employment, social security benefits, among others. It runs a special telephone hotline – *Save Our Ship (SOS) immigrant* – where immigrants can be informed about their rights and where a service on translation into forty-seven different languages is provided. The Commissioner has several local centres for the support of immigrants. These centres are inspired by the philosophy of 'one-stop shop' and have been internationally recognized as a good practice for the integration of immigrants in local communities. They provide assistance and counselling in several areas, such as labour law, immigration, consumer law, access to schooling, healthcare, housing, employment, entrepreneurship, training and qualifications recognition. These services may also refer the immigrant to the competent services of the Portuguese Public Administration. This body also promotes several activities aimed at developing the social inclusion of the immigrants, and at maintaining a permanent dialogue with the immigrants' associations. It organizes courses on Portuguese language, as well as conferences, seminars, and workshops. Socio-cultural mediators of various origins, with competences in several languages (twelve different languages and dialects), are chosen through protocols negotiated with the migrants' associations and with NGOs working in the field of human rights of immigrants, to work with the HCM.

50. Other entities may also intervene in migration procedures. That is the case of entities that may be required to issue documents or who will be responsible for accommodating foreigners. For example, schools and universities, institutions where the foreigner aims to develop a voluntary work, or even private institutions, like private banks and employers, can intervene in order to attest that the foreigner will enter the territory in order to study/develop a research/make an investment or work on their behalf.

II. Judicial Authorities

51. Courts play a paramount role in the development of migration law in Portugal. The Portuguese judiciary is organized into two branches: judicial courts and administrative courts. Both are independent jurisdictional institutions, composed of judges, public prosecutors and lawyers, and have three jurisdiction levels, although not every case can accede to the Supreme Courts. In both cases, courts decide according to a judicial adversary procedure.

52. These two different branches may play a role in immigration cases.

53. Administrative courts deal with the State's administrative activity. They are competent to review the legality of administrative decisions or regulations, to condemn the Public Administration to decide in a certain way or to perform a certain act, and, among other things, may also decide to adopt a wide range of precautionary measures. As regards the IL, they are competent to review the legality of SEF's administrative decisions – for example, a decision of administrative expulsion or of refusal to issue a visa, as well as the decisions on international protection.

54. Judicial courts, on their turn, are competent to decide all matters related to detention and criminal aspects of Immigration Law. For example, all foreigners that are detained by the SEF, according to the IL, for being irregularly staying in the national territory, must be presented before a criminal judge, who will decide on whether such person must be maintained in detention or whether another coercive measure shall be applicable.[53] Also, it is up to the criminal judge to apply an ancillary expulsion penalty to foreigners who have committed a crime, in the cases foreseen in the penal code.

55. Despite this important role of the judicial courts, its important control function may be impaired due to some dubious practices that have been adopted in 2018–2019, as regards detention of irregular migrants and asylum seekers at the border posts. Stays which exceed forty-eight hours in the temporary centres located in these areas must be authorized by the competent court. However, as it results from the Ombudsman's reports, authorizations are requested by fax to the competent court, which responds by the same means, without hearing the detainee in person.[54] This practice is not consistent with an effective right to access to justice. Moreover, it may preclude a broad understanding of the personal circumstances of the detainees, including accompanying family members, their possible consideration as 'especially vulnerable persons', etc. It may also prevent the application of alternative measures to detention.

56. Although courts mainly apply domestic laws – both the Immigration and Asylum Law – and also the Constitution – they naturally have to resort as well to the applicable EU law and have to apply directly all pertinent binding international instruments – namely on protection of human rights – as they prevail over the law and are directly applicable. For example, the Administrative Court stressed that Article 13 of the Universal Declaration of Human Rights was not disrespected where a permission of stay was refused to an immigrant who claimed economic reasons to stay in Portugal.[55] Also, taking into consideration the ECtHR's case law, the Administrative Court considered that the refusal to regularize a migrant's status who was registered in the Schengen Information System (SIS) for non-admission purposes was not considered contrary to Article 8 of the Convention.[56] The Supreme Administrative Court also decided that a four-year-long procedure that rejected an application for an extraordinary regularization of the immigrant's stay did not disrespect the right to a fair trial enshrined in Article 6 of the ECHR.[57]

57. The Supreme Court of Justice is deeply inspired by the ECtHR's case law in its decisions concerning judicial expulsions. In this context, it has systematically affirmed that any decision on expulsion can only be taken after taking into account the respect for the migrant's private and family life, enshrined in Article 8 of the

---

53. Article 38/4 IL.
54. Contribution of the Portuguese Ombudsman on the Implementation of the Convention against Torture and Other Cruel, Inhuman or Degrading Treatment or Punishment in the Process of Review of the Seventh Periodic Report submitted by Portugal under Art. 19 of the Convention pursuant to the optional reporting procedure, October 2019, p. 12.
55. Ruling dated 09/07/2002, procedure n. 048438.
56. Ruling dated 24/09/2003, procedure n. 047977 and Ruling dated 11-03-2003, procedure n. 047978.
57. Ruling dated 04-06-2002, procedure n. 046551.

ECHR.[58] Thus, it considers that any decision on expulsion can only be taken where proved to be 'necessary in a democratic society', and after achieving a fair balance between the individual interests and the interest of the State to maintain the public order.[59]

58. Finally, it is important to mention that foreigners have the right to a lawyer and to request legal aid when necessary. The Law on Access to Courts[60] shall be applicable, as the Constitutional Court has stressed several times. Nevertheless, there are some practical obstacles in this area. First, according to Article 7 of the Law on Access to Courts, only foreigners who hold a valid residence permit in Portugal or in another EU Member State may have access to legal aid. Foreigners without a valid residence permit in any EU Member State may only have a right to legal protection under conditions of reciprocity. That is to say, then, that some foreigners without financial means may be excluded from this protection, namely if they are willing to challenge an administrative decision on entry refusal – unless the principle of reciprocity applies. Second, the Public Administration has been adopting a questionable interpretation of the right to access a lawyer. It considers that the foreigner may only be accompanied by an attorney after having been the object of a refusal of entry. This may have serious impacts on enforcing an effective right to make an asylum request, as the applicant may not always be aware of how to exercise this right.[61]

III. Ombudsman

59. Finally, it is also important to mention the important role of the Ombudsman in the field of migration. This institution is completely independent from the Government, and directly elected by the Parliament. It has competence to receive complaints from any person, regardless of nationality or legal status, against the Public Administration. It mediates the complaints with informal means, by reaching out directly to the administrative institution, or with formal means, by recommendations to the competent bodies. Although the Ombudsman does not have the power to enforce its decisions, the prestige that it receives from the society at large allows for a broad respect of its positions by the Public Administration. In the last years, the number of complaints against the SEF has increased significantly – mostly due to serious delays in residence permits' renovations or attributions.[62]

---

58. Ruling dated 12-06-1996, procedure n. 96P303, ruling dated 19-06-1996, procedure n. 96P046, ruling dated 05-02-1997, procedure n. 96P1059, ruling dated 19-02-1997, procedure n. 96P1042, ruling dated 05-03-1997, procedure n. 96P1011.
59. Rulings dated 06-09-2006, procedure n. 06P1391, and n. 06P2663, ruling dated 27-09-2006, procedure n. 06P2802.
60. Law n. 34/2004, of 29 July, as amended by Decree-Law n. 120/2018, de 27/12.
61. *See* Ombudsman,.
62. Provedor de Justiça, *Relatório Nacional à Assembleia da República*, 2018 e 2019, available at htt p://www.provedor-jus.pt/.

60. Besides dealing with complaints, the Ombudsman also acts as the National Preventive Mechanism, designated for the purpose of the Optional Protocol of the United Nations (UN) Convention Against Torture and Other Cruel, Inhuman or Degrading Treatment or Punishment. Under this competence, it visits all places of deprivation of liberty, including migrants' detention centres. Its annual reports have been of the utmost importance to improve the detention conditions of migrant citizens in Portugal, as they point out several risk factors and shortcomings that characterize detention centres.[63] Finally, the Ombudsman is the National Human Rights Institution, fully complying with the Paris Principles. In this quality, it often engages with the international bodies and mechanisms, such as the several UN committees, where it provides alternative reports and takes the opportunity to advocate internationally for an improvement of the domestic treatment of foreigners.

§4. Overview of International Legal Instruments Applicable in Portugal

I. Legally Binding Multilateral Instruments

61. As regards the protection of migrants' human rights, the most important sources can be found at supralegal level. Portugal has ratified almost every convention on the UN system. Particularly relevant in this context is that Portugal is party to the following instruments:

Instrument	*Date*	*Date of Entry into Force in Portugal*
Slavery Convention	1926	1927
Supplementary Convention on the Abolition of Slavery, the Slave Trade, and Institutions and Practices Similar to Slavery	1956	1959
Convention for the Suppression of the Traffic in Persons and of the Exploitation of the Prostitution of Others	1949	1992
Geneva Convention on the Status of Refugees	1951	1960
Convention Relating to the Status of Stateless Persons	1954	2012
Convention on the Reduction of Statelessness	1961	2012
International Convention on the Elimination of All Forms of Racial Discrimination	1965	1982

63. Provedor de Justiça, *Relatório à Assembleia da República 2018 e 2019 – Mecanismo Nacional de Prevenção,* available at http://www.provedor-jus.pt/?idc=107.

Instrument	*Date*	*Date of Entry into Force in Portugal*
International Covenant on Civil and Political Rights and Its Protocols	1966	1978
International Covenant on Economic, Social and Cultural Rights and Its Protocol	1966	1978
Convention on the Elimination of All Forms of Discrimination Against Women and Its Protocol	1979	1980
Convention Against Torture and Other Cruel, Inhuman or Degrading Treatment or Punishment and Its Optional Protocol	1984	1989
Convention on the Rights of the Child and Its Protocols	1989	1990
United Nations Convention Against Transnational Organized Crime and Its Protocol	2003	2004

62. Portugal is also party to several United Nations Educational, Scientific and Cultural Organization (UNESCO) Conventions which are pertinent to matters of inclusion of migrants in the territory:

Instrument	*Date*	*Date of Entry into Force in Portugal*
Convention Against Discrimination in Education and Its Protocol	1960	1981
Convention on the Protection and Promotion of the Diversity of Cultural Expressions	2005	2007

63. Some instruments of the International Labour Organization (ILO) relating to the migration context are also applicable in Portugal:

Instrument	*Date*	*Date of Entry into Force in Portugal*
Migration for Employment Convention (N. 97)	1949	1979
Convention on Discrimination on Employment and Occupation (N. 111)	1958	1960
Migrant Workers Convention (N. 143)	1975	1979

64. Several Council of Europe instruments with decisive impact on the domestic migration law were also ratified by Portugal, such as:

Instrument	*Date*	*Date of Entry into Force in Portugal*
European Convention on Human Rights (and Protocols n. 1, n. 4, n. 6, n. 7, n. 11, n. 13, n. 14)	1950	1978
European Agreement on Regulations Governing the Movement of Persons Between Member States of the Council of Europe	1958	1984
European Agreement on the Abolition of Visas for Refugees	1959	1981
European Convention on the Suppression of Terrorism	1977	1982
European Convention on the Legal Status of Migrant Workers	1977	1983
European Convention on Nationality	1977	2002
European Agreement on Transfer of Responsibility for Refugees	1980	1992
Convention for the Protection of Individuals with regard to Automatic Processing of Personal Data and Its Additional Protocol	1980	1992
European Convention for the Prevention of Torture and Inhuman or Degrading Treatment or Punishment and Its Protocols	1987	1990
Framework Convention for the Protection of National Minorities	1995	2002

Instrument	*Date*	*Date of Entry into Force in Portugal*
Revised European Social Charter and Its Protocol	1996	2002
Council of Europe Convention on Action Against Trafficking in Human Beings	2005	2008

65. Despite the large number of international instruments to which Portugal is party, some conventions with relevance to migration matters were not ratified. That is the case of the 1990 International Convention on the Protection of the Rights of All Migrant Workers and Members of Their Families. Like all other EU Member States, Portugal has been avoiding its signature – thus contributing to the lack of global success of this document. In the context of the Council of Europe, two other Conventions related to the rights of foreigners are not part of domestic law either: the 1992 Convention on the Participation of Foreigners in Public Life at Local Level and the 2006 European Convention on the Avoidance of Statelessness in Relation to State Succession.

II. Legally Binding CPLP Instruments

66. Besides being party to all the mentioned instruments, enacted under the auspices of international organizations, Portugal is also party to several treaties and agreements celebrated under the auspices of the Community of Portuguese-speaking Countries (CPLP).

67. The constitutive statements of the CPLP, signed in Lisbon on 17 July 1996, stated among the objectives to be pursued, 'the strengthening of ties (…) between all the Peoples who have the Portuguese Language as one of the foundations of their specific identity and, in this sense, to promote measures that facilitate the movement of the citizens of the Member Countries within the CPLP space', as well as 'coordination and reinforcement of cooperation in the field of immigration policies'.[64]

68. Some bilateral agreements have already pursued this aim: first, the Convention on Equal Rights and Duties of Brasilian and Portuguese citizens, signed on 7 September 1971 and revised by the Porto Seguro Agreement, signed on 22 April 2000, which provides for the exemption of visas for periods up to ninety days for entries for cultural, business, journalistic or tourist purposes (Article 7). In addition, several agreements were signed in Brasilia on 30 July 2002, aimed at facilitating

64. Declaração Constitutiva da CPLP, available in https://www.cplp.org/id-3869.aspx.

movement within the CPLP space. It is worth mentioning in particular the agreements on temporary visas for medical treatment (approved by Decree n. 32/2003, of 30 July), the agreement on the granting of multiple-entry visas for certain categories of people, approved by Decree n. 34/2003, of 30 July (which provides for a special visa granting regime for business people, professionals, scientists, researchers, sportsmen, journalists and artists from CPLP countries), and finally the Treaty of Friendship, Cooperation and Consultation between the Portuguese Republic and the Federative Republic of Brazil, which provides for special rules of entry and permanence and the possibility of granting equal status to citizens of one of the countries who have their usual residence in the other.

69. In 2021, Member States of the Community of Portuguese-speaking countries signed the Agreement on Mobility, aimed at providing 'greater mobility and circulation within the CPLP area'. It is a framework agreement that establishes the legal basis on which Member States will be able to sign additional mobility partnerships, having the freedom to choose the mobility modalities they intend to apply. Several types are indeed foreseen, such as the CPLP Short-Term Stay, the CPLP Temporary Stay, the CPLP Residence Visa and the CPLP Residence. It foresees, thus, a flexible and variable system that meets the particularities relating to each State.

III. Global Compact for Safe, Orderly and Regular Migration

70. The approval of the Global Compact for Safe, Orderly and Regular Migration, in Marrakech in 2018, indicated a new international approach to international migration management.[65] Eight months after the endorsement of the Global Compact, the Portuguese Government adopted a national plan aimed at implementing it in the national territory.[66] This plan follows the twenty-three-objective framework of the Global Compact, in order to cover all relevant dimensions of the migration phenomenon. Several implementation measures are defined for each objective, identifying the respective implementation deadlines and the governmental areas involved. The Plan is therefore conceived as an operational document, oriented to practical and accurate results. It is organized according to twenty-three objectives:

(1) to collect and use accurate information on migration for evidence-based policymaking;
(2) to minimize adverse and structural factors that force people to leave their home country;[67]

65. *See*, on the Global Compact, AA.VV., *The relevance of migration for the 2030 Agenda for Sustainable Development: The Global Compact for Safe, Orderly and Regular Migration*, Constança Urbano de Sousa (org.), 2019.
66. Resolução do Conselho de Ministros n. 141/2019.
67. In this context, important measures are foreseen, such as the adoption, in a cross-cutting manner, measures to promote sustainable development, including through Strategic Cooperation Programme, Non-governmental Development Organizations' Project Finance Lines, Cooperation Agreements, among others.

(3) to provide accurate and up-to-date information at all stages of migration;[68]
(4) to ensure that all migrants have proof of their legal identity and proper documentation;[69]
(5) to foster legal migration pathways;[70]
(6) to facilitate a fair and ethical recruitment of migrant workers and safeguard conditions that guarantee decent work;[71]
(7) to address and reduce migration vulnerabilities;[72]
(8) to save lives and undertake coordinated international efforts to deal with missing migrants;[73]
(9) to strengthen the transnational response to illegal migrants' smuggling;[74]
(10) to prevent, combat and eradicate the trafficking of human beings in the context of international migration;[75]
(11) to manage borders in an integrated, secure and coordinated manner, namely through collaboration with neighbouring countries and through the development of joint inspections;
(12) to strengthen security and predictability in screening, assessment and referral of migrants at the border, namely through the development of management systems;

---

68. This information is expected to be provided through the Ministry of Foreign Affairs' website, which centralizes information on migration policy, namely in matters such as obtaining visas, labour legislation, professional qualification, internships and education, costs and living conditions, reception and integration of migrants and answers to frequently asked questions. A widely distributed national and international *Welcome Guide for Migrants* is also foreseen. Finally, the Government shall also be responsible for promoting information sessions on the mechanisms available for regular and organized migration, including the risks associated with illegal migration. These sessions shall be organized prior to the migrants' departure from their countries of origin and in cooperation with local authorities, diplomatic and consular missions and civil society organizations.
69. Some measures are drawn in this regard, such as: (1) to simplify visa and residence permit procedures by creating a one-stop shop at consulates, so that potential immigrants can access the services they need in one place; (2) to promote the rights of migrant children in schools; and (3) to pay particular attention to especially vulnerable persons.
70. In particular, by celebrating bilateral agreements, namely with Portuguese-speaking countries, and by promoting circular migration and fostering family reunification processes. The Plan also mentions the creation of new types of visas, such as the 'StartupVisa' and the 'TechVisa', as well as other measures aimed at promoting initiatives to raise human capital. The elimination of intermediaries associated with illegal migration and facilitating are also highlighted.
71. For this purpose, the Plan mentions the need to make effective the regularization procedures already foreseen in the law, and also to enhance labour inspection activities, reevaluate the quotas for the purpose of labour migration and develop the mechanisms aimed at assisting migrants to be included in the labour market (labour inclusion delegations).
72. Several measures are foreseen in this regard, namely in what regards the migrants' access to justice, developing support and care to special vulnerable migrants, provide several professionals with training on identification of potential victims of trafficking of human beings, supporting the creation of migrants' associations and finally making the family reunification more effective.
73. For this purpose, the enhancement of the cooperation between the institutions which are responsible for maritime rescue is foreseen.
74. Namely through police cooperation with the countries of origin and transit.
75. Important measures are designed for such purpose, such as the definition of procedures for the prevention, detention and protection of child victims of trafficking in human beings, celebration of partnerships with countries of origin and transit, reinforcement and training of personnel on victim's identification.

(13) to use detention only as a measure of last resort and work to find alternative measures;[76]
(14) strengthening consular protection, assistance and cooperation throughout the migration cycle, also focusing on Portuguese Migrants living abroad;
(15) providing access to basic services for migrants, namely through the local services for migrants' support, and developing the rights to healthcare and housing;
(16) to empower migrants and societies to achieve full social inclusion and cohesion;[77]
(17) to fight against all forms of discrimination and promote fact-based public discourse in building perceptions about migration, including through professional training of journalists;
(18) investment in skills and mutual recognition of abilities and qualifications;
(19) developing ways for migrants and diasporas to contribute fully to sustainable development in all countries, including programmes aimed at attracting Portuguese emigrants to maintain and reinforce ties with the Portuguese community, including through trade, investments, business and research activities;
(20) to promote faster, safer and cheaper remittance transfers and foster financial inclusion for migrants;
(21) to cooperate for safe and decent return and readmission facilitation and sustainable reintegration, namely through the development of links with the International Organization for Migration and bilateral agreements;
(22) to design mechanisms for portability of social security rights and vested benefits, and
(23) to strengthen international cooperation and global partnerships for safe, organized and regular migration, namely through the participation in international fora and the Community of Portuguese-speaking Countries.

IV. Importance of International Instruments in the Domestic Legal Order

71. International treaties ratified by Portugal play a very important role in the domestic order. That role is two-fold. First, as already mentioned, according to Article 8(2) of the Portuguese Constitution, they are immediately applicable in the national legal order, with no need to be transposed by a specific law. While being applicable in the national legal order, provisions of international and European law do not lose their international nature: the Portuguese Law does not convert them into domestic law. International law norms can be directly invoked before courts, and all public bodies may decide directly on the basis of an applicable Treaty.

---

76. For this purpose, the Plan foresees measures aimed at informing and facilitating the procedures for regularization of irregularly staying migrants. However, nothing is said as regards the detention of those whose entry into the territory is denied or detention of asylum seekers.

77. Very diverse measures are planned, such as the development of intercultural, interreligious and inclusive education programmes, the increase of classes on Portuguese language. Access to microcredit is also foreseen, with the aim to strengthen the inclusion of migrant communities.

72. Moreover, Article 16 of the Portuguese Constitution 'opens the door' of the fundamental rights catalogue to rights enshrined in international instruments by claiming that: 'The fundamental rights enshrined in the Constitution shall *not exclude any others set out in applicable international laws* and legal rules.' Even as regards rights that are expressly mentioned in the Constitution, Article 16(2) highlights that they 'must be interpreted in harmony with the Universal Declaration of Human Rights'. The Constitutional Court understands this provision broadly, as meaning that such rights must be read in harmony with *other international instruments of Human Rights Law* to which Portugal is part. As these sources of law are interpreted by specific institutions, namely the European Court of Human Rights and the Court of Justice of the European Union (CJEU), one must bear in mind the correspondent case law while applying these instruments and interpret Portuguese fundamental rights accordingly.[78]

73. Second, obligations stemming from the international conventions, in particular those which have monitoring bodies, often lead to important amendments to the legislation. If this can be obvious in the context of Treaties with clear obligations that lead to recommendations from the monitoring bodies, it is also true as regards decisions taken in individual cases, even where Portugal is not involved. The clearest example is the case law of the ECtHR. For instance, to respect the right to family and private life, guaranteed in Article 8 of the ECHR, and to avoid convictions (like those that were being applied to other State Parties), Portugal decided to reinforce the protection awarded to this right in Article 135 IL, foreseeing several limits to expulsions of migrants, in order to protect their family and private life – and, thus, avoid convictions from the ECtHR.

78. On this topic, *see* David Szymczak, *La Convention Européenne des Droits de l'Homme et le Juge Constitutionnel National,* Bruylant, 2007, p. 162 e ss., and Constance Grewe. Cf. 'Le Juge Constitutionnel et l'interprétation Européenne', AA.VV., L'interprétation de la Convention Européenne des Droits de l'Homme, Fréderic Sudre (dir.) Bruylant, 1998, p. 199. This understanding is not very recent and was affirmed, for example, in Ruling n. 222/90 de 20/06/1990, where the Constitutional Court interpreted the right to access to Courts in the light of Art. 6 of the ECHR.

Part I. Border Control and Entry

Chapter 1. Organization of Border Control

74. Portugal signed the Convention implementing the Schengen Agreement (hereinafter 'Implementing Convention') on 25 June 1991. Subsequently, as of 26 March 1995, the Schengen acquis was fully applied in Portugal.

75. Pursuant to the EU legislation, the Portuguese IL defines 'external borders' as the borders with third States, airports (with respect to flights originating in or destined for the territories of States not bound by the Implementing Convention), as well as seaports, except regarding connections in Portuguese territory and regular transhipment connections between States Parties to the Schengen Implementing Convention (Article 3(1)(o)). As for 'internal borders', they encompass the common land border with Spain, as well as airports (with respect to flights exclusively and directly to or from the territories of States Parties to the Implementing Convention) as well as seaports, about the regular connections of ships carrying out transhipment operations exclusively from or destined for other ports in the territories of the States Parties to the Implementing Convention, with no call at ports outside those territories. As other State Parties to the Schengen Agreement, Portugal is bound to remove all obstacles to fluid traffic flow at road crossing-points at internal borders, in particular any speed limits not exclusively based on road-safety considerations (Article 24 of the Schengen Borders Code – hereinafter 'SBC').[79] Third-country nationals who have entered the Portuguese territory must inform national authorities of their presence. This is not applicable to residence permit holders nor to foreigners who will be installed in a hotel or other tourist accommodation.[80]

76. Article 6 IL sets forth that entry into and exit from Portuguese territory shall take place in the recognized border posts during working hours, and every person who enters or leaves the territory must be subjected to border controls whenever they come from, or head to, States that are not Parties to the Implementing Convention. The same applies, naturally, to those individuals travelling in a flight that

79. Regulation (EU) 2016/399 of the European Parliament and of the Council of 9 Mar. 2016 on a Union Code on the rules governing the movement of persons across borders (SBC).
80. However, in this case, they are required to fill out an accommodation form. In case third-country nationals fail to respect these duties, they incur an administrative offence, and may be subjected to the payment of a fine (from EUR 100 to EUR 2,000).

makes internal stopovers, yet has departed from, or heads to, States that are not Parties to the Implementing Convention. Moreover, border checks can be carried out on board ships while travelling, following a request of the ship's captain or of the shipping agent and on payment of a fee.[81]

77. According to Article 8 SBC, all persons shall undergo a minimum check aimed at proving their identities, based on a mere presentation of their travel documents. This check shall be minimum when EU citizens are considered. In these cases, the control only involves a rapid and straightforward verification of information on stolen, misappropriated, lost, and invalidated documents or fraud. However, on a non-systematic basis, border guards may consult national and European databases in order to ensure that such person does not represent a genuine, present and sufficiently serious threat to the internal security, public policy, international relations or a threat to the public health of the Member State.

78. As for third-country nationals, they shall be subject to thorough checks. Articles 9 and following IL develop the SBC's rules in this realm. Border guards must analyse several factors, such as the conditions for entry, documents authorizing residence, travel documents, visas, stamps on the travel documents, the purpose of the stay, the existence of sufficient means of subsistence and the means to return to the country of origin. Border guards may consult the SIS to evaluate whether the person represents a menace to the public order or national security. If the third-country national holds a visa, border guards must verify the identity of its holder and the authenticity of the visa, by consulting the Visa Information System (VIS) in accordance with Article 18 of Regulation (EC) n. 767/2008. The SBC foresees that such thorough checks must be carried out in a private area if requested by the third-country national. All persons who might be subjected to a thorough second-line check shall be given written information in a language they understand or may reasonably be presumed to understand, or in another effective way, on the purpose of, and the procedure for, such a check. The third-country national may request the name or service identification number of the border guards carrying out the thorough second-line check, the name of the border crossing point and the date on which the border was crossed.

81. After performing the exit check of a ship or vessel, SEF issues an exit clearance, without which the ship may not leave the harbour.

Chapter 2. Right to Enter the Country

79. As in other States, we cannot strictly speak of 'a right to enter' in Portugal, as there is no 'human right to immigration'.[82] The Constitutional Court has already confirmed that a 'fundamental right to immigration' is not protected under the Constitution.[83] But we can also argue that the law does not protect such right: the IL (as the EU instruments) does not set forth *conditions for enjoying a subjective right to entry.* Instead, it establishes minimum conditions that must be mandatorily respected to have access to the territory – *but only if the authorities so authorize.* That is to say that, even if the foreigner fulfils all the required conditions, they may still be denied entry on discretionary grounds. The exceptions may only concern those cases where the migrant wants to enter in order to enforce a human or fundamental right – e.g., family reunification, right to asylum. In this latter situation, the State's sovereignty may indeed preclude a discretionary decision on entry refusal.[84]

80. Moreover, those who enjoy a fundamental right to free movement are also subjected to other rules, as we will see further below in Part II, Chapter 1, §1. Thus, this chapter is only applicable to those who, falling in the realm of IL, do not have a 'right to enter' the Portuguese territory as such.

§1. Conditions for Entering the Territory

81. In order to enter the Portuguese territory, foreign citizens must fulfil several conditions, which we will address separately.

I. Travel Document

82. First, foreign citizens must hold the necessary travel documents (Article 9 IL) in order to be admitted to enter the national territory. The period of validity of the travel document must be larger than the duration of the stay, exception made to foreign residents who are reentering the country. Some foreign citizens are exempted from presenting a travel document and may enter with a simple identity card or equivalent document: that is the case of nationals of States with which Portugal has signed international conventions for that purpose, of citizens covered by relevant conventions between the States Parties to the North Atlantic Treaty, of

82. *See*, on this topic, Ana Rita Gil, *Imigração e Direitos Humanos*, Petrony, 2017, pp. 131 et seq.
83. In its ruling 442/93, the Constitutional Court mentioned that 'foreigners do not have constitutionally guaranteed, for example, the right of entry, nor the right of residence or establishment in Portugal (*maxime* the right to settle here)'.
84. *See*, on this topic, Ana Rita Gil, *Imigração e Direitos Humanos* … , cit., pp. 292 et seq.

holders of a *laissez-passer* issued by authorities of their home countries,[85] of holders of a flight licence or a crew membership certificate as provided for by the Convention on International Civil Aviation, of holders of a seafarer's identity document as provided for in ILO's n. 108 Convention when on duty and, finally, of nationals of States with which Portugal has international conventions under which entry is permitted with a maritime identity card when on duty.

83. Every foreigner – including minors – must present a valid passport to enter the Portuguese territory (Article 9 IL). The principle of 'one person – one passport' has been in force in Portugal since 2001. However, the application of such principle could be improved by inserting the name of the child's legal guardian in the passport. The consultation of databases at the disposal of the SEF does not always provide enough information to establish the minor's parenthood or legal guardianship.[86] Children willing to enter or exit the national territory must present a written authorization of the legal guardian, authorizing the trip. For that purpose, SEF must confront the children's ID, which, in principle, mentions their parents' names. However, the legal guardian may not correspond to one of the child's parents.

II. Valid Visa

84. Second, foreign citizens willing to enter the territory must hold a valid visa – which must be adequate to the purpose of the entry (Article 10 IL). Valid visas are issued by the Portuguese competent authorities or by other States Parties to the Schengen Agreement. A visa may be annulled by the issuing authority abroad, by the SEF on the national territory or at the border posts when the visa holder has been the subject of an alert for purposes of refusal of entry in the SIS or in SEF's Integrated Information System, or if the foreign citizen has provided false information in the visa application.

85. Some categories of foreign citizens are exempted from holding a visa. That is the case of: (i) foreign citizens holding a valid residence permit, an extension of stay permit or an identification document issued by the Portuguese Ministry of Foreign Affairs (among others, diplomatic or consular agents accredited in Portugal) and (ii) foreign citizens falling under the scope of visa-exemption international conventions to which Portugal is a party or any other special scheme created under the CPLP Agreement on Mobility. Article 29 IL also exempts students who are third-country nationals and reside on the territory of other EU Member States from holding a visa, provided that they are travelling in the context of a school trip properly

85. A *laissez-passer* may also be issued by countries that represent them. It is valid solely for transit, and, when issued in Portuguese territory, only allows its holder to exit the country. Foreign citizens may also leave Portuguese territory if in possession of a safe-conduct or when holding a travel document for purposes of expulsion.

86. Ana Rita Gil & Nuno Piçarra, *Study on the legal requirements specific to minors travelling alone or accompanied, legally entering or leaving the Member States, focusing on EU/AC minors and with a separate section on third-country minors*, Ramboll, 2012.

organized by an officially recognized educational establishment. According to Article 6 SBC, foreigners not subjected to a visa requirement may move freely within the territories of the Schengen States for a maximum period of 90 days within 180 days period following the date of first entry, provided that they fulfil the other entry conditions.

86. Finally, the State may grant a visa at the border for humanitarian reasons or national interest. This possibility corresponds to a sovereign power of the State, which may provide protection to whoever it wishes.

87. The Portuguese IL foresees four types of visas: short-stay visas (which correspond to the so-called Schengen visas), temporary visas, residence visas and visas for job search.

88. Schengen visas are 'uniform visas' valid for the entire territory of the Schengen Area and may be issued for visits not exceeding three months. Temporary visas (also known as 'long-stay visas' under the Schengen Implementing Convention) are valid from ninety days to one year. Residence visas are issued for periods of more than one year. Finally, the new visas for job search are valuable for 120 days, extendable for another 60 days (Article 57-A IL).

89. Some rules apply to all types of visas. Pursuant to Article 52 IL, visas shall only be granted to third-country nationals who: (i) were not the object of a removal measure and the reentry ban period has not yet passed; (ii) are not the subject of an alert in the SIS[87] for purposes of refusing entry; (iii) are not subject of an alert in SEF's Integrated Information System for purposes of refusing entry; (iv) hold sufficient means of subsistence, as defined by the Government; (v) hold a valid travel document; (vi) are covered by a travel insurance; (vii) holds a parental or guardian's authorization, in case of minors who are not accompanied by the legal guardians. For the granting of a short-stay visa, a temporary-stay visa or a visa for job search, the applicant must also present a ticket for the return travel. Finally, a visa may be refused to any person that may represent a serious threat to the public order, public safety, or public health. Foreigners must also declare the purpose of their entry into the national territory.

---

87. The SIS is regulated by Regulation n. 2018/1861 of the European Parliament and of the Council of 28 Nov. 2018. According to its Art. 24, the Member States shall enter an alert for refusal of entry and stay when the presence of that third-country national on its territory poses a threat to public policy, to public security or to national security, and the Member State has consequently adopted a judicial or administrative decision in to refuse entry and stay and issued a national alert for refusal of entry and stay; or the Member State has issued an entry ban in accordance with procedures respecting Directive 2008/115/EC in respect of a third-country national. The first situations arises where the third-country national has been convicted in a Member State of an offence carrying a penalty involving the deprivation of liberty of at least one year; there are serious grounds for believing that a third-country national has committed a serious criminal offence, including a terrorist offence, or there are clear indications of his or her intention to commit such an offence in the territory of a Member State; or a third-country national has circumvented or attempted to circumvent the law on entry into and stay on the territory of the Member States.

90. The 2022 amendments to the IL have created special conditions for granting visas to nationals of Member States of the Community of Portuguese-speaking countries that have Mobility Agreements with Portugal. According to the new Article 52-A IL, in those cases, visas shall be issued without a prior opinion of the SEF and the competent services may only refuse them if there is indication of an entry and stay ban in the SIS, or if the applicants are minors and do not have the necessary authorizations signed by their guardians. This amendment has created a real 'subjective right to a visa' for these categories of persons, as consular authorities may only deny the requested visas in the expressly mentioned cases.

91. Apart from these general rules, special rules apply to the different types of visas.

III. Short-Term Visas

92. As with other EU Member States, the regulation of the Schengen visa falls under the competence of the European Union – being addressed by the Community Code on Visas (generally known as Visa Code – VC).[88] The Schengen visa is an authorization issued by a Member State for the purpose of an airport stopover, transit or short stay in the territory of one or more Member States. Regulation (EU) 2018/1806 sets forth the list of countries whose citizens need to hold a valid visa to enter into a Schengen State.[89]

93. The Schengen visa is intended for short stays of up to 90 days in each period of 180 days and can be granted for the purposes of tourism, family visits, business, seasonal work, transit, among others. Article 51 IL sets forth that a short-stay visa is a visa that enables its holder to enter Portuguese territory for any (legitimate) purposes that does not justify the granting of another type of visa, such as the transit to the other Schengen States, tourism and visiting or accompanying family members who hold a temporary-stay visa. A short-stay visa may be granted with a validity period of one year and for one or more entries, provided that neither the length of a continuous stay nor the total length of successive stays exceeds 90 days in 180 days to be counted from the date of the first entry through an external border. In duly substantiated cases, 'and when it serves the best interests of the Country', a multiple-entry visa for one year or more may be granted to certain persons by decision of the members of the Government responsible for internal and foreign affairs.

94. Foreign citizens who have been admitted under a short-stay visa not issued at the border checkpoints (or have been admitted into the country without the need

---

88. Regulation (EC) No 810/2009 of the European Parliament and of the Council of 13 Jul. 2009 establishing a Community Code on Visas.
89. Regulation (EU) 2018/1806 of the European Parliament and of the Council of 14 Nov. 2018 listing the third countries whose nationals must be in possession of visas when crossing the external borders and those whose nationals are exempt from that requirement (codification).

for that visa) and wish to remain in Portugal for a period which exceeds the one initially allowed may be granted an extension of stay up to 90 days, with the possibility of extension for another ninety-day period (Article 72(1)(d) IL).

IV. Temporary Visas

95. Article 54 IL foresees the so-called temporary visas which, not being short-term visas, enable third-country nationals to stay in Portuguese territory provisionally, until one year. These visas can only be awarded for the purposes foreseen in the IL: (a) to pursue a medical treatment in official or officially recognized health establishments or to accompany a family member for that purpose; (b) to nationals of States Parties to the World Trade Organization, within the scope of providing services or taking part in vocational training in Portuguese territory; (c) to carry out an employed or self-employed activity of temporary nature, in cases where the duration does not exceed six months (in the case of an employed activity, the stay is granted for the time of the contract's duration); (d) to conduct a scientific research in research centres, a teaching activity in a higher education establishment, or a highly qualified activity for less than one year; (e) to undertake an amateur sporting activity certified by the respective federation, provided that the club or sports association provides accommodation and healthcare; (f) to stay in the Portuguese territory for a period of more than three months, in certain exceptional and duly substantiated cases, including for the purposes of pursuing studies in an education establishment, a pupil exchange scheme, an unpaid internship or a voluntary activity during one year or less, for the purpose of compliance with international agreements in the framework of the World Trade Organization or other international conventions and agreements of which Portugal is a party; (g) to develop seasonal work for a period longer than 90 days; (h) to attend educational or vocational training.

96. The 2022 amendments have introduced two new temporary visas to Article 54 IL. The first type is the temporary visa for remote work. This visa is aimed at allowing persons who work remotely in foreign companies, or who are self-employed and work remotely, to temporarily reside in Portugal and work from there. The other new type of temporary visa is aimed at promoting the right to family unity to those who come to Portugal with a temporary visa. Family members of those who hold a temporary visa – of any kind, with the sole exception of visa for seasonal work – may, themselves, be issued with a temporary visa for the mere purpose of accompanying their family. With this new type of visa, Portugal shows its commitment to the protection of the right to family life, independently of the migrants' aim to establish permanent residence in the territory.

V. Residence Visas

97. The residence visa enables its holder to enter Portuguese territory with a view to apply for a residence permit. Such a visa is valid for two entries into the

Portuguese territory and enables its holder to remain there for a period of four months. A residence visa can be granted to a third-country national for the following purposes:

(a) Visa for taking up employment (Article 59).
(b) Visa for taking up a self-employed activity or for entrepreneurs (Article 60 IL).
(c) Visa for conducting scientific research in an officially recognized research centre (whenever the third-country national has been admitted in a higher education at doctoral level or as researcher) and for the purpose of teaching in a higher education establishment or for conducting a highly qualified activity (whenever the third-country national has an employment contract, a promissory employment contract, an invitation letter or a contract for provision of services) (Article 61 IL).
(d) Visa for highly qualified activity, provided that the third-country national holds an actual or promissory employment contract with a validity of at least one year, establishing an annual remuneration of at least 1.5 times the average gross annual salary or three times the Social Support Index, or as regards regulated professions, that he or she holds the professional qualifications required to access and carry out the occupation (Article 61-A IL).
(e) Visa for the purpose of residing in Portugal while remotely working to foreign entities (Article 61-B).
(f) Visa for purposes of studying, participating in a secondary level pupil exchange scheme, in an unremunerated traineeship or voluntary service, provided that, in the case of being a minor, the third-country national holds an authorization from whoever holds parental responsibilities to remain in Portugal for the period of stay; the third-country national who applies for a residence visa for obtaining a residence permit for the purpose of carrying out an unremunerated traineeship must be accepted as trainee by a company or an officially acknowledged vocational training institution (Article 62 IL).
(g) Visa for the participation as a student in higher education in an EU or bilateral exchange programme or as student who has been admitted in a Member State for no less than two years and applies to continue in Portugal a part of the course (Article 63 IL).
(h) Visa for the purpose of family reunification (Article 64 IL).

According to Article 24 IR, a resident visa can also be requested by third-country nationals who are retired, pensioners, who live on income from personal property, real estate, intellectual property, or financial investments.

VI. Visas for Job Search

98. The 2022 legal amendments introduced a new, very important type of visa: the visas for job search. This measure aimed at opening new channels for legal immigration, which can be seen as an important measure for fighting against smuggling and trafficking of human beings. According to the new Article 57.º-A IL, this visa allows their holders to enter and remain in Portugal for the purposes of finding work. It is only valid for one entry. It also allows them to work, until the end of the visa or until acquiring a residence permit. The visa is valid for 120 days, extendable for 60 days more. For this purpose, the visa automatically sets forth a date for a meeting with the Foreigners and Borders Service after the end of the initial period. In cases where the foreigners have concluded a work contract during this period, they will have the right to apply for a residence permit, provided that they fulfil the general conditions for having residence in Portugal. On the contrary, if migrants failed to find a job, they shall abandon the country and may only request a new visa for job search after one year.

VII. Means of Subsistence

99. Foreigners must also prove that they have sufficient means of subsistence to remain in the Portuguese territory during the period of stay. The Portaria n. 1563/2007 sets forth the amount of these means of subsistence, which amounts to EUR 75 for the entry, plus EUR 40 for each day of stay (Article 2(3)). All income shall be considered, including grants, scholarships, contracts or promises of employment contract (Article 12-A IR).

100. Foreign citizens who prove that they have accommodation and food during the stay, or who present a term of responsibility from a sponsor, may be exempted from this requirement. The acceptance of the sponsor's term of responsibility depends on a proof of their financial capacity (Article 12 IR).

VIII. Purposes and Conditions of Stay

101. Article 13 IR sets forth that, whenever deemed necessary to prove the objective and conditions of stay, border authorities may require adequate proof from the foreign citizen of the stay's purpose.

IX. Entry Refusals

102. Foreigners who do not fulfil the conditions mentioned above are refused entry to the Portuguese territory. Entry shall also be refused to those who have been the object of an alert in the SIS or in SEF's Integrated Information System[90] for that

90. Alerts for purposes of refusing entry are entered into SEF's Integrated Information System, regarding foreign citizens: (a) who have been subject to a forced return or expulsion measure; (b) who have been returned into another country under a readmission agreement; (c) in relation to whom there are strong evidences of having committed serious criminal acts; (d) in relation to whom there are clear indications that they intend to commit serious criminal acts or pose a serious threat to the public order, national security or to the international relations of a European Union Member State, as well as to those of States that have adopted the Implementing Convention; (e) of citizens who have been sentenced through a final and binding decision to imprisonment for more than one year, even if such sentence has not been served; or who have been subject to identical punishment more than once, even if the enforcement of the penalty has been suspended (Art. 33 IL).

purpose, as well as to those who have been indicated in the SIS for the purpose of being returned to their country of origin and were also object of an entry ban (Article 32 IL). However, the latter can be authorized to enter the territory if they show that they have left the territory of the Member States in compliance with the respective return decision and have completed the period of the ban on entry and permanence.

103. Moreover, Article 32 IL also foresees that entry shall be denied to those who represent a danger or a serious threat to public order, national security, public health[91] or to the international relations of EU Member States, as well as to those of States that have adopted the Implementing Convention. Protection against these threats is a permanent 'exception clause' in legal regimes concerning foreigners' entry or residence in the territory. However, they afford a large scope of discretion to border authorities, and do not provide legal certainty to applicants. This discretionary power may, however, also work the other way around. As already mentioned, according to Article 5 SBC, States have the right to authorize entry into their territories to those who do not fulfil the mentioned conditions, on humanitarian or national interest grounds, or even due to international obligations.

104. Following the ECtHR's case law with respect to private and family life enshrined in Article 8 of the ECHR, the Portuguese Law sets forth other limits to decisions on entry refusals. Some categories of persons cannot be refused to enter the territory, precisely due to their rights to family or private life (Article 36 IL). That is the case of: (a) foreign citizens who were born in Portuguese territory and reside regularly therein; (b) foreigners who are parents of minor Portuguese children of or foreign children with legal residence in Portugal, over whom they effectively exercise parental responsibilities and to whom they provide for their livelihood and education. In the original version of this provision, these limits had an absolute nature – *irrespective of the reason for the refusal*, these persons would always be guaranteed the right to enter the territory. However, due to security measures that were introduced following the 2015 Charlie Hebdo terrorist attacks in France, this provision was amended. So, when more serious threats to public order or national security are concerned, even these persons may be denied access to the Portuguese territory, irrespective of their right to family and private life. That may happen, according to Article 36 IL, if the foreigner was subject to a forced return or expulsion measure; there is strong evidence that he or she has committed serious criminal acts or intends to commit serious criminal acts or poses a serious threat to the public order, national security or to the international relations. However, in these

91. The refusal of entry on grounds of public health may only be based on diseases that have been defined in the applicable instruments of the World Health Organization, or on other infectious or contagious parasitic diseases which have been object to protection measures in the national territory. A medical exam may be required to a third-country national in order to establish that he/she does not have any of the above-mentioned diseases, as well as to determine any adequate medical measures (Art. 32(2) and (3) IL).

cases, obviously, the State is still bound to balance the respect for the alien's private and family life with the public interests at stake.[92]

X. Entry of Minors

105. In order to prevent trafficking of children, the IL sets forth that border authorities must refuse entry into the country to foreign citizens who are less than 18 years old when not accompanied by their legal guardian, unless there is a Portuguese citizen or a legal resident who is responsible for their stay. In the latter case, there must be an appropriate valid authorization issued by the legal guardian attesting that this person may take care of the child. All other elements must also be evaluated, and SEF must proceed with all procedures aimed at identifying the child and, if necessary, confirm the situation with the legal guardians (Article 31 IL and Article 8 IR).[93] In case of entry refusal, the child must be returned by the carrier to the country of origin and handed over to their legal guardian, or to an organization to whom they can be entrusted. It is our opinion that these rules must be read together with the principles on protection of unaccompanied minors according to which the public authorities shall not send back unaccompanied minors before it is confirmed that they will be received by their legal guardians in the country of origin.

106. Following this general rule, entry into the territory must also be refused if the legal guardian or someone who is duly in charge is not authorized to enter the country. The IL, however, sets forth that this rule may be derogated in 'very exceptional circumstances', although it does not define these circumstances (Article 31(2) IL). Similarly, if the foreign minor is not accepted into the national territory, the entry of the accompanying adult must also be refused.

107. However, Article 31(4) IL sets forth that both Portuguese and foreign children who are not accompanied by those who hold parental responsibilities or legal guardianship cannot be authorized to leave the territory, unless they carry an authorization, with the signature of the responsible person legally certified.

§2. Administrative Procedures and Documents

108. It is important to analyse the administrative procedures and the documentary requirements regarding entry into the Portuguese territory on two different moments: (1) the procedures at the border and (2) the procedures when issuing a visa.

92. *See*, for example, *Maslov v. Austria*, 23/06/2008, app. n. 1638/03. On this topic, *see* Ana Rita Gil, *Imigração e Direitos Humanos …* , cit., p. 486 and following.
93. In cases where minors are involved in organized trips or youth exchange programmes, there may be an exception to this rule.

I. Administrative Procedures and Documents at the Border

109. Border guards are the first administrative interaction that foreigners have when entering the territory. They are responsible for confirming that all requirements for the entry are fulfilled, and also for checking whether there are any grounds for refusing the entry.

110. According to Article 8 SBC, all persons undergo a minimum check in order to establish their identities on the basis of the production or presentation of their travel documents: 'such a minimum check shall consist of a rapid and straightforward verification, where appropriate by using technical devices and by consulting, in the relevant databases, information exclusively on stolen, misappropriated, lost and invalidated documents, of the validity of the document authorising the legitimate holder to cross the border and of the presence of signs of falsification or counterfeiting'. When in doubt as to the authenticity of documents issued by Portuguese authorities, SEF may access the information available in the application that led to the issuing of a passport, identity card, or any other document used for crossing the borders (Article 35 IL).

111. The minimum check shall be the rule for persons enjoying the right of free movement under EU law. By contrast, third-country nationals are subjected to thorough checks both on entry and exit. Thorough checks on entry shall comprise verification of the conditions governing entry explained above and, where applicable, of documents authorizing residence and the pursuit of a professional activity. According to Article 8(3) SBC, this shall include a detailed examination of, e.g., the entry and exit stamps on the travel document, verification of the point of departure and the destination, sufficient means of subsistence for the duration and purpose of the intended stay, for the return and means of transport. Such verification shall include direct consultation of the data and alerts on persons and, where necessary, objects included in the SIS and in national data files. If the third-country national holds a visa, the thorough checks on entry shall also comprise verification of the identity of the holder of the visa and of the authenticity of the visa through the consultation of the VIS.

112. When the refusal of entry is grounded on the presentation of a travel document that is false, forged, someone else's, or fraudulently obtained, it will be seized and forwarded to the national or foreign competent authority, in accordance with the applicable provisions. In all cases where there is doubt as to the identity of the holder of the visa and/or the authenticity of the visa, the VIS shall also be consulted (Article 8(3) SBC).

113. Lack or forgery of the necessary documents, an alert in the SIS or in the SEF's Integrated Information System, as well as a threat to public order, national security, and national health or to the international relations of EU Member States, as well as to those of States that have adopted the Implementing Convention leads, as mentioned above, to an entry refusal – unless the State decides otherwise on humanitarian or national interest grounds, or due to international duties.

114. Traditionally it was considered that the foreigner would not be recognized as a holder of specific rights when faced with an entry refusal decision made at the border, as it was traditionally understood that the State was exercising a sovereign prerogative. Only basic human rights should be respected (such as prohibition of torture, or the right to life). This opinion was aggravated by the idea that, at the border, the foreigner had not entered yet into the territory and, thus, other fundamental and legal rights protected domestically would not yet be applicable to them. These theories began to be questioned following the case law of the ECtHR, namely as regards pushbacks at the borders.[94] This case law opened the door to considerations that not only minimum human rights but also procedural rights should be guaranteed to migrants at the borders.

115. As for other 'core' human rights, the SBC expressly sets forth that 'border guards shall, in the performance of their duties, fully respect human dignity, in particular in cases involving vulnerable persons'. Any measures taken in the performance of their duties shall be proportionate to the objectives pursued by such measures. Moreover, it forbids discrimination on grounds of sex, racial or ethnic origin, religion or belief, disability, age, or sexual orientation during border checks (Article 7). This last prohibition undoubtedly aims to fight against racial, ethnic and religious profiling. Human dignity; prohibition of torture; right to life, personal integrity, dignity; and prohibition of discrimination would be minimum guarantees that would derive from Human Rights Law, independently from any written legal norm. As in Portugal International Law Conventions are directly applicable, foreigners would always benefit from these rights. The same could be said for the right to a fair procedure.[95] However, procedural rights would require a certain level of detailed normative detail – which is enshrined in the SBC.

116. According to Article 14 SBC, an entry may only be refused by a substantiated decision stating the precise reasons for the refusal. The decision shall be taken by an authority empowered by national law – the SEF, in Portugal. Although the SBC sets forth that the decision shall be automatically effective, the Portuguese IL requires, according to the general administrative procedures' regulations, that the decision is only issued following a hearing of the foreign citizen (Article 38). This hearing represents, for all purposes and effects, a hearing of the interested party, and shall be immediately reported to the diplomatic or consular representation of that person's country of origin.

117. The decision shall be notified to the person in a standard form, as set out in Annex V, Part B SBC. The IL expressly sets forth that the notification shall be made in a language that the foreigner presumably understands, with the indication of the grounds that lead to such decision.

---

94. According to the ECtHR, these acts would amount, *inter alia*, to a collective expulsion, being, thus forbidden by Protocol 4. *See*, among others, *Sharifi and Others v. Italy and Greece*, 21/10/2014, appl. 16643/09. For further developments, Ana Rita Gil, *Imigração e Direitos Humanos …* , cit., pp. 617 et seq.

95. Ana Rita Gil, *Imigração e Direitos Humanos …* , cit., pp. 622 et seq.

118. Pursuant to Article 26 of the Implementing Convention and Council Directive 2001/51/EC, if third-country nationals who were refused entry are brought to the border by a carrier, the SEF shall order the carrier to take charge and transport them without delay to the third country from which they were brought, to the third country which issued the document authorizing them to cross the border, or to any other third country where they are guaranteed admittance.

119. Pending onward transportation, the border authority shall take appropriate measures to prevent third-country nationals who have been refused entry from entering irregularly. In practice, these foreigners shall wait in the international area for a returning flight, in a temporary accommodation centre located in the airport's international area. Whenever the foreign citizen's removal is not possible within forty-eight hours, the criminal judge shall be informed for the purpose of deciding on the citizen's detention in the airport's accommodation facility.

120. Foreign citizens that remain temporarily in the airports' international area must be granted all rights enshrined in Article 40 IL: (1) the right to communicate with the diplomatic or consular representation of their country, or with any person of their choice; (2) to receive the assistance of interpreters, as well as healthcare, including medical visits, when necessary, and all material support to meet his/her basic needs;[96] (3) legal assistance by a lawyer, at his/her own expense, or when requested, access to legal protection.[97] As we will analyse in Part IV, Chapter 3, these 'accommodation' centres may be considered as true 'detention centres' and may pose some risks in terms of inhuman and degrading treatments.

121. Foreigners whose entry was refused have the right to appeal before the administrative courts – although the appeal will not have suspensive effect on the decision to refuse entry (Article 39 IL). In order to guarantee that the foreigner is in the possibility to exercise this right, the SEF must provide written material with the information regarding the right to appeal and respective procedures.[98]

122. In cases where the Court decides that the decision was ill-founded, the entry refusal is cancelled, and foreigners may have right to a compensation if they demonstrate that they have suffered a damage.

96. Some reports of the Portuguese Ombudsman, acting as National Preventive Mechanism, demonstrate, however, that these rights are not guaranteed in practice. Provedor de Justiça, *Relatório à Assembleia da República 2018 e 2019 – Mecanismo Nacional de Prevenção*, available at http://www.provedor-jus.pt/?idc=107.

97. In this case, the Law on Legal Aid is applicable – Act 34/2004, of 29 July.

98. The above-mentioned reports of the National Preventive Mechanism mention that the right to have the decision explained to migrants in a language that they presumably will understand is not always guaranteed. Moreover, there are severe difficulties to speak to a lawyer during the border procedure.

II. Administrative Procedures and Documents for the Purpose of Issuing a Visa

123. As already mentioned, the Portuguese IL sets forth several types of visas. It is therefore important to address the procedures applicable to these different types of visas.

Short-Stay Visas

124. Portuguese permanent consular posts and consular sections abroad are the authorities normally competent to issue short-stay visas. If such visas are 'applied by holders of diplomatic, service, official and special passports or travel documents issued by international organisations', the competent authorities are the Portuguese embassies and permanent consular posts (Article 48 IL). These authorities may request all information and additional elements which may be necessary for processing the applications.

125. According to Article 9 of the VC, applications shall be lodged no more than 6 months before the start of the intended visit, and, as a rule, no later than fifteen calendar days before the start of the intended visit. Articles 10–15 of the same Regulation regulate in detail all documents and biometric data that must be provided.

126. Articles 18 VC et seq. set forth the decision procedure. First, the consular authority shall verify whether it is competent to examine and decide the request. If the consulate is not competent, it shall, without delay, return the application form and any documents submitted by the applicant, reimburse the visa fee, and indicate which consulate is competent. Second, the competent consulate shall verify whether the application has been lodged within the required delay and if all data were collected. That being the case, the application will be considered as admissible. Otherwise, the application shall be deemed as inadmissible, and the consulate shall, without delay, return the application form and any documents submitted by the applicant, destroy the collected biometric data, reimburse the visa fee, and cease its analysis. However, by way of derogation, an application that does not meet the requirements set out in paragraph 1 may be considered admissible on humanitarian grounds or for reasons of national interest. When an application is admissible, the competent consulate shall stamp the applicant's travel document.

127. Article 21 VC regulates the phase of certification of entry conditions and risk assessment. In this phase, particular consideration shall be given to assessing whether the applicant presents a risk of illegal immigration or a risk to the security of the Member States and whether the applicant intends to leave the territory of the Member States before the expiry of the visa. During this assessment, consulates may call the applicant for an interview and request additional documents. The SIS and the VIS shall be consulted. According to Article 20(9) VC, a previous visa refusal shall not lead to an automatic refusal of a new application.

128. In some cases, the SEF must issue a prior opinion before the consular decisions. According to Article 53 IL, this shall happen: on grounds of national interest, for internal security reasons, or for preventing illegal immigration and related crimes. Whenever the applicant has been punished in Portugal with a sentence of imprisonment for more than one year, the SEF shall issue a negative opinion.

129. Pursuant to Article 23 of the VC, applications shall be decided within fifteen calendar days after the day of the lodging of an application deemed admissible. This period may be extended up to a maximum of thirty calendar days in individual cases, notably when further scrutiny of the application is needed, or in cases where the SEF must be consulted. Exceptionally, when additional documentation is needed, the period may be extended up to a maximum of sixty calendar days.

130. Unless the application has been withdrawn, a decision shall be taken to: (a) issue a uniform visa; (b) issue a visa with limited territorial validity; (c) refuse a visa; or (d) cease the analysis and transfer it to the relevant authorities.

131. The visa shall be refused pursuant to Article 32 of the VC if the applicant: (i) presents a false or forged travel document; (ii) does not provide justification for the purpose and conditions of the intended stay; (iii) does not provide proof of sufficient means of subsistence for the duration of the stay and for the return; (iv) has already stayed for ninety days during the current 180 days period on the territory of the Member States on the basis of a uniform visa or a visa with limited territorial validity; (v) is a person for whom an alert has been issued in the SIS for the purpose of refusing entry; (vi) is considered to be a threat to public policy, internal security or public health or to the international relations of any of the Member States, in particular where an alert has been issued in the national databases for the purpose of refusing entry on the same grounds; or (vii) does not provide proof of holding adequate and valid travel medical insurance, where applicable; or, also if there are reasonable doubts as to the authenticity of the supporting documents submitted by the applicant or the reliability of the statements made by the applicant.

132. The decision on refusal and the reasons on which it is based shall be notified to the applicant by means of the standard form set out in Annex VI of the VC. Also, the consulate of the representing Member State shall inform the applicant of the decision. As with decisions on entry refusal, applicants who have been refused a visa shall also have the right to appeal. The appeal shall be made before the administrative courts. The applicant must be informed of the procedure to be followed in the event of an appeal.

133. Finally, information on a refused visa shall be entered into the VIS in accordance with Article 12 of the VIS Regulation.

134. There is an exception to the procedure described above. On exceptional grounds, foreseen in the Portuguese legislation, short-stay visas may be granted at the border checkpoints to foreign citizens who, by unexpected reasons, were unable to apply to the competent authorities for a visa (Article 67 IL). For that purpose, the applicant shall: (a) hold a valid travel document enabling border crossing; (b) not be subject to an alert in the SIS or in the national alert system for purposes of refusal of entry; (c) not represent a threat to the public order, to the public security or to the international relations of a European Union Member State; and (d) ensure the return to the country of origin. Short-stay visas issued in these conditions are granted for one single entry, and their validity must not exceed fifteen days.

Temporary-Stay Visas

135. As already seen above, temporary-stay visas, as regulated in Articles 54 and following. IL are valid for periods inferior to one year, and for multiple entries. However, they are only valid in the Portuguese territory.

136. As with short-stay visas, applications for temporary-stay visas must be submitted by the third-country national at the Portuguese consular posts and consular sections. At the time of the application, information on the legally required documents, as well as on the rights, duties and guarantees, must be provided to the applicant. If the information or documentation submitted by the applicant is incomplete or insufficient, the analysis of the application is suspended, and the necessary information or documents are requested, which must be made available within ten days – which is the general administrative term foreseen in the Portuguese Administrative Procedures Code.

137. The documents that shall be presented by the applicant depend on the purpose of the visa (Articles 18 et seq. IR):

(a) *Medical treatment and accompanying family members* (Article 18 IR): the applicant must present proof that a health establishment guarantees a hospitalization or an outpatient treatment; the accompanying family member must present proof of the family ties (in case of spouse, partner, parent, child, or other family members); or, in the case of minors or incapacitated persons without a family, that he/she is in charge of the patient. Means of subsistence can be waived or reduced if the treatment was paid in advance, if the internment is provided under a cooperation agreement, or if the applicant proves that he/she has secure accommodation and food, or a term of responsibility signed by a national or foreign resident.
(b) *Transfer of nationals of States Parties to the World Trade Organization, within the scope of providing services or talking part in vocational training in the Portuguese territory* (Articles 19 IR and 55 IL): the applicant must present documents that prove that his/her transfer will be done between branches of the same company or group of companies, and that the branch located in the Portuguese territory provides the same services as those provided by the company of origin.[99]
(c) *Employment or self-employment activity of temporary nature for which duration does not exceed, as a rule, a six-month period*: according to Article 19-A

99. The transfer only covers partners or employees who have been, for at least one year, in a branch located in another State Party to the World Trade Organization, and who fall into one of the following categories: (i) those who hold decision- making competences, hold senior positions and act as managers of an branch or department, under general guidance from the administration board; those

IR, the application is accompanied by a contract, a promissory contract, or a service contract in the context of an independent professional activity of a temporary nature and, when applicable, a declaration issued by the competent authority to verify the requirements for the exercise of a profession that, in Portugal, is subject to special qualifications.

(d) *Scientific research in research centres, teaching activity in a higher education establishment, or a highly qualified activity for less than one year*: the applicant must present (a) proof that he /she was admitted for the purposes of taking part in a research centre which is duly recognized by the Ministry of Education and Science, by means of an actual or promissory employment contract or a research grant for scientific purposes; or (b) proof that he/she holds an actual or promissory employment contract, or a written job offer for purposes of teaching in a higher education establishment, or carrying out a highly qualified activity in the national territory.

(e) *Amateur sporting activity certified by the respective federation*: the applicant must present a document, issued by the respective federation, confirming the exercise of the sporting activity, as well as the term of responsibility subscribed by the sports association or club, assuming the responsibility for the accommodation and for the payment of eventual healthcare and repatriation expenses (Article 22 IR).

(f) *Staying in the national territory for a period of more than three months, in certain exceptional and duly substantiated cases*: the applicant must present proof of the exceptional situation, namely: a document issued by the educational establishment, proving acceptance of the enrolment, proof of reception by family and proof of accommodation; document issued by an officially recognized company or professional training body attesting admission to the internship; document issued by the responsible organization in Portugal for the officially recognized volunteer programme; or service contract and certificate of possession of the technical qualifications required for the service (Article 23 IR).

(g) *Seasonal work longer than ninety days*: the applicant must present a contract or a promissory of employment contract, which identifies the place, time and type of work, duration, remuneration and paid vacations to which the worker is entitled; proof of health insurance, accommodation or term of responsibility of the employer; and, when applicable, a declaration issued by a competent entity to verify the requirements of the exercise of profession that, in Portugal, is subject to special qualifications (Articles 17-A and 23-A IR).

(h) *Course attendance at an educational or vocational training establishment*: the applicant must have a document issued by an officially recognized educational or vocational training establishment that proves the applicant's admission to a course of less than one year and proof of means of subsistence and accommodation.

---

who hold specific technical knowledge crucial to the activity, its research equipment or the techniques or management thereof; and those who must receive vocational training in a branch located in the national territory.

138. The maximum period for reaching a decision regarding a temporary-stay visa is thirty days, from the beginning of the examination of the visa application (Article 54(3) IL). For all these types of temporary visas, in case of refusal, the decision shall be notified in a written form, stating the grounds for the refusal. Rules on judicial appeal to the administrative courts shall be applicable.

Residence Visa

139. As already mentioned, the residence visa is meant to allow its holder to enter into the Portuguese territory to apply for a residence permit. It is valid for two entries and entitles its holder to stay there for a period of four months. Application conditions depend on the purpose intended with the establishment of residence, which will be analysed further below in Part III.

Part II. Residence Rights

Chapter 1. General Rules

140. After analysing the general conditions that foreigners must respect to enter into the Portuguese territory legally, we will now study the legal requirements that they must fulfil in order to be authorized to *reside* in the territory.

141. First, interested persons must acquire a residence visa. This visa is conferred under Article 58 IL, and aims precisely at authorizing the entry into the national territory for the purpose of applying for a residence permit or accompanying a family member who is making an application. It allows two entries and a period of stay of four months. With the granting of a residence visa, a residence 'pre-authorization' is issued. It contains the provisional assignment of tax, social security and national health service identification numbers.

142. In the context of the Immigration Law, there are two types of residence permits according to their length: temporary and permanent permits. Temporary titles are valid for a two-year period and are renewable for successive periods of three years.[100] By contrast, as its name points out, the permanent residence permit has no time limit. However, it must be renewed every five years or whenever there is any change to the foreigner's relevant data (Articles 75 and 76 IL).

143. The IL sets forth some *general* conditions that migrants must fulfil in order to obtain a temporary residence permit, irrespective of its grounds. These conditions are foreseen in Article 77 IL: (a) they must hold a valid residence visa, granted for one of the purposes established as grounds for taking legal residence in the territory; (b) there must not be any fact that, if known by the competent authorities, could preclude the granting of that visa; (c) they must be present on the Portuguese territory; (d) they must hold sufficient means of subsistence; (e) they must have accommodation; (f) they must contribute to the Portuguese social security, whenever applicable; (g) they must not have been convicted for any crime punishable by imprisonment for more than one year; (h) they must not be subjected to an entry ban into the national territory, for having been ordered to return to their country of origin: (i) they must also not have been object of any alert in the SIS; (j) or of any

100. The 2022 legal amendments extended these periods. Before these changes, the initial period of a temporary residence period was of one year, renewable for periods of two years.

alert in SEF's Integrated Information System. Moreover, the already mentioned general exception clause may be applied: a residence permit may be refused on grounds of public order, national security, or public health.[101]

144. Article 78 sets forth the conditions for the renewal of a temporary residence permit. It must be requested up to thirty days before its expiry, and are only renewed if the immigrants prove that they have: (a) sufficient means of subsistence; (b) accommodation; (c) fulfilled their tax and social security obligations; and (d) have not been convicted of a punishment or penalties that, individually or cumulatively, exceed one year in prison or for terrorism, violent or organized crimes. As for the issuance, also the renewal may be denied for reasons of public order or public security. As for public health, the IL sets forth that the appearance of illnesses after the issuance of the first residence permit does not constitute sufficient grounds to justify the refusal to renew the residence permit. Similarly, the IL also foresees some *general conditions* for the issuance of permanent residence permits. Migrants may acquire a permanent status provided that they meet cumulatively the following requirements: (a) they hold a temporary residence permit for at least five years; (b) they have not been sentenced for any crime punishable by imprisonment that, individually or cumulatively, exceeds one year[102] during the last five years of residence in Portuguese territory; (c) they have sufficient means of subsistence; (d) they have accommodation ensured and (e) they prove to have sufficient basic knowledge of Portuguese language.

145. As regards procedural rights, the IL sets forth that the application for a residence permit shall be decided within ninety days, and the application for renewing a residence permit shall be decided within sixty days. In the absence of a decision within these periods, for reasons that are not attributable to the applicant, the decision is considered favourable, and the residence title shall be immediately issued (Article 82 IL). This may seem a very generous provision, but in practice there are some doubts as to how a migrant can prove that he or she holds a residence permit which was tacitly approved.[103] In cases where the administration does not provide a timely decision to the applicant, this situation may lead to the impossibility of migrants to lead a dignified life in society: it is more difficult for them to prove that they have the documents to take up an employment, to rent a house or to enjoy social benefits. Pursuant to Article 81 IL, during the decision of the request, the applicant may develop a professional activity. This norm was enacted due to the

101. The refusal of residence permit on grounds of public health may only be based on diseases that have been defined in the applicable instruments of the World Health Organization, or on other infectious or contagious parasitic diseases which have been object to protection measures in the national territory. A medical examination may be required for this purpose, however not on a systematic basis.

102. This shall be applicable even if they have been convicted of an intentional crime or were somehow related to that crime, or crime of terrorism, violent crime or particularly violent crime or highly organized crime – and the sentence has been suspended.

103. In 2019, the Portuguese Ombudsman received several complaints of migrants that could not prove that their residence permit was renewed or that a residence permit was conferred. *See* Provedor de Justiça – *Relatório à Assembleia da República – 2019*, available in http://www.provedor-jus.pt/site/public/archive/doc/Relat2019_web.pdf.

delays in the decisions, which were very frequent, and could result in deprivation of rights to the applicants. Therefore, the right to work is only admissible if the delay of the decision is not the applicant's responsibility. Article 81(6) IL sets forth that foreigners whose household includes minors of school age or dependent children of age, in both cases attending an educational establishment in the Portuguese territory, have preference in submitting their applications for residence. This provision is also extremely important, for giving primacy to the best interests of migrant children.[104]

146. In case where the application is rejected, the decision shall be communicated to the applicant, informing the grounds for refusal, as well as the right to appeal and respective time limit for that action (Article 82(3) IL).

147. These conditions are not applicable to persons falling under the Asylum Law (AL) or the Law on Free Movement of Persons, which have different and autonomous requirements, as will be explained in Chapter 1 and Chapter 7 below.

104. These delays have been subjected to several communications made by the Portuguese Ombudsman. *See*, among many others, the interview dated 10/12/2022 to the *Expresso* weekly journal, entitled: 'Ombudsman admits «serious problems» in the delay in residence permits'. Available in: https://expresso.pt/nosection/foruns/forum_sociedade/2022-12-10-Imigracao-Provedora-de-Justica-admite-problemas-graves-na-demora-nas-autorizacoes-de-residencia-f7146668.

Chapter 2. Nationals with Preferential Treatment

§1. EU Citizens

148. Act 37/2006 of 9 August regulates the right of EU citizens and respective family members to move and to reside freely within Portuguese territory. This Act transposes Directive 2004/38/EC of the European Parliament and of the Council of 29 April 2004 on the right of citizens of the Union and their family members to move and reside freely within the territory of the Member States to the Portuguese legal order. Hereinafter we will refer to this Act as 'Law on Free Movement' (FML).

I. No Problem of 'Reverse Discrimination'

149. The Portuguese Law on Free Movement is applicable both to EU citizens and to *Portuguese citizens* – irrespective of whether they have exercised their right to free movement. By adopting this solution, the Portuguese Law avoided a criticism that was commonly directed to Directive 2004/38/CE: the reverse discrimination. This was an undesirable effect of the enactment of the Directive, which would only be applicable to EU citizens that make use of their right to free movement – and not to national citizens that would remain in the national territory. In some cases, citizens who were moving had more rights than national citizens, as the Directive's standards would be applicable, and could be more favourable than domestic standards. This effect was particularly important for family reunification purposes: in some cases, the concept of family enshrined in the national law was narrower than the concept of family foreseen in the Directive. As a result, EU citizens who would move to that particular country could bring with them more family members than what was allowed for national citizens. That could amount to reverse discrimination. As mentioned, the Portuguese FML is applicable both to EU citizens who are exercising their right to free movement and to Portuguese citizens alike. That being so, no problem of reverse discrimination affects the Portuguese citizens.

150. To these conclusions, we must add that the legal provisions referring to the citizens of the Union are understood to cover nationals of States Parties to the Agreement on the European Economic Area (EU countries, Iceland, Liechtenstein and Norway) and nationals of Switzerland.

II. Right to Enter the Territory

151. Contrarily to what was said above as regards third-country nationals, who do not enjoy a 'right to enter', as such, in the Portuguese territory,[105] EU citizens do

105. *See* above Part I, Ch. 2.

enjoy a fundamental right in this realm – as a consequence of the fundamental right of free movement guaranteed in Article 45 of the EU Charter of Fundamental Rights.

152. Article 4 of the Portuguese FML, such as Article 5 of the Free Movement Directive[106](FMD), regulates this right to enter. EU citizens may enter any Member State territory with a valid identity card or passport without any further requirement. Third-country nationals who are family members of Union citizens are admitted to the national territory by presenting a valid passport, being subject only to the entry visa requirement under the rules in force in the European Union. Every support shall be given to them for obtaining the necessary visas. Such visas shall be issued free of charge as soon as possible and on the basis of an accelerated procedure. In cases where family members hold a residence permit, they are exempted from presenting a visa.

153. After entering, family members who are third-country nationals shall report their presence in the territory. In case they fail to do so, they are subjected to the sanctions foreseen in the IL.

III. Right to Residence

154. According to the FML, EU citizens and their family members have the right to reside in the Portuguese territory. This is a fundamental right foreseen in Article 45 of the EU Charter on Fundamental Rights. Nevertheless, it is important to mention that such a right is always an exception to the general rule that characterizes international law: every State has the right to control who enters and remains in their territory. European Union Law confers an actual fundamental right to anyone who is an EU citizen, to live in another Member State. Such a right can only be limited in very restricted situations, which we will analyse below.

155. The Law on Free Movement (LFM) foresees, such as the Directive, three types of residence rights: residence for a period of up to three months, residence for a period longer than three months and permanent residence. EU citizens who wish to take residence in another Member State for a period of up to three months do not need to fulfil any conditions or any formalities other than the requirement to hold a valid identity card or passport (Article 6(1)). However, for taking up residence for a period longer than three months, they must respect conditions foreseen in Article 7 FML. Finally, permanent residence, extensive to their family members, is also possible if conditions set forth by Article 10 FML are respected. As we can see, this

106. Directive 2004/38/EC of the European Parliament and of the Council of 29 Apr. 2004 on the right of citizens of the Union and their family members to move and reside freely within the territory of the Member States.

right to free movement, although being characterized as a fundamental right, is subjected to some requirements, not being, thus, totally equivalent to the fundamental right, enshrined in Article 44 of the Portuguese Constitution, that national citizens have to enter and remain in the territory.

A. *Conditions for Taking Up Residence for a Period Longer Than Three Months*

156. As Article 7 of the FMD, Article 7 of the FML also sets forth the conditions that EU citizens may fulfil in order to reside in Portugal for more than three months. Conditions depend on whether they came to Portugal to work, to study or just to live with any other (or no specific) purpose.

157. In the first case, the FML, as the FMD, does not demand any other requirement, besides the exercise of a professional activity. As for students, they must be enrolled at a public or private establishment, accredited by the Portuguese State, hold health insurance cover (as long as the same is demanded in their country of origin from Portuguese citizens as well) and assure that they have sufficient resources for themselves and their family members. Finally, all EU citizens that have sufficient resources for themselves and their family, as well as a health insurance cover (as long as the same is demanded in their country of origin to Portuguese citizens as well), may reside in Portugal for more than three months, irrespective of any specific reason.

158. Article 7(3) FML (such as Article 7(3) of the FMD) foresees a right to residence to EU citizens that are no longer workers or self-employed persons. They may retain the status of worker or self-employed in cases where they are temporarily unable to work as the result of an illness or accident or duly documented involuntary unemployment. The same can be said in cases where workers are enrolled in vocational training.

159. If we compare the Portuguese norms with the Directive's, we may reach the conclusion that the Portuguese FML has almost the same reading as the FMD. However, there is a specific mention in the FMD that appears in almost all provisions, but to which the FML does not make any reference: as regards sufficient means of subsistence, the Directive highlights permanently that the EU citizen 'shall not become a "burden" to the social security of the host EU Member State'. However, the same is not mentioned in the Portuguese Law, even where it requires 'sufficient means of subsistence'. In this context, we must highlight that Article 9(3) FML sets forth that recourse to the Portuguese social security system by a citizen of the Union, or his family does not automatically result in the loss of the right of residence. Article 14(3) FMD sets forth that an expulsion measure shall not be the automatic consequence of Union 'citizens' or their family 'members' recourse to the social assistance system of the host Member State. However, paragraph 2 of the same Article sets forth that Union citizens and their family members shall have the right of temporary residence, as long as they do not become an unreasonable burden on the social assistance system of the host Member State. It seems, thus, that the Portuguese FML provides for a higher standard of protection.

B. Conditions for Taking Up Permanent Residence

160. Like Article 16 of the FMD, Article 16 of the Portuguese FML foresees the right to acquire permanent residence to Union citizens who have resided legally for a continuous period of five years in Portugal (Article 16). The continuity of the residence can be attested by any admissible means of proof.

161. The Portuguese Law has adopted provisions that are totally equivalent to the Directive's in this regard. Thus, continuity of residence shall not be affected by temporary absences not exceeding a total of six months a year, or by absences of a longer duration for compulsory military service, or by one absence of a maximum of twelve consecutive months for important reasons such as pregnancy and childbirth, serious illness, study or vocational training, or a posting in another Member State or a third country. Once acquired, the right of permanent residence shall be lost only through absence from the host Member State for a period exceeding two consecutive years. Furthermore, the FML provides that the continuity of residence is interrupted by any valid decision to remove the person in question.

162. There are some cases where the EU citizen may acquire the right to permanent residence before having completed the five years period. According to Article 17 of the FML (which, again, has almost transposed the FMD verbatim), the following categories of persons shall acquire such possibility: (a) workers or self-employed persons who, at the time that they have stopped working, have reached the age laid down by the Portuguese Law for entitlement to an old age pension, or workers who cease to develop a paid employment to take early retirement, provided that they have been working in Portugal for at least the preceding twelve months and have resided there continuously for more than three years; (b) workers or self-employed persons who have resided continuously in Portugal for more than two years and stopped working there as a result of permanent incapacity to work; and (c) workers or self-employed persons who, after three years of continuous employment and residence in Portugal, work in an employed or self-employed capacity in another Member State, while retaining their place of residence in Portugal, to which they return, as a rule, each day or at least once a week.

163. SEF shall issue to EU citizens with the right of permanent residence, on their request, a document which shall certify permanent residence (Article 16 FML). The family members of EU citizens who are nationals of a third State and have the right to permanent residence shall also be issued a permanent residence card (Article 17 FML).

C. Family Unity and Protection of Family Members

164. The Portuguese FML adopts an enlarged concept of family. According to Article 2(2), 'family member' encompass the following persons: (a) the spouse; (b) the partner with whom a Union citizen lives in a de facto union, established under the law, or with whom the Union citizen has a permanent relationship duly certified by the competent entity of the Member State where he/she resides;[107] (c) the direct descendants of the migrant or the spouse or partner, who are under the age of 21 or are their dependants; (d) the direct relatives' dependents in the ascending line and those of the spouse or partner.

165. According to Article 3(2) FML, entry and residence of other family members is facilitated, regardless of nationality, pursuant that these family members are in charge of the EU citizen in the country of origin, or that they live together, or when the citizen of the Union must take personally care of these persons for reasons of serious health.[108] In these cases, the decision regarding the entry and residence of the persons can only be taken after analysing all the relevant personal circumstances, and any refusal to enter or to grant a residence permit must be substantiated.

166. The FMD provides special protection to family members of EU citizens, even in the event of death or divorce. Contrary to the other norms, this one does not aim primarily at facilitating the free movement of persons. Its main concern is, indeed, to protect the human rights of non-EU citizens. For this purpose, Article 12 FMD sets forth that the Union citizen's death shall not entail the loss of the right of residence of their family members who are not nationals of a Member State and who have been residing in the host Member State as family members for at least one year before the Union citizen's death. However, according to Article 8 of the Portuguese FML, both the Union citizen's death and his or her departure from the host Member State, as well as the divorce, marriage annulment, or separation (in cases of partnerships), do not affect the right of residence of the family members who are not nationals of a Member State. However, before acquiring the right of permanent residence, these family members must be able to show that they are workers or self-employed persons or that they have sufficient resources for themselves and their family members and health insurance. Finally, the Union citizen's departure from Portugal or their death shall not entail loss of the right of residence of their children or of the parent who has actual custody of the children, irrespective of nationality, if the children reside in the host Member State and are enrolled at an educational establishment, for the purpose of studying there, until the completion of their studies. Further to this protection of family members, Article 12(2) FML (just as Article 17(4) FMD) sets forth that if the workers or self-employed persons die while still working but before acquiring permanent residence status, their family members who are residing with them shall acquire the right of permanent residence, on condition

107. In this context, the Portuguese Law made use of the voluntary provision of Art. 3(2) of the Directive.

108. Here, also, the Portuguese Law made use of the voluntary provision of Art. 3(2) of the Directive.

that: (a) the worker or self-employed person had, at the time of death, resided continuously on the territory for two years; or (b) the death resulted from an accident at work or an occupational disease; or (c) the surviving spouse had lost the Portuguese nationality following marriage to the worker or self-employed person.

D. Exceptions

167. The right to residence of EU citizens may be subject to restrictions for reasons of public policy, public security or public health. This clause is foreseen in Article 27 and beyond of the FMD, which were transposed by the FML, also into its Article 27. The FML's wording is imperative: free movement can only be restricted for reasons of public policy, public security or public health. Furthermore, and like the FMD, it implements the broad CJEU's case law on this matter. In this context, it sets forth clearly that reasons for public order, public security and public health cannot be invoked for economic purposes. Moreover, such reasons must comply with the principle of proportionality and be based exclusively on the behaviour of the person in question, which must constitute a real, current and sufficiently serious threat that affects a fundamental interest of the society. Thus, justifications that are not related to the individual case or based on general prevention reasons cannot be used. Moreover, as the CJEU has repeatedly highlighted, previous criminal convictions cannot, by themselves, serve as a basis for restriction on the grounds of public order.

168. In order to ascertain whether the person concerned represents a danger for public policy or public security and if deemed necessary, when issuing the registration certificate or residence card, information concerning the criminal record of the person in question may be requested from the Member State of origin and, if need be, other Member States (Article 22 FML).

169. Finally, the only diseases justifying measures restricting the freedom of movement of EU citizens or their family members shall be diseases with epidemic potential as defined by the relevant instruments of the World Health Organization and other infectious diseases or contagious parasitic diseases if they are the subject of protection provisions applying to Portuguese citizens (Article 24 FML).

§2. Long-Term Residents

170. The long-term resident status is also an instrument designed in the context of the EU migration policy, created by the Council Directive 2003/109/EC of 25 November 2003 concerning the status of third-country nationals who are long-term residents. It has the aim to contribute to the objective, affirmed in the Tampere European Council's, to provide a 'fair treatment of third country nationals who reside legally on the territory of its Member States', namely by approximating the 'legal status of third country nationals to that of Member States' nationals'.[109] Moreover, it is also an instrument aimed at implementing Article 45(2) of the EU Charter of Fundamental Rights, whereby 'Freedom of movement and residence may be granted, in accordance with the Treaty establishing the European Community, to nationals of third countries legally resident in the territory of a Member State.' The Directive was one of the first instruments to be adopted by the EU on immigration and asylum, and aims, precisely, to provide an 'ersatz of free movement' to third-country nationals who have resided for a considerable period of time in one of the EU Member States. One of the most important and impressive rights of this status is, indeed, the recognition of a mitigated 'right to free movement' to its holders. Such right, however, is still not equivalent to the fundamental right to free movement of EU citizens. The third-country national acquires such status in a first EU-Member State, after residing therein for the necessary period. After acquiring such status, the third-country national may move to another EU Member State. However, this second Member State must, on its turn, recognize the long-term resident status that was acquired in the first. For that purpose, it may require additional conditions.

171. That being the case, there are two different issues to be considered under the Portuguese national law: on the one hand, the attribution of a long-term residence status to a third-country national who is residing in Portugal. On the other, the recognition of a long-term residence status of a foreign citizen that has acquired such status in another EU Member State and wants to move to Portugal. We will begin by analysing the first situation, under Articles 125 to 133 of IL, which have transposed the Long-Term Residents Directive (hereinafter 'LTD').

I. Acquisition of a Long-Term Resident Status in Portugal

A. *Conditions*

172. According to IL's Article 126, a long-term resident status must be granted to third-country nationals who: (i) have a legal and uninterrupted residence in Portugal for at least five years before submitting the application, or in case where they are beneficiaries of international protection, since the date of submission of the application of international protection;[110] (ii) hold stable and regular resources without having recourse to the solidarity subsystem;[111] (iii) have health insurance; (iv) have accommodation and (iv) prove proficiency in basic Portuguese language.

109. *See* Tampere European Council, 15 and 16 October 1999, Presidency Conclusions, §18-21.

110. According to Art. 126(4), periods of absence from the national territory may be counted for the calculation, provided that they are shorter than six successive months, and do not exceed, in total, ten months of the mentioned period. However, in the calculation of the period of five years, the periods resulting from detachment for work purposes, more specifically as regards a cross-border provision of services, shall be taken into account.

111. Article 126(6) sets forth that the resources are assessed by their nature and regularity, taking into consideration the level of minimum wages and pensions, before submitting the application for acquiring a long-term resident status.

173. Article 125(2) sets forth that third-country nationals do not qualify for the long-term resident status if they: (i) hold a residence permit for purposes of study, unremunerated professional traineeship or voluntary service; (ii) are authorized to reside in the national territory under temporary protection or have submitted an application for a residence permit for that reason and are awaiting a decision on their status; (iii) stay in Portugal only for temporary reasons, as seasonal workers, workers posted by a service provider for the purposes of cross-border provision of services, or as a cross-border provider of services; (iv) enjoy a legal status under the Vienna Convention on diplomatic relations of 18 April 1961 or under the Vienna Convention on consular relations of 24 April 1961.

B. Procedure

174. Article 129 IL deals with the procedure for acquiring a long-term resident status – which shall be dealt with by the SEF's delegation in the applicant's area of residence. The application shall be accompanied by documents demonstrating that the third-country national fulfils the conditions to benefit from a long-term residence status, as well as a valid travel document. The decision must be taken 'as soon as possible, and, in any event, within six months'. This period can be extended for three more months.

175. The long-term resident status is permanent. Their holders are issued with an EU long-term residence permit, which is valid for five years, and is automatically renewed, upon request, at the end of the expiry period (Article 130 IL).

C. Refusals on the Grounds of Public Order or Public Security

176. The status of long-term resident can be refused, even where all requirements were met, for public order or public security reasons (Article 127 IL). Portugal decided to use the optional clause foreseen in Article 6 LTD – thus, economic reasons cannot give rise to refusals. The severity or type of offence, the danger that the person's stay represents, as well as the length of residence and the existence of links to Portugal are factors that shall be taken into consideration for that decision. The IL adopted the exact reading of the LTD in this regard – which, on its turn, has adopted the case law of the ECtHR on protection of private life in cases of foreigners' expulsions.[112] However, it is still discussed whether the concept of public order adopted in the context of free movement of persons, as explained above, shall also be applicable in the present context. Although we cannot assume that the debate around this question is closed, it seems that the CJEU's case law on the concept of public policy on free movement purposes may be transposed to the context of long-term residents.[113]

112. *See*, for example, *Maslov v. Austria*, cit.
113. Ruling dated 11/06/2020, *WT*, C-448/19.

D. Holders of a Long-Term Resident Status Acquired in Other EU Member States

177. Holders of a long-term resident status acquired in another EU Member State who stay in Portuguese territory for more than three months have the right of residence in Portugal, provided that they are employed, self-employed, pursue a course of study or vocational training or present a strong motive to set up residence in the national territory (Article 116 IL).[114]

178. The long-term resident shall submit to the SEF an application for residence permit within three months as from the date of entry into the national territory.[115] The decision on an application for a residence permit shall be rendered within three months, although this period may be extended with a period not exceeding three months. In the absence of a decision within six months, the application is considered approved (Article 117(8) IL).

179. A residence permit is granted to family members as well,[116] which shall have an identical length as the one granted to the long-term resident.

E. Limits: Public Order and National Security

180. According to Article 119 IL, the application for a long-term resident permit submitted in accordance with this section can be refused when the person concerned represents a threat to public policy or public security. The decision must take into consideration the seriousness or type of offence to public policy or security committed by the long-term resident or his/her family member, or the dangers that might result from that person's stay in the national territory. These obligations of balancing the different interests at stake would derive from the ECtHR, even in case where the law would not expressly mention them.[117]

181. Refusal of long-term resident status cannot be grounded on economic reasons. The application may also be rejected if the person concerned represents a threat to public health. These reasons also justify a cancellation and non-renewal of the residence permit (Article 120 IL).

---

114. This is not applicable to employees posted by a service provider for the purpose of cross-border service providers (Art. 116(2) IL).
115. The application shall be accompanied by documents confirming that the applicant fulfils the conditions for exercising his/her right to residence, the long-term resident title and a valid travel document or certified copies of those documents.
116. For this purpose, 'family members' are those recognized as such by the provisions on family reunification, as explained below (Ch. 4).
117. ECtHR case law, mentioned in the General Introduction, §4, 4.

Chapter 3. Students, Interns and Volunteer Workers

182. The Portuguese IL was amended in 2018 to transpose the Directive (EU) 2016/801 of the European Parliament and of the Council of 11 May 2016 on the conditions of entry and residence of third-country nationals for the purposes of research, studies, training, voluntary service, pupil exchange schemes or educational projects and au pairing.

183. According to Article 62 IL, students of higher or of secondary education, interns or volunteers who want to develop their activities in Portugal must require a residence visa, which will allow them to enter the territory and apply for a residence permit. The visa is granted if the applicant presents, besides the general documents for entry purpose, a health insurance, or equivalent, with coverage for the whole expected duration of the stay. Besides that, they must comply with special conditions depending on the purpose of the stay. Only after acquiring a visa may they apply for a temporary residence permit.

§1. Residence Visa for the Purposes of Studies, Internship or Voluntary Work

I. Visa for Higher Education Students

184. Higher education students must be accepted by a higher education institution to attend, as a main activity, a full-time study programme leading to an academic degree or a recognized higher education title, namely a diploma, a certificate, or a PhD, which may include a preparation course for such studies or compulsory training within the programme of study (Article 3(m) IL). They must prove that they fulfil the admission conditions or have been accepted in a higher education institution to attend a study programme and that they have sufficient resources to attend it (Article 62 IL).[118]

II. Visa for Secondary School Students

185. According to Article 3, n) IL, a third-country national student who wishes to reside in Portugal in order to attend a recognized education programme equivalent to levels 2 and 3 of the International Standard Classification of Education, within the framework of a student exchange programme or through individual admission to an educational project carried out by a recognized educational establishment, can be admitted to the Portuguese territory for that purpose.

118. If the student was admitted to a higher education institution officially recognized for this purpose, exempted from presenting some of the documents, namely the proof of having sufficient resources (Art. 90(5) IL).

186. In order to obtain a residence visa for this purpose, students must comply with the conditions established in Article 62(6)IL: (a) having the minimum age of 14 and not exceeding the maximum age of 21;[119] (b) having been accepted by the educational establishment; and (c) during the period of the stay, being welcomed by a family or have accommodation in suitable facilities, within the educational establishment or other suitable institution.

III. Visa for Trainees

187. Article 3(l) IL defines who can be considered as a trainee for the purposes of immigration: a third-country national who holds a higher education diploma, or who attends a cycle of studies in a third country aimed at obtaining a higher education diploma, and who has been admitted to the Portuguese territory to attend a training programme in an unpaid professional context.

188. In order to obtain a residence visa, the trainee must prove that he or she has been accepted as an intern by a certified host organization and must present a contract for theoretical and practical training in his or her field of studies. This document must state the description of the training programme (namely its educational objectives or learning components), its schedule and duration, the location and conditions for the internship supervision, and the type of the relationship between the intern and the host entity. It must also mention that the internship is not a job post and that the host entity is responsible for reimbursing the State for the expenses of stay and removal if the intern remains irregularly on the national territory (Article 62(7) IL).

IV. Visa for Volunteer Workers

189. Finally, volunteer workers must also comply with some specific visa requirements. According to Article 3(r) IL, a 'volunteer program' is a programme recognized by the competent authorities or by the European Union, which pursues general interest goals, in favour of a non-profit cause or a solidarity cause. Its activities are not remunerated, except for the purpose of reimbursement of expenses and/or pocket money, including voluntary activities under the European Voluntary Service.

190. The volunteer who requires a visa must present several documents, the first of which is a contract with the host entity responsible for the volunteering programme. This contract must contain a description of the content and the duration of the volunteering programme, its schedule, the conditions of supervision and the guarantee of coverage of food and accommodation expenses, including a minimum

119. *See* Portaria 1079/2007 of 10 December of the Minister of Education and the Minister of the Interior.

sum of allowances or pocket money. Second, the host organization must take a civil liability insurance, except in the case of volunteers participating in the European Voluntary Service (Article 62(8) IL).

§2. Residence Permit for the Purposes of Studies, Internship or Voluntary Work

I. Residence Permit for Higher Education Students

191. The student of higher education who holds a residence visa issued in accordance with the provisions of Article 62 IL, explained above, and who fulfils the general conditions mentioned in Article 77 IL, is granted a residence permit, provided that he/she presents the following documents: (a) proof of enrolment in a higher education institution; (b) payment of tuition fees, if applicable;[120] (c) means of subsistence; and (d) coverage by the National Health Service or health insurance (Article 91 IL). This provision sets forth a right of the student and a duty for the State: those who fulfil the mentioned conditions must receive a residence permit without interference of a discretionary power.

192. The residence permit for study in a higher education institution is valid for three years and is renewable for equal periods if its holder continues to fulfil the concession conditions (Article 91(2) IL). If the duration of the studies is less than three years, the permit is issued for its precise duration.

193. The Immigration Law also foresees situations where residence permits may be granted to higher education students who do not hold a residence visa issued under the terms of Article 62. We may consider that to be a case of 'legal status regularisation', for study purposes. As we will see, there are several cases foreseen by the IL, where migrants' legal status may be regularized, pursuant to some objective criteria. As for the case of higher education students, Article 91(4) sets forth the right to regularization to those who have legally entered into the national territory and fulfil the other conditions set out in that article. However, this provision does not establish a 'right to be regularized', contrary to other situations foreseen in the IL. One may indeed conclude that regularization in this context is dependent on a discretionary administrative decision.

II. Mobility for High Education Students

194. Higher education students who hold a residence permit granted by another EU Member State and covered by a European Union or multilateral programme

120. Higher education students admitted to an approved higher education institution under the terms of the ordinance of the members of the Government responsible for the areas of internal administration and higher education are exempted from presenting documents proving the payment of tuition fees and livelihoods (Arts 91(6) IL and 57(3) IR).

with mobility measures, or by an agreement between two or more higher education institutions, are authorized to enter and remain in the Portuguese territory to carry out part of the studies (Article 91-A IL).

195. The SEF may not authorize entry or stay when the person concerned represents a threat to the public order, public security, or public health. It may also oppose the mobility when the required conditions are not met (e.g., when the maximum period of 360 days is exceeded).[121]

196. In case of non-opposition, the SEF issues a declaration that certifies that the student is authorized to remain in the national territory and to enjoy the rights provided for by law.

III. Residence Permit for Secondary Education Students

197. The secondary school student holding a residence visa is granted a residence permit, if he or she is enrolled in an educational establishment and is covered by the Portuguese National Health Service or by a health insurance. The residence permit may not exceed one year, renewable for equal periods, as long as the conditions for granting it are maintained.

198. Although, as a rule, the student must hold a residence visa in order to benefit from a residence permit, Article 92(3) IL sets forth that those who have entered and remained legally in the national territory request a residence permit. All other conditions established for acquiring this type of residence permit must, nonetheless, be verified.

IV. Residence Permit for Trainees

199. The intern holding the correspondent residence visa and other requirements demanded by Article 77 is granted with a residence permit, provided that he or she is covered by the National Health Service or by a health insurance (Article 93 IL).

200. The residence permit granted to interns is valid for six months, or for the duration of the internship programme when it is shorter than six months – in which case it is valid for the period of the programme plus three extra months. For long-term traineeships, a two-year residence permit is issued. In this case, the permit can be renewed once, for the remaining traineeship period (Article 93(2) IL).

121. The opposition shall be transmitted, in writing, to the interested party and to the authorities of the Member State that granted him the residence permit, within thirty days.

201. A possibility of 'regularisation' is also foreseen for trainees. In cases where they have entered and remained legally in the country – on any other grounds – and comply with the requirements specially foreseen for interns, they may be issued a trainees' residence permit.

V. Residence Permit for Volunteer Workers

202. Finally, those who hold a visa for the purpose of developing volunteer work may also acquire a residence right. The same requirements as to health insurance and general conditions apply. The residence permit is also valid for one year, or for the duration of the volunteer work, and cannot be renewed (Article 94).

Chapter 4. Researchers

§1. Residence Visa for the Purposes of Research Activities

203. Researchers' residence is also regulated under the IL pursuant to the Directive (EU) 2016/801. As with other residence permits mentioned before, researchers must hold a residence visa for the purposes of acquiring a residence permit. The general conditions for acquiring the visa are those established in Article 62, already explained above (Part III, Chapter 2). However, the researcher is exempted from presenting a health insurance when the hosting institution is an officially recognized investigation centre or high education institution. Besides these general requirements, the researcher must have an employment contract or a hosting agreement with a research centre or higher education institution or must have been admitted to one of these organizations. Moreover, he or she must present proof of having their expenses covered, whether by a scholarship, grant research or a term of responsibility signed by the institution that guarantees their admission, as well as the expenses for their stay. However, in cases where the researcher was admitted to work in an officially recognized institution, they are also exempted from presenting these elements (Article 63 (3) IL).[122] Some general requirements for obtaining visas, foreseen in Article 52 IL, are not required either, such as sufficient subsistence means and travel insurance. To sum up, researchers must be in one of the following situations: (1) have an employment contract or a hosting agreement with a research centre or higher education institution; (2) have been admitted to a research centre or higher education institution and hold a scholarship or grant research; or (3) present a term of responsibility signed by the research centre or higher education institution that guarantees their admission, as well as the expenses for their stay.

204. A residence visa is not always required. As it stems from Article 91-B (9), where the researcher has entered legally into the territory, he or she is exempted from presenting a visa, and may acquire the residence permit directly.

§2. Residence Permit for the Purposes of Research Activities

205. Article 91-B IL sets forth the conditions for a researcher to obtain a residence permit. Such residence permit shall be granted to third-country nationals who, besides meeting the general conditions laid down by Article 77 IL, were admitted to collaborate in an officially recognized research centre, namely through: (1) work contract, (2) service provision contract, (3) scientific research grant or (4) hosting agreement.

206. As was the case with visa requirements, some general conditions for acquiring residence permits in Portugal are not applicable either to researchers who will conduct their activity in an officially recognized institution. That is the case of

122. According to Art. 91-B, this official recognition is requested by the institution, and must be preceded by a favourable opinion issued by the SEF (n. 3). It is valid for five years.

paragraphs (d) (proof of having sufficient means of subsistence), (e) (adequate housing) and (f) (inscription in the social security) of Article 77 IL.

207. The researchers' residence permit is valid for two years (Article 91-B (6) IL), renewable for equal periods, unless the hosting agreement has a shorter duration. However, residence permits granted to researchers under European Union or multilateral programmes, which include mobility measures, are valid for two years or for the duration of the hosting agreement.

Chapter 5. Labour and Economic Migration

§1. Labour Employment: General Scheme

208. The Portuguese Immigration Law sets forth several types of immigration titles for labour purposes. We will start by analysing the 'general residence scheme' of immigration for labour employment.

209. As a rule, a residence permit for labour employment is issued when the applicant holds a visa issued for the purpose of acquiring the respective residence permit. However, the Portuguese Law foresees some cases of 'regularisation' of migrant workers – that is to say, residence permits for migrants who do not hold a visa and are already in the territory. We will analyse these two situations separately.

I. Visa and Residence Permits for Labour purposes

A. Visa and Residence Permit to Exercise Subordinate Professional Activity

210. Until 2022, the granting of a visa for dependent work was subjected to a protectionist clause: this visa was conditional upon the existence of job opportunities that had not been taken by Portuguese nationals, by workers who were nationals of EU Member States, of the European Economic Area, or by nationals of third States with which the EU has signed an agreement on free movement of persons, as well as by third-country nationals who were already residents. For such purposes, the Council of Ministers, with the prior opinion of the Permanent Commission for Social Coordination, had to annually approve a resolution that would set forth a number of employment opportunities presumably not filled by the workers referred to above. Only exceptionally could a visa be issued to third-country nationals without taking into account the number of employment opportunities. The interested person had to already have an employment contract and also had to prove that the job offer was not filled by the mentioned workers.

211. The 2022 amendments have deeply simplified the granting of work visas by completely eliminating these protectionist clauses. Currently, for acquiring a visa for the purposes of exercising a subordinate professional activity, it is sufficient for the migrant to be in one of the two following cases: (1) to hold a work contract or a promise of work contract *or* (2) to present a 'declaration of interest' from an employer and hold the necessary qualifications and competences for the exercise of the correspondent activity (Article 59(5)(b) IL). The migrant does not need to show that the job offer was not filled by 'preferable workers'. The new law demonstrates the complete willingness of the Portuguese system to open legal channels for migration, as the EU itself has been so largely advocating.

212. The IL also sets forth that the Institute of Employment and Vocational Training, I. P. (Instituto de Emprego e Formação Profissional, I. P.), as well as the regions' competent services shall maintain an information system, available to the general public through the Internet, that will permanently publish updated information on available job offers. This is an important legal provision that follows some of the measures foreseen in the Global Compact for Migration, regarding information on migration opportunities (namely on labour migration).[123]

B. *Visa and Residence Permit for the Exercise of Independent Professional Activity or for Enterprising Immigrants*

213. Under the Portuguese IL, a visa to obtain a residence permit for the exercise of an independent professional activity may be granted to third-country nationals who fulfil the following conditions: (i) have a service contract or a written proposal to that effect in the framework of liberal professions; (ii) and being entitled to carry out the independent activity where applicable (Article 59(1), paragraphs (a) and (b) IL).

214. Furthermore, a residence visa is granted to enterprising immigrants wishing to invest in Portugal, provided that they: (i) have carried out investment operations; (ii) prove to have financial means in Portugal, including those arising from financing obtained from a financial institution in Portugal, and demonstrate, by any means, the intention to carry out an investment operation within the Portuguese territory; (iii) or develop an entrepreneurial project, including the creation of an innovative base company as defined by the Government (Article 60(2), paragraphs (a), (b) and (c) IL).

C. *Visa and Residence Permit for Teaching, Highly Qualified or Cultural Activity*

215. Without prejudice to the application of the 'EU blue card' scheme,[124] a residence permit is granted to a third-country national for the performance of teaching in an educational or vocational training institution or highly qualified or cultural activity if he/she fulfils the general conditions set forth in Article 52 IL and has: (i) an employment contract or promise of employment contract, or service contract; (ii) an invitation letter issued by an educational or vocational training institution; (iii) or a term of responsibility of a certified company in accordance with the terms defined by a Government's Decree; (iv) or an invitation letter issued by a company or entity carrying out in the national territory a cultural activity recognized by the

123. Global Compact's Objective 5 calls upon States to 'enhance availability and flexibility of pathways for regular migration'. Under this objective, the Global Compact urges States to 'work towards inclusive labour markets and full participation of migrant workers in the formal economy by facilitating access to decent work and employment for which they are most qualified, in accordance with local and national labour market demands and skills supply'.

124. *See* §3 of this chapter.

member of the Government responsible for the area of culture as of interest to the country, or as defined in the law; (v) or an invitation letter issued by a research centre [Article 61 (1), al. (a) to (e)].

216. The deadline for deciding on the visa application is of thirty days (Article 60(2) IL).

D. Visa and Residence Permit for Highly Qualified Activity Carried Out by a Subordinate Worker

217. A residence visa is granted for the exercise of a highly qualified activity carried out by a subordinate worker to third-country nationals who: (i) hold a valid employment contract or promissory employment contract valid for at least one year, corresponding to an annual remuneration of at least 1.5 times the national average gross annual salary or three times the Indexing Value of Social Support (IAS); (ii) in the case of a regulated profession, hold the necessary professional qualifications for access and exercising the profession; (iii) in the case of a non-regulated profession, hold high professional qualifications appropriate to the activity or sector specified in the employment contract or promise of employment contract (Article 61-A, als. a) to c) IL).

218. When there is doubt as to the framework of the activity and for the purpose of verifying the adequacy of the professional experience of the third-country national, the ministries responsible for the areas of employment and education and science issue an opinion prior to the granting of the visa (Article 61-A (3) IL).

E. Residence Permit with Residence Visa Exemption

219. The IL introduced a mechanism aimed at awarding residence permits to foreigners that are present in the Portuguese territory who do not hold residence visas for work purposes. This scheme – foreseen in Article 88 – can be considered as a case of regularization of foreigner workers' legal status. However, its first readings foresaw very narrow possibilities of 'regularisation'. They would not correspond to a real subjective right of the applicant but, instead, to a discretionary power of the Ministry that could be awarded only to those who would fulfil the strict requirements that Article 88 demanded.[125]

125. Regarding the previous wording of Art. 88 IL, *see* the ruling delivered by the Central Administrative Court of the South (TCAS), which states: ' (...) the expression of interest presented by the foreign citizen does not have the virtuality to trigger, that is, to initiate the administrative procedure, contrary to what happens in the particular procedures, in which the request of the person concerned is, on a practical level, the very act of opening the procedure' (cf. Judgment of the TCAS, of 03-02-2017, case n. 1523/16.5 BELSB, reported by Catarina Jarmela; accessible in: www.dgsi.pt).

220. After the IL's 5 amendment,[126] some changes in the wording of Article 88(2) were introduced. These amendments represented a very important evolution in the legalization of undocumented immigrants. The granting of a residence permit for labour purposes to third-country nationals, who maintained a properly proven employment relationship in Portuguese territory, but without being provided with their work visa, ceased to be an exceptional and discretionary procedure.[127] From then on, the regularization procedure would be only dependent on a mere expression of interest from the applicant submitted through the SEF website or directly in one of its regional delegations.

221. Regularization would be awarded to applicants who gathered the following requirements: (i) hold an employment contract or a promissory employment contract or an employment relationship proven by a trade union or by a representative of migrant communities belonging to the Council for Migration or by the Authority for Labour Conditions; (ii) have entered legally into the national territory; (iii) were registered in the social security, except in cases where the document submitted by the applicant was a promissory employment contract.

222. This is to say that, under the new legal wording, those who fulfil the conditions demanded by Article 88 IL would acquire a subjective right to regularization.

223. Through this amendment, the law seeks to circumvent a practical difficulty under the first regime that was very problematic or even impossible to overcome: having at their service illegal labour and this situation being prohibited and sanctioned by the IL (cf. Article 198 – A), employers avoided the celebration of employment contracts, for fear of being persecuted by the public inspection authority (SEF). However, having a legal contract was one of the conditions, under the previous regime, that was necessary to obtain regularization of the stay. This would lead to practical difficulty to benefit from the regularization possibility. Moreover, the previous legal solution also required that those applying for the work residence permit should have another type of regular residence in the national territory. This requirement often led to very distressing situations because it required foreigners to be already staying in a regular situation due to the possession of another administrative status. This is to say that those who lived outside the law – without any status – would be condemned to economic exploitation and social unprotection of the

---

126. Amendment operated through Law n. 59/2017 of 31 July. Accessible in: https://dre.pt/application/file/a/107784629.

127. According to the previous wording of Art. 88(2) IL, 'exceptionally and upon proposal of the national director of the SEF or on the initiative of the member of the Government responsible for the area of internal administration, the ownership of a valid residence visa for one of the purposes provided for by law could be waived, provided that the foreign citizen, in addition to the other general conditions legally provided for, fulfilled the following conditions: (i) have an employment contract or an employment relationship proven by a trade union, by an association with a seat on the Advisory Board or by the Authority for Working Conditions; (ii) had legally entered and legally resided in national territory; (iii) was registered and had its situation regularized in the social security'.

State, with virtually no possibility of access to the most basic public services (health, justice, education, etc.). So much so that the administration itself often decided, however, to make an abrogatory interpretation of such legal provision in the part in which it prescribes the need for regular residence in the national territory, but in a discretionary manner, in a manifest prejudice to legal certainty and security: when the number of annual regularizations seemed excessive, the SEF would again suddenly require the verification of the requirement of legal stay![128]

224. In the interim Law 28/2019, of 29 March, the seventh and last amendment to the IL, came into force. On the one hand, it had the purpose of revising the policy on control of migration flows and to combat illegal immigration, and, on the other hand, it aimed to promote the integration of those foreign citizens who, although having irregularly entered the national territory, were integrated into the labour market – even though in the informal sector – and were contributing to the national social security. In this regard, paragraph 6 of Article 88 IL established that, for the purposes of fulfilling the requirements for regularizing their stay in the territory, all migrants that were integrated into the labour market and contributing to the social security should be presumed to have entered legally in the national territory. Therefore, from then on, applicants who were in this situation would not need to prove to the SEF their legal entry into the country to obtain a residence permit, as long as they have worked in the national territory and have their situation regularized before social security for at least twelve months.[129]

225. Despite the development of these successive technical mechanisms to regularize the legal status of foreigners irregularly staying in the territory – an important mechanism to guarantee access to basic human rights to all those that contributed to social security – it is important to underline that this change was naturally accompanied with a substantial increase of applications, and a practical inability of the services to respond to this enormous evolution. These situations resulted in numerous delays in requests and in a chaotic system in the functioning of the SEF, motivating an odd number of complaints to the Portuguese Ombudsman, as its annual reports demonstrate.[130]

---

128. In this regard, *see* Ana Rita Gil, 'Breve Nótula sobre as recentes alterações à Lei dos Estrangeiros, aprovadas pelas Leis n. 59/2017, de 31 de julho, e n. 102/2017, de 28 de agosto', *in* AA.VV., *O contencioso de direito administrativo relativo a cidadãos estrangeiros e ao regime da entrada, permanência, saída e afastamento do território português, bem como do estatuto de residente de longa duração,* Sofia David (coord.), Centro de Estudos Judiciários, 2017, pp. 47-54. Available in: http://www.cej.mj.pt/cej/recursos/ebooks/Administrativo_fiscal/eb_estrangeiros_2ed.pdf.
129. It should be noted that, unless the law prohibits it, the legal presumptions may be rebutted by proof on the contrary (cf. Art. 350(2) of the Portuguese Civil Code), leaving it open the possibility of the SEF to prove, during the regularization process, that the applicant's entry into the national territory was carried out irregularly.
130. Provedor de Justiça – *Relatório à Assembleia da República – 2018*, available in http://www.provedor-jus.pt/site/public/archive/doc/Relat2018_web.pdf.

§2. Special Schemes

I. Special Scheme for Company Relocation

226. According to Article 123 – A (1) IL, a residence permit shall be granted to the owners, managers or workers of companies that have their registered office, or main or secondary establishment, in a State of the European Economic Area (EEA). The same can be applied when the worker comes from a State defined by the Portuguese Government when the company has established its registered office or principal or secondary establishment in Portugal. In these cases, the transferee worker may exercise his or her activity in Portugal provided that they meet the following conditions: holding a residence authorization or a valid residence permit in the state of the EEA where the company's registered office or principal or secondary establishment is located; they do not constitute a threat to public order or public security and fulfil the conditions of Article 77(g)–(j) IL.

227. The request for a residence permit for company relocation must be made by the interested parties to the SEF and must be accompanied by the following documents: an updated business registration certificate; the work contract or service agreement contract or other document proving the quality of the holder of the company or of a social body; proof of social security registration; residence permit of the country of origin; certificate of criminal record of the country of previous residence and an authorization to consult the Portuguese criminal record (cf. Article 62 – A IR).

228. The SEF must recognize the foreign residence and issue a similar residence permit valid in the Portuguese territory (Article 123 – A (2) IL). This scheme is also applicable to members of the worker's family or employee's family (Article 123 – A (3) IL).

II. Residence Permit for Workers Transferred Within the Company: 'ICT Residence Authorization'

229. A residence permit for intra-corporate transferees enables its holders to reside and work in Portuguese territory within the scope of an intra-corporate transfer (ICT) in a company or company group.[131] This scheme is a transposition of

131. However third-country nationals who fall in one of the following cases cannot apply for this residence permit: (1) have requested or are holders of residence authorization for research, pursuant to Art. 91-B; (2) benefit from free movement rights equivalent to those of European Union citizens under agreements signed between the European Union and its Member States with the person's third country of origin or in whose territory the person's company of employment is established; (3) are posted pursuant to Directive 96/71/EC of the European Parliament and of the Council of 16 December 1996; (4) are independent workers; (5) are parties to an agreement signed with temporary employment agencies or any other agencies providing professional workers under third-party supervision and direction; (6) have residence authorization for the purposes of short-term traineeships or studies integrated into curricular programmes (cf. Art. 124 – A (2) IL).

Directive 2014/66/EU of the European Parliament and of the Council of 15 May 2014 on the conditions of entry and residence of third-country nationals in the framework of an intra-corporate transfer.

230. The IL allows the granting of a residence permit for intra-corporate transferees to carry out the professional activity of manager, specialist[132] or trainee, provided that they fulfil the general conditions to obtain a residence permit established in Article 77 IL and the specific conditions set out below: (i) they prove that the host company and the company established in the third country belong to the same company or company group; (ii) they prove that they have worked at the same company or same company group for at least 3 to 12 consecutive months as a manager or specialist, or 3 to 6 consecutive months as a trainee, immediately prior to the date of transfer; (iii) they have an employment agreement with the company or company group to which the host company belongs, specifying their position as a manager, specialist or trainee; (iv) they submit a document issued by the employer mentioning the host company, remuneration and other conditions of employment during the transfer period; (v) they prove that they have professional experience and qualifications compatible with the duties of manager or specialist to be performed at the host company, or the appropriate higher education diploma in the case of trainees; (vi) they prove, in the case of a regulated profession, that they meet the conditions for practising the profession under national legislation; (vii) they have a valid travel document, whose validity covers the planned duration of the intra-corporate transfer; (viii) they prove that they have requested health insurance, under conditions applicable to Portuguese citizens, for periods in which they do not benefit from this type of coverage, or have corresponding payments related to or resulting from the work to be carried out; (ix) they provide a guarantee, by the host company, of compliance with legislation, during the transfer, concerning work conditions and the payment of remuneration not less than that paid to Portuguese workers with identical employment duties.

231. Notwithstanding, workers transferred within a company to a host company belonging to the same certified company or certified company group shall be exempt from submitting documents proving the conditions referred to in (ii), (iii), (v), (viii) and (ix), being also facilitated the issue of a visa allowing their entry into Portuguese territory (cf. Article 124 – B (3) IL).

232. The decision of granting (or not) this residence permit is the responsibility of SEF National Director, with the power to delegate. In case of concession, the permit shall be valid for one year, or for the duration of the transfer to Portuguese territory, subject to renewal for equal time periods, up to a maximum of three years for managers and specialists and one year for trainees, provided that the conditions for its granting are upheld (cf. Article 124 – A (3) and Article 124 – B (7) IL).

132. According with Art. 3(ii) of IL 'specialist' is a highly qualified worker belonging to a regulated profession, with specialized knowledge and adequate professional experience essential to the host entity's specific business, technical or management.

III. Residence Permit for Remote Work

233. The 2022 legal amendments to the Immigration Law introduced a new residence permit for foreigners who work remotely for foreign entities and wish to reside in Portugal. This novelty was a development brought after the Covid-19 pandemic crisis in 2020, where remote work became generalized, and it was broadly accepted that professionals could develop their activity while residing anywhere in the world. Under this new reality, Portugal wished to attract new residents that could contribute to the Portuguese society while maintaining their works in their countries of origin. Foreign residents who wish to migrate to Portugal for this purpose shall acquire a residence visa for remote work (Article 61-B IL) and must present a proof of their work relation or activity.

§3. 'Blue Card' Residence Permit

234. The 'EU blue card' residence permit corresponds to the transposition of the EU Directive 2009/50/EC on Conditions of entry and residence of non-EU nationals for the purposes of highly qualified employment and is regulated by Articles 121-A to 121-K IL. The new Directive (EU) 2021/1883 of the European Parliament and of the Council of 20 October 2021 on the conditions of entry and residence of third-country nationals for the purpose of highly qualified employment was not yet formally transposed.

235. The 'blue card' residence permit is defined as a residence title which enables its holders to reside and carry out a highly qualified activity in the Portuguese territory and to enjoy equal treatment with the national citizens although not so widely as the long-term residents if we compare Article 121-H with the abovementioned Article 133.

236. The 'EU blue card' residence permit shall be granted to third-country nationals who: (i) produce a work contract compatible with carrying out a highly qualified activity, for not less than one year, with a salary of at least 1.5 times the average national gross annual salary or a salary of at least 1.2 times the average national gross salary in professions which are in particular need of third-country national workers; (ii) have health insurance or submit proof that they are covered by National Health Service; (iii) are registered with the social security system; (iv) for unregulated professions, submit the documents establishing the relevant higher professional qualifications in the activity or sector specified in the work contract binding job offer; (v) for regulated profession specified in the work contract or binding job offer, submit documents establishing professional certification, where applicable (Article 121-B).

237. Article 121-A(3) specifies that 'EU blue card' shall not be granted to third-country nationals who: (i) are authorized to reside in a Member State on the basis of temporary protection or have applied for a residence permit on that basis, as well as beneficiaries of international protection in accordance with Act 27/2008, or have applied for that protection and are awaiting a decision on their application; (ii) are family members of EU citizens in accordance with Act 37/2006; (iii) have applied for or are holders of a residence permit for purposes of pursuing a research activity; (iv) enjoy a long-term resident status in a EU Member State; (v) are temporarily staying in Portugal in order to carry out investment-related trading activities, as seasonal workers or posted within the framework of a provision of services; (vi) pursuant to an agreement concluded between the EU and the third country of nationality, enjoy rights of free movement equivalent to those of EU citizens; or (vii) whose expulsion has been suspended for reasons of fact or of law. An application for a 'EU blue card' shall also be rejected: (i) if the employer has been sanctioned for irregularly employing foreign workers in the last five years; (ii) for reasons of public policy, public security or public health (Article 121-B(4)IL).

238. The 'EU blue card' is initially valid for two years and is renewable for successive periods of three years. Such renewals must be requested by the interested party up to thirty days before the expiry of the document's validity period (Article 121-E). For the first two years of legal employment in the Portuguese territory, access to the labour market shall be restricted to the exercise of paid employment activities which meet the conditions set out in Article 121-B (Article 121-G). The 'EU blue card' shall be only renewed when its holder cumulatively: (i) meets or continues to meet the conditions of entry and residence, or when the same conditions which enabled the issuing of the document are maintained; (ii) has sufficient resources to maintain him/herself without having recourse to social security assistance, exclusion made to employment benefit; (iii) has not been convicted of a crime with punishment or penalties which, individually or collectively, exceed one-year imprisonment; (iv) does not cause any risk to public policy, public security or public health (Article 121-F(2)).

239. The 'EU blue card' shall be cancelled whenever: (i) it has been obtained on grounds of false or fraudulent declarations, or false or forged documents, or through fraudulent means; (ii) there are 'strong reasons' to believe that the holder of such card has 'committed serious criminal acts, or there is strong evidence that he/she intends to commit acts of the same nature, specifically in EU territory'; (iii) there are reasons of public policy, public security or public health (Article 121-F(1)).

240. The provisions of Articles 125 to 133 shall apply *mutatis mutandis* to holders of 'EU blue card' acquired in Portugal who wish to benefit from the long-term resident status (Article 121-I). If they meet the necessary conditions, they shall be issued with an EU long-term resident permit (Article 121-J). Moreover, the 'EU blue card' holder who has resided for at least eighteen months as such in the Member State that first issued the title may, together with his/her family members, move to Portugal for the purpose of highly qualified employment (Article 121-K).

§4. SEASONAL WORKERS AND TEMPORARY WORKERS

241. The IL considers as 'seasonal worker' the third-country national who resides outside Portugal and remains legally and temporarily in the national territory to perform seasonal work, under the terms of a fixed-term employment contract concluded directly with an employer established in Portugal (Article 3(1) (cc) IL). In turn, 'seasonal work' is defined by IL as an activity dependent on the seasons, namely the activity that is linked to a certain period of the year by a recurring event or pattern of events associated with seasonal conditions, during which there is a significant increase in the labour required for the usual tasks (Article 3(1) (dd) IL).

242. The temporary work regime for seasonal purposes was introduced in the IL by Law 102/2017 of 28 August, which transposed to the domestic legal order several directives, including Directive 2014/36/EU, adopted in February 2014, which lays down the conditions for entry and residence of third-country nationals for seasonal work purposes. The Directive aims to contribute to the effective management of migration flows in the specific category of seasonal temporary migration and to ensure decent working and living conditions for seasonal workers.[133]

243. The Government member responsible for the area of employment provides after consultation with the social partners the list of employment sectors where seasonal work exists, which shall be further communicated to the European Commission. The list, in force since January 2018, results from a quantitative and qualitative sectoral analysis of the volume of job vacancies raised by the Public Employment Service and the volume of employment applications registered by this body.[134] According to paragraph 1 of this Order, the sectors of activity where there is a need for seasonal work on the Portuguese mainland are as follows: (a) agriculture, animal production, hunting, forest, and fishing; (b) accommodation and hotels, catering, and the like; (c) food, beverage, and tobacco industries; (d) wholesale and retail trade; (e) construction; (f) land transport.

244. Seasonal workers can obtain a short-term visa or a long-term visa according to the duration of the seasonal work to be carried out within the national territory. The first one is granted when the seasonal work is performed during a period equal or no longer than ninety days (cf. Article 51-A IL), and second one when the seasonal work exceeds that period (cf. Article 56 IL).

133. As mentioned in para. 7: 'This Directive should contribute to the effective management of migration flows for the specific category of seasonal temporary migration and to ensuring decent working and living conditions for seasonal workers, by setting out fair and transparent rules for admission and stay and by defining the rights of seasonal workers while at the same time providing for incentives and safeguards to prevent overstaying or temporary stay from becoming permanent. In addition, the rules laid down in Directive 20052/EC of the European Parliament and of the Council will contribute to avoiding such temporary stay turning into unauthorised stay' (cf. Directive 2014/36/EU of the European Parliament and of the Council of 26 Feb. 2014 on the conditions of entry and stay of third-country nationals for the purpose of employment as seasonal workers).

134. The list was published in the national official journal through Order n. 745/2018, issued by the Office of the Secretary of State for Employment. Cfr. Despacho n. 745/2018, of 17 Jan. 2018.

I. Short-Term Visa for Seasonal Work for a Period of Ninety Days or Less

245. A short-term visa for *a period of ninety days* or less is granted to third-country nationals who, without prejudice to Article 52 IL, fulfil the following conditions: (i) hold an employment contract or a promissory employment contract valid for performing the seasonal work, concluded with a temporary employment agency or employer established in the national territory identifying the place, time and type of work, as well as its duration, the remuneration to be paid and the duration of paid leave to which it is entitled; (ii) have adequate protection in the event of illness, in the same way as nationals, or health insurance, or benefits corresponding to the professional or work to be carried out, as well as occupational accident insurance made available by the employer; (iii) have an adequate accommodation, by lease or equivalent, or accommodation provided by the employer in accordance with Article 56 – D (3) and (4); (iv) in the case of a regulated profession, fulfil the conditions laid down in national legislation for the exercise thereof; (v) hold a valid transport ticket ensuring his return to his/her country of origin (Article 51 – A, paragraphs (a)–(e)).

246. The short-stay visa for seasonal work authorizes its holder to engage in seasonal work for a period of ninety days or less, being valid as a work permit whenever the holder is exempt from a visa to enter the national territory (cf. Article 51 – A (3) IL).

II. Temporary Stay Visa for Seasonal Work for a Period Longer Than Ninety Days

247. A temporary-stay visa for seasonal work for a period longer than ninety days is granted to a third-country national who: (i) in addition to the general conditions prescribed in Article 52 IL; (ii) fulfils the conditions prescribed in Article 51 – A (a) (d); (iii) and owns a valid travel document, during the period of validity of the visa.

248. The temporary-stay visa is valid for the period of the employment contract, but may not be higher than nine months over a period of twelve months. If the validity of the visa is less than nine months, the stay may be extended up to a limit of nine months within a period of twelve months (cf. Article 71 – A IL)[135].

135. The IL authorizes the extension of residence for seasonal work, without prejudice to the relevant provisions of the Community VC, to third-country nationals who have been admitted to the national territory in accordance with Art. 51 – IL and wish to remain in Portugal for a period longer than originally authorized (not exceeding nine months), if the conditions that allowed the admission of the seasonal worker remain unchanged (not taking into account the possible change of the employer) (Art. 71(1)(2) IL).

§5. Self-Employed Activities

I. Residence Visa for the Exercise of Independent Professional Activity

249. A visa to obtain a residence permit for the exercise of an independent professional activity may be awarded to third-country nationals who: (i) fulfil the general conditions for granting residence visas (provided for in Article 52(1) IL); (ii) have a contract or a written offer of a service agreement in the framework of liberal professions; (iii) and are entitled to carry out the independent activities, where applicable, such as doctors, engineers, and lawyers. The latter requirement shall be established by means of a declaration issued by the competent authority competent to check the requirements for the exercise of the profession when such profession is subjected to special qualifications.[136]

250. Article 60 IL could be problematic, in so far as it does not cover all situations in which a liberal activity may be exercised, nor does it fall within the definition of 'independent professional activity' adopted by that law. In fact, according to Article 3(1)(b) IL, an 'independent professional activity' consists of any activity carried out personally, in the context of a service agreement, relating to the exercise of a liberal profession or in the form of a corporation. However, the IR sets forth that the application for a visa for the exercise of an independent activity must be accompanied by a company agreement or a provision of services agreement or a written proposal for a provision of services agreement[137] – which substantially expands the possibilities contemplated in Article 60 IL.

II. Residence Permit for the Exercise of Independent Professional Activity

251. A residence permit for the exercise of an independent professional activity is granted to third-country nationals who meet the general requirements prescribed in Article 77(1) IL for the granting of a temporary residence permit and the following specific requirements: (i) have established a company, in accordance with the law; have submitted a statement of startup of activity to the Tax and Social Security Administration as a natural person or concluded a service agreement for the exercise of a liberal profession; (ii) are qualified to pursue an independent professional activity, where applicable; (iii) have means of subsistence; (iii) and, where required, submit a declaration of the professional order that they fulfil their registration requirements.[138]

252. As we have seen with regard to subordinate workers, since the 2017 amendments to the Immigration Law, self-employed workers may also apply for

136. Cf. Art. 31.º (1)(b), IR.

137. That would be the case, for example, of a doctor who wants to open an office or a lawyer, a writer, among other professions, that can be exercised without a subordinate work relationship attested by a contract.

138. Cf. Art. 89(1) als. a) to d) IL. These conditions must be proven through the relevant documentation, depending on the applicant's particular situation (Art. 55(1), als. a) a c) IR).

their regularization. They must meet the following conditions for that purpose: (i) the general requirements for granting temporary residence permit prescribed in Article 77(1) IL (excepting the visa) (ii) have legally entered into the national territory.

253. The regularization procedure begins with the submission of an 'expression of interest' by the applicant through the SEF website or directly in one of its regional delegations. The applicant must add to its request an application for exemption from residence visa and proof of legal entry into the national territory.[139] After the analysis of the expression of interest, SEF communicates to the applicant the possibility of making an appointment at a SEF service delegation, and the latter can choose a date, place, and time of his convenience according to the availability of vacancies at national level. If granted, the residence permit has an initial validity of two years and can be renewed for successive periods of three years.[140]

254. In addition, the last amendment to the IL, introduced in 2019, has simplified even more the granting of a residence permit for the exercise of independent professional activity through regularization, establishing a legal presumption that the third-country national has entered legally into the national territory in cases where he/she: (i) holds a service agreement or has an independent professional activity in the national territory; (ii) has fully complied with tax and social security obligations; (iii) in both cases, for at least twelve months (cf. Article 89(5) IL).

255. Finally, the holder of a residence permit for the exercise of an independent professional activity may pursue a subordinated professional activity by replacing the residence permit (cf. Article 89(3) IL).

§6. Investment Activities

I. Residence Visa for Enterprising Immigrants

256. The specific provision of a residence visa for enterprising immigrants willing to invest in Portugal pursued the goal – shared with several other EU countries – of attracting immigrants who could boost the national economies.

257. For the granting of this visa, it is necessary that the applicant: (i) has made investment operations in Portugal or (ii) proves to have financial resources available in Portuguese territory, including those arising from a financial institution in Portugal, and demonstrate, by any means, the intention to carry out an investment operation in the national territory.[141]

139. Cf. Art. 55(2) IR.
140. This period has recently been extended by an amendment to Art. 75(1) IL ('Temporary Residence Permit'), introduced by Law 75-B/2020 of 31 December, which approves the State Budget for the year 2021.
141. Cf. Art. 60(1)(2) IL.

258. The IL requires evidence of each of these situations, whether it is the realization of investments or the availability of financial resources in Portugal. Accordingly, the applicant must provide proof that he has carried out investment transactions or that he/she has available financial resources in Portugal, including those obtained from a financial institution, and the intention to carry out an investment transaction in Portuguese territory.[142]

II. 'Startup Visa'

259. Law n. 102/2017 of 28 August, which made the 5th amendment to the IL, introduced the 'Startup Visa'. This residence visa may be granted to a third-country national who has developed an entrepreneurial project, including the creation of an innovative base company, in a startup certified in accordance with the terms of the Government members responsible for the areas of internal administration and the economy (Article 60(2)(c) IL).

260. Following this amendment to the Portuguese IL, several legal acts were enacted, such as Ordinance n. 344/2017, of 13 November, which regulates the role of startups in the reception, framing and support of immigrant entrepreneurs and their business projects, Legislative Order n. 4/2018, of 2 February, which regulates the procedure, to be processed electronically, of the 'Startup Visa' programme.

261. Entrepreneurs applying for a start-up visa must enter an 'incubation contract' with a certified incubator, pursuant to Ordinance n. 344/2017. They must meet a number of requirements, as to their administrative, financial and entrepreneurial potential, at the time of the application.[143] Certified incubators function as host entities, which provide support in the creation and equipment of companies, and access to all the benefits that are included in the programme (e.g., financial support and tax benefits).

262. The 'Startup Visa' programme takes place in two phases: the 1st phase of 'incubator certification' aims to ensure that these entities can welcome third-country nationals. The Agency for Competitiveness and Innovation (IAPMEI) is responsible for the analysis, selection and certification of applications, as well as for monitoring the implementation of the programme. In the 2nd phase, the entrepreneurs must submit their application through an online platform provided by IAPMEI.

263. In order to obtain a residence visa for enterprising, immigrants must meet a number of requirements at the time of submitting their application for the 'Start-Up Visa' programme, such as: not have permanent residence in the Schengen Area; fully comply with tax and social security obligations (where applicable); have no criminal record; are at least 18 years old; have their own financial and subsistence

142. Cf. Art. 31(2)(b)(c) IR.
143. Cf. Art. 7 of Legislative Order n. 4/2018.

resources – which must be equivalent to twelve times the Social Support Index, proven by a banking document; and also a proof of interest of one or more certified incubators.[144] To obtain this declaration of interest, the entrepreneur must contact the certified incubators that are on a public list on the programme's electronic platform.

264. If the IAPMEI decides in favour of the application submitted to the Startup Visa programme, an incubation contract with a certified incubator shall be concluded, whether one that has shown interest or another. The contract will set forth the obligations of the entrepreneur and the obligations and services provided by the incubator.[145]

III. Residence Permit for Enterprising Immigrants

265. The 'Startup Visa' may not be necessary for the granting of a residence permit to enterprising migrants. Such permit may be directly granted to third-country nationals who developed an entrepreneurial project, including the creation of an innovative base company, integrated with a certified incubator, provided that they meet the other requirements required by law, such as the presence in Portuguese territory, the possession of means of subsistence, accommodation, absence of a conviction for a crime which in Portugal is punishable by a custodial sentence of more than one year and absence of indication in the SIS and the SEF Integrated Information System for the purpose of non-admission.[146]

266. The entrepreneur may be granted a temporary residence permit by presenting the IAPMEI statement, demonstrating the conclusion of an incubation contract with a certified incubator. This permit is valid for a period of two years and is renewable for successive periods of three years.[147]

IV. Residence Permit for Investment Activity ('Golden Visa')

267. The residence regime for Investment Activity is in force since the 2012 amendments to the IL. According to this regime, third-country nationals may have a residence permit for investment activity with a visa waiver to enter into the Portuguese territory.[148] They must, however, hold a valid Schengen visa and fulfil the other requirements foreseen in Article 77 IL.

---

144. Cf. Art. 5(1)(2) of Legislative Order n. 4/2018 of 2 February.
145. Cf. Art. 7 of Legislative Order n. 4/2018 of 2 February.
146. Cf. Art. 89(4) and Art. 77(1) IL.
147. According to the changes introduced by law 75-B/2020 which approves the State Budget for the year 2021 and which has simplified the procedures for the granting and renewal of residence permits.
148. Cf. Art. 90 – A (1) (a) IL.

268. In order to acquire this residence permit, the third-country national must exercise – whether personally or through a limited liability company – an investment activity in the national territory. For this purpose, the IL sets forth an array of actions that shall be considered as 'investment activities':[149]

(a) a capital transfer to a Portuguese Bank account of at least EUR 1 million;[150]
(b) the creation of at least ten job positions;[151]
(c) the purchase of real state valued at least EUR 500.000 or at least EUR 350.000 in the case of renovation of properties with construction dating back of more than thirty years or located in urban redevelopment areas;[152]

149. Cf. Art. 3(1)(d) IL.
150. This investment may be proven through the presentation of the following documents: (i) declaration of a credit institution authorized or registered in the national territory with the Bank of Portugal, attesting the ownership, free of encumbrances and charges, of deposit accounts with a balance equal to or greater than 1 million euros, resulting from an international transfer, or a share in the same amount when collective accounts are involved; (ii) in the case of the acquisition of public debt instruments of the Portuguese State, namely treasury bonds, savings certificates or treasury certificates, a certificate attesting ownership, free of encumbrances and charges, issued by the Treasury and Public Debt Management Agency, for instruments with a value equal to or greater than 1 million euros; (iii) in the case of the acquisition of book-entry securities, a certificate proving ownership, free of encumbrances and charges, issued by the respective registering entity under the terms and for the purposes of paras 1 and 2 of Art. 78 of the Securities Code Furniture; (iv) in the case of the acquisition of bearer-titled securities deposited with the depositary under the terms of Art. 99 of the Securities Code, a certificate proving ownership, free of encumbrances and charges, issued by the depositary; (v) in the case of non-integrated nominative securities in a centralized system, a certificate proving their ownership, free of encumbrances and charges, issued by the respective issuer; (vi) in the case of the acquisition of securities integrated into a centralized system, a certificate proving their ownership, free of encumbrances and charges, issued by the financial intermediary with whom the respective account is opened in a centralized system; (vii) in the case of acquisition of shareholding not covered by the preceding points, certificate of the updated commercial register, attesting the holding of the shareholding, and the contract by which the acquisition took place, indicating the acquisition value (cf. Art. 65 – D (1) als. a) to g) IR).
151. This requirement must be evidenced through the presentation of the employment contracts concluded with the workers (cf. Art. 65 – D (2) IR).
152. The investment in real estate preview in this and in the following point must be certified by the investor through the presentation of the adequate documentation to each situation: (i) purchase deed or precontract agreement of real estate; (ii) declaration of a credit institution authorized or registered in the national territory with Bank of Portugal, attesting the international transfer of capital for the acquisition of real estate or for payment, as a sign in the precontract agreement, with a value equal or superior than the legally required; (iii) up-to-date certificate from the land registry office, with the registers, endorsements and inscriptions in force, showing ownership of the real estate, free of encumbrances and charges; or certificate from the land registry stating the valid provisional registration of the precontract agreement, whenever legally feasible, with a signal equal to or greater than the amount legally required; (iv) real estate booklet of the property, whenever legally possible (cf. Art. 65 – D, als. a) to d) IR. This type of investment must also be evidenced with the following documentation: (i) prior notice or licensing request for the realization of the urban rehabilitation operation or contract for the realization of rehabilitation works in the properties object of acquisition, signed with a legal entity that is duly qualified by the Institute of Public Markets, Real Estate and Construction, IP; (ii) proof of completion of the construction of the real estate(s) at least 30 years ago if this does not result from the land registration certificate; or declaration by the competent entity attesting that the property is located in an urban rehabilitation area (cf. Art. 65 – D, als. (e), (h) and (i) IR).

(d) a capital transfer of at least EUR 350.000 for investment in research activities conducted by public or private scientific research institutions involved in the national scientific or technological system;[153]
(e) transfer of EUR 250,000 or more in capital which is invested in artistic production, restoration or maintenance of national cultural heritage, through direct central and peripheral administrative services, public institutes, entities from the public business sector, public foundations, private foundations with public utility status, inter-municipal entities, entities belonging to the local business sector, municipal associations and public cultural associations pursuing functions in the area of artistic production, restoration or maintenance of national cultural heritage;[154]
(f) transfer of EUR 350,000 or more in capital for the acquisition of holdings in investment funds or venture capital funds for corporate capitalization, established under Portuguese Law, with at least five years' maturity at the time of the investment, and with at least 60% of the investment amount in commercial companies based in Portuguese territory;[155]
(g) transfer of EUR 350,000 or more in capital to incorporate a commercial company based in Portuguese territory, together with the creation of five permanent job positions, or as capital input for an existing commercial company based in Portuguese territory, together with the creation or maintenance of job positions, with a minimum of five permanent positions, and for a minimum of three years.[156]

269. The application for a 'Golden Visa' must be made online on the SEF website (an online pre-registration is mandatory). Alternatively, the application may be

153. This requirement must be certified through a declaration issued by a public or private scientific research institution integrated with the national scientific and technological system, attesting the effective transfer of that capital (cf. Art. 65 – D (7) al. b) IR).
154. The applicant must certify the fulfilment of this requirement by presenting the following documents: (i) declaration issued by the beneficiary entity, attesting the effective transfer of the legally required capital; (ii) declaration issued by the Cultural Strategy, Planning and Evaluations Office, after hearing the service of the cultural area with attributions in the sector, attesting the nature of investment or support to artistic production, recovery, or maintenance of the national (Art. 65 – D (8) (a) (b) IR).
155. This investment must be evidenced by: (i) a certificate proving ownership of the participation units, free of charge, issued by the entity responsible for maintaining an updated register of the participation unit holders, under the terms of the law, the respective management regulation or contractual instrument; (ii) a declaration issued by the management company of the respective investment fund, attesting the viability of the capitalization plan, the maturity of at least five years, and application of at least 60% of the investment in commercial companies based in the national territory (Art. 65 – D (9) (a) (b) IR).
156. The applicant must present a certificate proving the incorporation of a commercial company with share capital equal to or greater than the legally required and the respective updated commercial registration certificate or, in the case of acquisition of shareholding, updated commercial registration certificate, attesting the ownership of the share, and contract through which the respective acquisition was made, with an indication of the acquisition value, being SEF the responsible by the verification unofficially of his/her situation before social security (cf. Art. 65 – D (10) IR).

made by the applicant's legal representative, duly authorized for this purpose (after registration, the representative must submit to the SEF his or her forensic power of attorney).

270. The request shall be formalized by the applicant, upon presentation of an oath statement, attesting to the fulfilment of the minimum quantitative and temporal requirements of the investment activity in the national territory.[157]

271. Moreover, at the time of the request for a residence permit to carrying out an investment activity, the applicant must prove that he/she is up-to-date with his/her tax and social security contributions, which can be done by the presentation of an updated negative debt statement issued by the Tax Authority and by the Social Security or, in its impossibility, through a declaration certifying the absence of registration with these entities.[158]

272. In addition to the documents referred to above, when the investment is realized through an international transfer of capital, the applicant must submit a declaration from the credit institution authorized or registered in the national territory with the Bank of Portugal, attesting the effective transfer of an amount equal to or greater than that legally required.[159]

273. The Residence Permit for the Investment Activity is initially a temporary residence permit, valid for a period of two years, renewable for successive periods of two years if the conditions which allowed its concession are maintained.[160] In addition to the conservation of the investments realized, the investors must also secure a minimum period of permanency in the Portuguese territory, which is of seven days, consecutive or interpolated in the first year of residence and of fourteen days in the subsequent periods of two years of residence.[161]

157. Article 65 – D (15) IR.
158. Cf. 65 – D (14) IR.
159. Cf. 65 – D (11) IR.
160. Cf. Art. 90 – A (2) of IL and 65 – E IR.
161. Cf. Art. 65 – C IR. The amendment introduced to Art. 75 IL by Art. 192 of Law n. 75-B/2020, of 32 December (State Budget for 2021), which prolongs the validity period of the temporary residence permits is not applicable, since there is a special provision for the investment's residence permits.

Chapter 6. Asylum

274. The right to asylum is a fundamental right, recognized first and foremost not only by the European Charter of Fundamental Rights but also by the Portuguese Constitution. Article 33(8) of the Constitution guarantees the right of asylum 'to foreigners and stateless persons who are the object, or are under grave threat, of persecution as a result of their activities in favour of democracy, social and national liberation, peace among peoples, freedom or the rights of the human person'. As mentioned in the General Introduction, the Portuguese Asylum Law (AL) is in force since 2008, and was only amended once, in 2014, in order to accommodate the changes of the EU Asylum Law. Thus, it has transposed the three most important EU Directives of the so-called Common European Asylum System (namely the 'Qualification Directive',[162] the 'Procedures Directive'[163] and the 'Reception Conditions Directive')[164]. Moreover, it also foresees some provisions aimed at implementing the Dublin Regulation.[165] As for the Temporary Protection scheme, the Portuguese Law has enacted a specific law that has transposed the Directive on Temporary Protection[166] – Law n. 67/2003 of 23 August.

275. In this chapter, we aim to analyse the conditions foreseen in the law to be granted asylum through the several statuses provided by the EU law – refugee status, subsidiary protection and temporary protection. According to Article 2(1)(b) of the AL, the first two categories grant their holder the status of 'beneficiary of international protection'. Through this status, the competent Portuguese authorities (essentially the SEFs' National Director) recognize that a foreigner or stateless person is authorized to remain in the national territory. In cases where the applicants hold multiple nationalities, asylum may only be granted when the reasons for persecution apply to all States of which they are nationals (Article 3(3) AL).

§1. Conditions

I. Refugee Status

276. The concept of Refugee enshrined in the AL follows strictly the notion recognized by EU law and, also, by the 1951 Geneva Convention on the status of

162. Directive 2011/95/EU of the European Parliament and of the Council of 13 Dec. 2011 on standards for the qualification of third-country nationals or stateless persons as beneficiaries of international protection, for a uniform status for refugees or for persons eligible for subsidiary protection, and for the content of the protection granted.
163. Directive 2013/32/EU of the European Parliament and of the Council of 26 Jun. 2013 on common procedures for granting and withdrawing international protection.
164. Directive 2013/33/EU of the European Parliament and of the Council of 26 Jun. 2013 laying down standards for the reception of applicants for international protection.
165. Regulation (EU) n. 604/2013 of the European Parliament and of the Council, of 26 Jun. 2013, establishing the criteria and mechanisms for determining the Member State responsible for examining an application for international protection lodged in one of the Member States by a third-country national or a stateless person.
166. Council Directive 2001/55/EC of 20 Jul. 2001 on minimum standards for giving temporary protection in the event of a mass influx of displaced persons and on measures promoting a balance of efforts between Member States in receiving such persons and bearing the consequences thereof.

Refugees, and also encompasses the concept of 'political Refugee' enshrined in the Portuguese Constitution. Thus, this concept is broader than the notion that would result from a literal reading of the Constitution.[167]

277. According to Article 3(1) and (2) and Article 4 AL, foreign nationals and stateless persons may acquire the refugee status where: (i) they are being persecuted or face serious threat of persecution, as a result of their activities in the State of origin (which can be the State of nationality or the State of residence), in favour of democracy, social and national liberties, peace among peoples, freedom and human rights; or (ii) well-grounded fear persecution on grounds of their race, religion, nationality, political opinions or membership in a particular social group,[168] and cannot, or due to such fear, do not wish, to return to the State of their nationality or residence. As one can see, the refugee definition in the AL includes both the notion that stems from the Portuguese Constitution: (i) and the notion that results from international and European law (ii). The concept foreseen in the Portuguese Constitution may indeed be broader, as it encompasses persecution due to ideas and activities that may not be considered, strictly speaking, 'political ideas'. That would be the case of persons working in favour of human rights, for example.

278. These notions encompass several elements which meaning is explained in detail in the law. Acts of persecution must be understood as those that, by their nature or repetition, represent a serious violation of fundamental rights. As detailed by Article 5(2) AL, the acts of persecution can be of different types, such as: (i) acts of physical or psychological violence, including sexual violence; (ii) legal, administrative, police or judicial measures, when discriminatory or applied in a discriminatory manner; (iii) denial of access to fair procedures, implying disproportionate or discriminatory sanctions; (iv) sanctions for refusing to perform military service in a conflict situation which would imply the practice of a crime against peace, war crimes, crimes against humanity, or other serious crimes; and (v) acts committed specifically on grounds of gender or against children.

279. Persecution can be made by: (i) the State; (ii) political parties or organizations which control the State or a significant part of the territory; (iii) non-State agents if it is proven that the former is incapable of or does not wish to provide protection against the persecution (Article 6 AL). Protection is considered to exist whenever the State or the controlling organizations' agents adopt appropriate measures to prevent, effectively and not temporarily, the practice of acts of persecution – namely through an effective legal system, capable of prosecuting and punishing those acts.

---

167. *See*, on this issue, Andreia Sofia Pinto Oliveira, *O Direito de Asilo na Constituição Portuguesa – Âmbito de protecção de um direito fundamental*, Coimbra Editora, 2009.

168. It is irrelevant that the applicant effectively has the characteristic associated with race, religion, nationality, social or political group that induces the persecution, provided that this characteristic is attributed to him by the agent of the persecution.

280. A well-grounded fear of persecution may be based on events that have occurred or activities that have been developed after the foreign national or the stateless person has left his/her State of origin, especially in cases where the activities serving as the basis of the application represent the convictions or orientations which have already been manifested by the person in that State (Article 8). This corresponds to the 'protection sur place'. However, this protection is not applicable if those circumstances were created by the applicant exclusively for the purpose of benefiting, without sufficient reason, from the status of refugee or subsidiary protection.

281. Foreign nationals or stateless persons may not benefit from the status of refugee when they fall under one of the 'exclusion clauses'. These clauses are aimed at protecting the Portuguese community, national security, and public order. Since we must understand these clauses as being restrictions to the right to asylum, they must be interpreted strictly and limited. Reasons that may justify an exclusion of protection are the following: (i) the applicant is suspected of having committed a crime against peace, a war crime or a crime against humanity, as defined by the competent international instruments; (ii) he/she is suspected of having committed an intentional common law crime punishable with a prison sentence of more than three years, before having been admitted in the Portuguese territory; (iii) he/she has committed acts which are considered as being against the United Nations; or (iv) he/she constitutes a danger or justified threat for internal or external security or for the public order.

II. Subsidiary Protection Status

282. International protection can also be granted through a subsidiary protection status. This status is granted to foreign nationals and stateless persons who do not qualify as refugees but are also prevented from returning to their country of origin. This happens due to other important reasons related to the protection of the applicant's paramount human rights. The Portuguese AL has transposed the reasons established in the EU Qualification Directive but has introduced some slight changes. Subsidiary protection can be awarded where there are systematic violations of human rights in the country of origin and also where the applicant runs the risk of suffering serious harm, such as: (i) death penalty or execution; (ii) torture, inhuman or degrading penalties or treatments; (iii) a serious threat to his/her life or physical integrity, resulting from indiscriminate violence in situations of international or internal armed conflict or widespread and indiscriminate violation of human rights (Article 7 AL). Article 15 of the Qualification Directive limits the latter clause only to indiscriminate violence in situations of international or internal armed conflict. The Portuguese Law has added the situation of 'indiscriminate violation of human rights' as a ground for acquiring subsidiary protection status. As with the refugee status, subsidiary protection may also be granted 'sur place'.

283. There are also 'exclusion' clauses of subsidiary protection. Besides circumstances applicable in the context of refugee status, foreign or stateless persons may not benefit from subsidiary protection when they have committed one or more crimes which would have been punishable with a prison sentence had they been committed in Portuguese territory and have left the country of origin solely with a view to avoid the penalties resulting from such crime or crimes (Article 9(2)(c) AL).

III. Temporary Protection

284. Temporary Protection is regulated under a special law Temporary Protection Law (TPL)[169] which – like its source (the Temporary Protection Directive) – was only activated in Portugal in 2022, in the context of the war in Ukraine. In general, temporary protection is dependent on the declaration of a 'mass influx of persons' by the Council of the European Union. However, the TPL also foresees a national situation where the Portuguese State may be confronted with a mass influx and be forced to take measures to deal with that challenge. In this case, the declaration must be made by the Council of Ministries, through a resolution (Article 4(3) TPL).[170] For this purpose, the Council of Ministries shall take into account the risks to displaced persons, the urgency and need for temporary protection and the consequences for the national public order and national security. Moreover, in case of a declaration made at the EU level, the Portuguese State may broaden the group of persons who are covered by the EU decision, and volunteer to receive other groups of people (Article 9 TPL).

285. In order to adequately manage the crisis, the Government must create an interministerial commission, which shall be competent to evaluate the country's reception conditions and govern the national responses in order to effectively respond to the persons' protection needs.

286. Exclusion clauses applicable to the refugee or subsidiary protection status are also valid for persons willing to receive temporary protection in Portugal. Special care must be taken in order to guarantee that any exclusion decision is only based on the person's individual behaviour (Article 6 TPL).

287. If the persons concerned fulfil all the requirements to receive temporary protection, then the applicant must receive a temporary protection title. All procedures related to visas and other documents shall be eased, and promoted quickly. In order to facilitate this procedure, some documents may be exempted in case of need. The procedure is free of costs (Article 10 TPL).

288. The temporary protection lasts for one year, and must be renewed for one more year if the reasons that have justified its declaration still exist (Article 7 TPL). However, during this period, those who are interested can apply for asylum, in one

169. Law n. 67/2003, of 23 August.
170. Resolution of the Council of Ministers n. 29-A/2022, of 1 March, which established the specific criteria for granting temporary protection to displaced persons from Ukraine.

of its modalities (Article 19 TPL). Until the end of the asylum procedure, the applicant retains his or her status as 'protected person' (Article 21).

289. When the temporary protection's time limit is reached, its holders must leave the Portuguese territory, or request a residence permit – being applicable, in this latter case, the IL (Article 22 TPL).

§2. Procedures

I. Asylum Procedure

290. A foreigner or stateless person who enters in the Portuguese territory seeking asylum must apply without delay to the SEF or to any other police authority (Art 13(1) AL). The application can be done in writing or orally. In the latter case, a written record to that effect shall be made. According to Article 10 AL, any international protection request must be understood as an asylum request – that means that the applicant does not need to expressly mention the word 'asylum', and the official must register an asylum application when it stems from the applicant's discourse that he or she is seeking asylum.

291. According to the Asylum Law, SEF shall immediately inform the United Nations High Commissioner for Refugees (UNHCR) representative in Portugal and the Portuguese Refugee Council (CPR) as a non-governmental organization acting on its behalf on the filing of the application for international protection. They may contact the applicant immediately upon receipt of such communication with the purpose to inform them about the procedure and its possible intervention, which depends on the consent of the applicant (Article 13(3) AL).

292. The Portuguese general asylum procedure is structured in two phases: the admissibility procedure (Article 14 AL) and the decision procedure (Art 21 AL). The first stage is aimed at analysing whether the application is admissible and whether it shall be decided.[171] Applicants must submit all documents possible, and their fingerprints are collected (Article 15(e)) if the applicant is aged above 14 years old. During this first stage, applicants are authorized to remain in the Portuguese territory – although no residence permit is yet issued. Claimants only receive a document that proves that they have made an application (Article 11 AL).

293. Applications can be deemed unfounded in several cases, foreseen in Article 19-A AL: (a) when the request is subjected to the special procedure aimed at determining the State responsible for examining the request for international protection, as provided for in the Dublin III Regulation; (b) when the applicant benefits from international protection status in another Member State; (c) when a country other than a Member State is considered a first asylum country; (d) when a country other

171. On this topic, *see*, Ana Rita Gil, 'O Papel do Advogado na defesa dos direitos das pessoas carecidas de proteção internacional', *Themis*, Ano XIX, n. 34, 2018, pp. 7-42.

than a Member State is considered a safe third country; (e) when a subsequent application was submitted in which no new elements or data related to the analysis of compliance with the conditions to benefit from international protection were presented; (f) when a person in charge of the applicant makes a second application without adequate justification.

294. Decisions on admissibility must be made within thirty days after the application. If no answer is provided to the applicant, then the request is deemed to have been decided as approved (Article 20(2) AL).

295. When the application is admitted, the applicant receives the formal status of 'asylum seeker', and is issued with a provisional residence permit, valid for six months from the date of the decision – which can be renewed (Article 27(1) AL). As 'asylum seekers', applicants have access to several rights – as required by the 'Reception Conditions Directive'. Applicants seeking international protection, having or not being issued a provisional residence permit, and who do not have economic and social resources, and members of their families are granted social support for accommodation and food. Also, all these persons are allowed to access the National Health Service. Minor children have access to the educational system in the same conditions as national citizens. Applicants who have already been issued a provisional residence permit are guaranteed access to labour market, pursuant to general legislation (Articles 51 et seq. AL).

296. The stage aimed at analysing whether the applicant is entitled to international protection begins after the decision of admissibility. According to Article 10(2) AL, while assessing applications for international protection, the competent authorities must determine, first and foremost, whether the applicant fulfils the conditions to benefit from the status of refugee. If that is not the case, then they can analyse whether he or she is eligible for subsidiary protection. The SEF has six months to investigate whether the applicant meets the grounds for protection. This deadline can be extended for three months. Unfortunately, these deadlines are sometimes not respected, due to the heavy workload affecting the SEF since 2017 and the lack of sufficient human resources. The UNHCR and the Portuguese Council for Refugees have the right to intervene during the procedure, namely by providing evidence, reports on the country of origin, and other relevant elements (Article 28 AL). The SEF may also request the cooperation of other experts. After the analysis phase, the administration must notify the applicant of the planned decision, and the asylum seeker may respond in ten days. The final decision must be then taken in eight days, and it must be notified to the applicant in a language that he or she might understand. The UNHCR and the CPR must also be notified (Article 29).

297. Besides the general procedure – which was so far explained – the AL also foresees special procedures. One of the most important – due to its broad application in practice – is the border procedure, regulated under Articles 23 et seq. This procedure is applicable to asylum seekers who submit their applications at border posts (Article 23). According to the AL, they shall remain in the international zone of the port or airport while awaiting notification of the decision – which must be taken in seven days – Article 24(4) AL. In practice, during the procedure, asylum seekers have to remain in the temporary detention centres located at international airports. This practice seems to go against the spirit of the EU 'Reception Conditions Directive', according to which 'Member States shall not hold a person in detention for the sole reason that he or she is an applicant' of international protection (Article 8). It is a fact that the Directive provides a wide range of exceptions to this rule, namely allowing detention 'in order to decide, in the context of a procedure, on the applicant's right to enter the territory' or that grounds for detention shall be laid down in national legislation. The Portuguese AL also foresees several exceptions in this realm – the most important of which corresponds precisely to the requests made at border posts – where, as said, applicants remain in 'temporary accommodation centres' located at the airports' international areas. As the National Preventive Mechanism has repeatedly reported, these areas correspond to detention centres, as asylum seekers do not have freedom of movement. Moreover, these centres do not offer sufficient conditions for the accommodation of asylum seekers, as they do not meet the requirements established in the 'Reception Conditions Directive' nor those foreseen in the Portuguese Law – namely allowing access to information, social and psychological support, leisure activities, education for children and maintenance of family unity[172] – as required by Article 35-B AL.

298. If a decision on an application made at the border is not taken within a maximum period of seven days, the applicant shall be allowed to enter the national territory (Article 26(4) AL). In practice, as it stems from the National Preventive Mechanism reports, the SEF takes the decision in seven days – but often at the cost of failing to inform the applicants, in a language that they understand, on the grounds of the decision. In most situations, however, applicants remain longer in the detention centre as they choose to challenge the decision judicially. In these cases, applicants remain in the border zone, at least until the judicial review decision or the expire of the maximum time of detention allowed by the Asylum Law (sixty days, according to Article 35-B AL).

299. The AL also foresees other special procedures, such as those enshrined in the Procedures Directive. One of these procedures is the accelerated procedure, applied where the applicant has presented false information or documents or withheld important information or documents, has made clearly inconsistent and contradictory statements, has provided manifestly false or obviously improbable information, has entered or remained irregularly in the national territory and did not submit an application for international protection as soon as possible, has submitted a subsequent application only with the intention of delaying or preventing the application of a previous or imminent decision which results in his removal, represents a danger to the public order or internal security or refuses to submit a mandatory registration of his fingerprints in accordance with the 'Eurodac' Regulation.[173]

---

172. *See* Provedor de Justiça, Mecanismo Nacional de Prevenção, *Relatório à Assembleia da República*, 2018, pp. 37 et seq. and *Relatório à Assembleia da República,* 2019, pp. 49 et seq.

173. Regulation (EU) n. 603/2013, of the European Parliament and of the Council, of 26 June, on the creation of the 'Eurodac' system of fingerprint comparison.

300. The AL upholds both the concept of 'safe country of origin' and of 'safe third country'. When asylum seekers are deemed to come from one of these countries, they are subjected to special rules.

301. According to Article 2(q) AL, a 'safe country of origin' is the country of which the applicant is national or, being stateless, resident, in relation to which the applicant has not given any serious reason to consider that it is not safe – taking into account the applicant's personal circumstances assessed on the basis of a set of sources of information (including from other Member States, the UNHCR, the Council of Europe and other relevant international organizations). Paragraph ii) clarifies that, in order to label a certain country as a 'safe country of origin', due consideration must be given to the particular circumstances of the applicant – and not only to the country's characteristics.

302. The same provision defines, on point (r), 'safe third country' as the country where the asylum seeker has remained or transited before reaching Portugal, and where the asylum seeker will not be subjected to threats to life and freedom, to risk of refoulement or of being exposed to torture or cruel, inhuman or degrading treatment. Moreover, in order to be a 'real' safe country, it must offer a real opportunity to apply for refugee status and to receive protection under the terms of the Geneva Convention. As with the concept of 'safe country of origin', the concept of 'safe third country' can be applied, taking into account the characteristics of a particular country or of a specific person, which requires an individual assessment, or a 'case by case security analysis', and, also, the consideration that the country is considered as generally safe.[174] Finally, there must, obviously, be a link between the asylum seeker and that third country. Such link shall allow the asylum seeker to return to that country. As with the qualification of a country as 'safe country of origin', considering a particular country as 'safe third country' also implies considering the particular circumstances of the applicant (paragraph iii). An individual analysis is, thus, always required in order to determine whether a particular country can be deemed as 'safe' in a particular case.

II. Review of the Decision Rejecting the Application for Asylum

303. As already mentioned above, according to the Portuguese Constitution, all persons subjected to the Portuguese jurisdiction have the right to an effective judicial remedy against all administrative decisions (Article 268(4) Constitution). That is the case of all decisions taken during the asylum procedure – irrespective of their nature, form, or stage. Deadlines seeking judicial remedies vary depending on the specific contested decision. The applicant must seek judicial review in eight days as

174. As regards the general qualification of that country to be safe, the asylum seeker must be allowed to challenge such qualification, on the grounds that he or she would be subjected to torture, cruel, inhuman or degrading treatment or punishment, if returned to it.

regards decisions on the admissibility phase (Article 22 AL), four days for decisions taken on border procedures (Article 25) and for decisions on accelerated procedures (Article 33, Article 33-A) and fifteen days for the final decision (Article 30 AL).

304. According to the AL, the administration must notify the applicants of their right to seek judicial review in all these cases (Article 24). This is, indeed, a paramount condition to effectively guarantee the right to an effective judicial remedy – which could be impaired due to lack of knowledge on such rights and on how to exercise them. This is especially important when we are dealing with foreigners – and often vulnerable persons – who, understandably, are not familiarized with the Portuguese judicial system. Thus, the first way of assuring an effective judicial review is to inform all persons of that right.

305. Almost all judicial reviews in the asylum context suspend the decision, irrespective of their nature. That is the case of unfavourable decisions taken during the admissibility phase (Article 22), in border procedures (Article 25) and in the main decision procedure (Article 30).[175] However, judicial appeals against the first court's decision do not always have suspensive effect, as it is the case of appeals against first court's decisions on subsequent applications (Article 33(1) AL).

306. All procedures are urgent and take place in administrative courts, under a special urgent procedure aimed at protecting fundamental rights, freedoms and guarantees. The judicial review is free of charge, which means that no judiciary costs are required by the courts (Article 84 AL). Asylum seekers also have the right to free legal aid when needed, when fulfilling the requirements established in the Portuguese Legal Aid Law.[176]

III. Unaccompanied Minor Asylum Claimants

307. The Asylum Law does not establish a comprehensive and systematic legal regime on protection of unaccompanied asylum-seeking children, as this topic is regulated throughout the Asylum Law in different sections.

308. When confronted with an unaccompanied asylum seeker child, the SEF shall immediately inform the UNHCR representative and the CPR on the filing of an application for international protection – although the law does not mention it expressly. This situation is also communicated to the competent Family and Children Court, for the purposes of designating a legal guardian, who will be responsible for representing the child in the asylum procedure. In practice, unaccompanied children are represented by the entity which holds their guardianship (generally, the CPR). However, in some cases identified by the National Preventive Mechanism

175. In this latter case, the asylum seeker keeps his or her right to work until a final decision is reached in the Courts (Art. 60 AL).
176. Lei n. 34/2004, of 29 July, as last amended by Law n. 2/2020, de of 31 March.

against Torture (NPM), the Court has designated the Borders Service itself as the child's legal guardian and representative – which raises severely important questions, as the representative and the decision-making entity are the same. The absence of a legal representative does not exempt the unaccompanied children from the personal interview aimed at determining their legal status (Article 79(5)) – which is also extremely questionable.

309. According to Article 79 AL, in case of doubt, when an asylum seeker claims to be a child, he or she is deemed to be a minor until there is a proof of the contrary. Pursuant to Article 79(6) AL, the SEF may use medical expertise through a non-invasive assessment for age determination. The child must be informed of the procedure and may refuse to perform it. In that case, the refusal cannot lead to a denial of international protection.

310. Article 79(14) foresees that, in order to protect the best interests of the unaccompanied child, the SEF, in liaison with the other entities involved in the procedure, and the Ministry responsible for foreign affairs, shall begin the process of finding the child's family members as soon as possible.

311. Detention of unaccompanied children is not expressly forbidden under the AL, although it mentions the last-resort nature of this measure. Temporary 'accommodation' of unaccompanied or separated minors is subject to special conditions, as internationally recommended, namely by UNHCR, United Nations International Children's Emergency Fund (UNICEF) and the International Committee of the Red Cross (Article 26(2) AL).[177] As far as possible, these children are entitled to housing in staffed institutions and facilities that take into account the personal needs of their age (Article 35(6) AL). In practice, the child can be accommodated in the detention facilities located in the airport, being transferred to the CPR's accommodation centre as soon as possible. Following an order issued by the Minister of the Interior in 2018, children aged below 16 can only be detained in the airport's detention centres for a maximum period of seven days. As for unaccompanied minors aged 16 and over, they can only be placed in adult care centres applying for international protection when this is in their best interest (Article 79(10) AL).

312. In practice, in most cases, unaccompanied children are accommodated in the CPR's children's accommodation centre. This centre is managed by a multidisciplinary team that provides cultural, social, legal and educational support. They shall also be granted access to education (Article 53 AL). The CPR has several protocols with different entities, such as the UNHCR, the Social Security Institute, and educational entities, which shall guarantee these rights. In practice, accompanied and unaccompanied children are systematically referred to public schools upon accommodation at CPR. According to the experience of CPR's Social Department, enrolment in local public schools is generally guaranteed within a reasonable

177. On detention of unaccompanied children, *see* Ana Rita Gil, 'O papel dos Tribunais Judiciais na proteção das crianças migrantes – exigências decorrentes do Direito Internacional e Europeu', *Julgar*, n. 37, 2019, pp. 109-142.

period, although the placement of students in secondary education (i.e., over the age of 15) can be problematic due to more demanding bureaucratic procedures and placement examinations.

313. Children who are deemed to have been victims of trafficking of human beings are accommodated in special homes for trafficked children, and benefit from special security measures. For example, the shelter's address is unknown, and the personnel receives specific training on trafficking of human beings.

314. The CPR's children's home and the home aimed at protection of trafficked children may only accommodate children temporarily – in practice, only for an average stay of seven months, until a long-term solution is found. This long-term solution shall be decided by the Family and Children Court, which will apply a protection measure under a promotion and protection procedure. These measures are dealt with by the Law on Protection of Children and Youngsters in Danger (LPCYD), which sets forth that unaccompanied migrant children found in the Portuguese territory must be considered as children in danger (Article 3(2)(h)). In every case, the measure is applied after a case holistic analysis, where the needs and personal circumstances of the unaccompanied minor are evaluated and balanced. The child as well as his or her legal representative or guardian are entitled to be heard and to participate in the acts and in the definition of the protection measure.

315. Article 78(3) of the Asylum Law foresees, as regards long-term solutions, that unaccompanied children shall be placed, by order of preference, with relative adults, in foster families and, only as last resort, with specialized juvenile housing centres. However, in Portugal, there are very few families registered as foster families. Thus, there is a high percentage of children that end up being institutionalized. An individual care plan for the child is then designed, containing the medical, educational and training measures, among others. The Plan is periodically reviewed and updated on the basis of a best interests assessment. Unaccompanied children who have been the object of an institutionalization measure according to the LPCYD may acquire Portuguese nationality through naturalization (Article 6(3) of the Nationality Law).

316. Sometimes an unaccompanied child is only found in the Portuguese territory after his or her entry into the territory. In that case, the local commissions for protection of children and youngsters in danger can apply for international protection on behalf of the child, as foreseen in Article 79(13).

317. According to Article 78(3) of the Asylum Law, competent authorities must ensure that minors who have been victims of any form of abuse, neglect, exploitation, torture, inhuman and degrading treatment must have access to rehabilitation services as well as psychological assistance.

§3. LEGAL POSITION

318. Those who enjoy the legal status of refugees are entitled to a residence permit valid for an initial period of five years, renewable for similar periods. Subsidiary protection holders, however, are granted a residence permit for an initial period of three years, renewable for similar periods. This renewal is preceded by an analysis of the evolution of the situation in the country of origin (Article 67 AL).

319. The refugee status is renewed unless a specific cause for loss of the status, foreseen in Article 41 of the Asylum Law, has occurred. As for subsidiary protection, renewal is dependent on an evaluation of the situation in the countries of origin. However, even in the cases where, due to the improvement of the situation in such countries, there is no reason to renew the status, the Portuguese Law provides a way to maintain the foreigner's right to reside in the territory. Such possibility is foreseen in Article 122 (f) of the Immigration Law, which provides that those who have ceased to enjoy the right to international protection in Portugal because of the reasons on which they obtained such protection have ceased, may receive a residence permit.[178] That residence permit is no longer perceived as a protection status, and is regulated under the Immigration Law.

320. Persons benefitting from the status of refugee and subsidiary protection enjoy the rights and are subject to the duties of foreign nationals residing in Portugal. This principle would stem directly from Article 15 of the Portuguese Constitution, as explained above. However, Articles 65 et seq. AL reaffirm the social rights that must be guaranteed to international protection holders in the Portuguese territory. These rights encompass access to Education (Article 70),[179] the Labour Market (Article 71),[180] Social Security (Article 72),[181] Health Care (Article 73),[182] Housing (Article 74) and integration programmes (Article 76). As we have already pointed out, migrants' integration in Portugal is seen as a public competence. Therefore, the HCM shall promote integration programmes in order to facilitate the integration of refugees and beneficiaries of subsidiary protection into the Portuguese society.

321. Another right that is important to highlight is the right to free movement in the Portuguese territory, under the same conditions as other legal residents (Article 75 AL). The guarantee of this right was particularly discussed during the refugee

178. *See* §4 of Ch. 6. for Art. 122 IL.
179. Article 70 AL states that: 'minors who are granted refugee or subsidiary protection status shall be granted full access to the education system, under the same conditions as nationals'.
180. Youngsters will benefit from the general measures, applicable to Portuguese citizens, as regards access to employment, under the aegis of the Employment and professional training Institute.
181. A monetary allowance is only provided for asylum seekers. After obtaining the international protection status, all migrants shall benefit from general social protection rules: according to Art. 72 AL, they are subjected to the same schemes as those applicable to Portuguese citizens. These change leads often to adverse reactions from the international protection holders, who see the end of the monetary allowance as a decrease of their rights in the Portuguese society.
182. Beneficiaries of refugee or subsidiary protection status and their family members have access to the National Health Service, under the same conditions as national citizens.

relocation system in the aegis of the 2015 European Agenda on Migration. Its application in Portugal depended on the allocation of an international protection holder to a specific part of the territory. Several refugees and subsidiary protection holders claimed that they would lose social benefits and support to housing if they would move to another part of the territory. However, the right to movement was not precluded itself, although a specific housing support could be lost. Thus, it was understood that these measures were not incompatible with the protection of the right to free movement.

§4. Position of Family Members

322. The right to family reunification is obviously recognized to international protection holders. According to Article 68 AL, they may ask to be reunited with the following family members: the spouse or the member of a de facto union, minor or incapable children in charge of the couple or of one of the spouses, applicant's or spouse's adopted minor children (according to a decision of the competent authority of the country of origin), ascendants in the straight line and in the first degree of the beneficiary of international protection, if he /she is a minor or, finally, in case of unaccompanied minors, the adults who are responsible for them.

323. The effects of refugee status or subsidiary protection are extended to these family members. This implies that family members of international protection holders receive a residence permit, the validity of which is identical to the refugee or subsidiary protection holder. Although the AL refers to the rules on family reunification foreseen in the IL, some requirements mentioned in the latter are not applicable to refugees, such as having adequate housing and sufficient resources.[183] Thus, family members enjoy the same social rights, such as access to labour market, education, social security, and professional training, that are enjoyed by the international protection holder.

183. *See*, *supra*, Ch. 4.

Chapter 7. Humanitarian Reasons

§1. Humanitarian Grounds

I. Concept and Grounds of Humanitarian Protection

324. It is a general principle of international law that States have a sovereign power to admit in their territory whoever they may want – irrespective of the fulfilment of legal requirements. That is what one normally calls *'ius includendi et excludendi'*. Traditionally, this power has been used to award protection to persons who, albeit not being eligible to asylum, need to receive protection due to other grounds, usually related to human rights or simply due to a State's 'act of grace'. Therefore, traditionally, this type of protection is only granted where the person's situation does not fall upon any grounds conferring a refugee status or subsidiary protection.

325. Traditionally, one may not consider that there is a 'right to humanitarian residence' nor a 'State's duty to grant a humanitarian protection'. Traditionally, this possibility falls upon a discretionary and free power belonging to the State.

II. Humanitarian Visas

326. According to Article 68 IL, a special visa for temporary entering and remaining in the Portuguese territory may be granted at border posts to foreign citizens that do not meet the legal requirements for that effect.[184] This may occur, precisely, due to humanitarian reasons or due to national interests. Although this possibility should be open-ended, due to its *ratio*, the grounds for conferring such visas must be foreseen in Government's regulations. This solution aims at providing some guidance to the border guards and at avoiding arbitrariness at the borders.

327. The visa shall be temporary[185] and, contrary to the short-term 'Schengen visa', is only valid in the Portuguese territory. This corresponds to what Article 25 VC refers. However, if the person to whom such visa is issued is subject to an alert in the SIS, his/her admission in Portugal shall be communicated to the competent authorities of other Schengen-Member States.

III. Humanitarian Residence Permits

328. Migrants who wish to apply for residence based on humanitarian grounds must enter into the Portuguese territory with a humanitarian visa. Nevertheless, the

184. When the beneficiary of such visa holds a diplomatic service, official or special service passport, or a travel document issued by an international organization, the Ministry of Foreign Affairs shall be consulted wherever possible (Art. 68(5) IL).
185. The special visa on humanitarian grounds may be extended exceptionally for up to sixty days, according to Art. 72(1)(b) IL and Art. 46 of Regulation 15-A/2015.

IL foresees the possibility of awarding a humanitarian residence permit even to those who have not entered legally into the territory. One may consider that this possibility represents a case of 'humanitarian regularisation'. This solution is established in Article 123 IL, under the title 'exceptional reasons'.

329. This type of residence permit is awarded upon a proposal of the SEF's National Director or by initiative of the member of the Government responsible for internal affairs. Normally, the interested person applies for such residence permit (through what the IR calls an 'expression of interest') – which will be analysed by the Government. Although this possibility leads, by its very nature, to a discretionary governmental power, Article 123(3) sets forth that the correspondent ministerial decisions shall be duly substantiated.[186]

330. The 'exceptional regime' may be used for an array of cases that surpass the literal and strict meaning of 'humanitarian grounds'. Indeed, this possibility is also employed to award residence for 'national interest reasons' and also to foreigners who provide important services to the State – in scientific, cultural, sports, economic or social domains.[187]

331. The IR has developed this regime, clarifying what may be considered as 'humanitarian reasons'. Law n. 71/2018 has amended this regulation and has enlarged substantially the concept quite beyond its original purpose. According to Article 62(2) of that regulation, SEF should consider as humanitarian reasons, according to the specific circumstances of the case, the applicants' inclusion in the Portuguese labour market for more than one year.

332. This change led to a substantial adjustment of the 'humanitarian grounds' concept – as it would now function to regularize those who are merely inserted in the work market and who would not – per se – correspond to a humanitarian pressing need, even though, it could be the case when other factors are present (e.g., development of strong ties with the Portuguese community).

333. Article 123 started to be used as an alternative to Article 88, as another way of regularization of migrant workers. This benefitted especially those who entered irregularly in the territory, as Article 88 only regularizes the status of those who had entered into Portugal through legal channels.

334. This amendment also led to a significant increase in requests made under Article 123. However, it did not change this article's nature: it continues to foresee a mere discretionary possibility – thus, even where the applicant has been working

186. *See* Nuno Piçarra and Francisco Borges 'Portugal – Exceptional grant of residence permits to irregular migrants' in *Policies on irregular migrants, Volume III – France, Portugal and Poland*, Council of Europe Publishing, 2010, pp. 93-114.

187. The Portuguese Nationality Law also sets forth a special regime for naturalization to those who provide relevant services to the Portuguese community. *See* Art. 6(6) Nationality Law.

in the national territory for more than one year, the Government may still deny discretionarily the residence permit. However, since Article 123 demands the decisions be duly grounded, one may control the respect for fundamental principles, such as the prohibition of discrimination on the basis of nationality, race, religion, and sexual orientation.

§2. Unaccompanied Minor Children

335. As seen above,[188] in order to prevent trafficking of children, the IL sets forth that border authorities must refuse entry into the country to foreign citizens who are less than 18 years old when not accompanied by their legal guardian, unless there is a Portuguese citizen or a legal resident who is responsible for their stay. In the latter case, there must be an appropriate valid authorization issued by the legal guardian attesting that this person may take care of the child. If that is not the case, the child must be returned by the carrier to the country of origin and handed over to their legal guardian, or to an organization to whom they can be entrusted. However, unaccompanied minors may only be returned to their country of origin or to a third-country which is willing to receive them *provided that there is a guarantee that, upon arrival, they will be given appropriate care and assistance* (Article 30(6) IL, which implements Article 10§2 of the EU Return Directive). This rule prevails over the provision on return – which is easily understandable due to the duty to protect the best interests of the child in every circumstance.

336. Indeed, the Convention on the Rights of the Child requires that in every decision that may affect children – including, thus, administrative migration decisions – the State must take into account, primarily, the best interests of the child. Returning an unaccompanied child to a country where he or she would not be received by his or her legal guardian would hardly be compatible with their best interests. Moreover, Article 69 of the Portuguese Constitution sets forth the State's duty to protect every child who is in the Portuguese territory. This implies, naturally, that the State must protect unaccompanied children who are present at the border.

337. Unaccompanied minors awaiting a decision on their admission into the national territory or on their repatriation shall be granted all material support and assistance necessary to meet their basic needs of food, hygiene, accommodation and medical assistance[189] (Article 30(5) IL). Normally, these children have been received in a shelter ran by the Portuguese Council for Refugees, which is specially aimed at accommodating unaccompanied children. However, in 2019, as the National Preventive Mechanism reports, this centre was often overcrowded. As a consequence, unaccompanied children have been sometimes received in detention

188. Part I, Ch. 2.
189. Nuno Piçarra, Ana Rita Gil, *Study on the requirements specific to Minors travelling alone or accompanied, legally entering or leaving the Member States/Associated Countries*, Ramboll, EurAsyllum, 2012.

centres run by SEF.[190] As the Portuguese Ombudsman has consistently recalled, this is incompatible with measures aimed at stopping the detention of migrant children, and also with their best interests.[191]

338. In cases where the State does not have guarantees that the child will be duly received in the country of origin, it must allow the child to enter and remain in the territory, for as long as needed. In these cases, the Family and Children Courts shall be notified as soon as possible so that they can decide a measure aimed at protecting the child. Protection measures are foreseen in the Law on Protection of Children in Danger, and encompass several possibilities, such as placement in an institution or family foster care.[192]

339. Article 123 IL, which, as studied in the point above, foresees an 'exceptional residence permit', was amended in 2018 to also encompass unaccompanied migrant children. According to n. 2, children who were admitted to a public, cooperative, social or private institution with a cooperation agreement with the State are considered to be in a humanitarian situation. Thus, they may acquire this residence permit. Although this measure is undoubtedly very important for protecting these children, the law could have broadened its scope in order to include unaccompanied children who were object to other protection measures, such as family foster care.

§3. Victims of Trafficking in Human Beings

340. The Portuguese legal order is in full compliance with the European standards on fighting against trafficking of human beings. It has transposed the EU Directive on fighting against trafficking of human beings and on protection of victims.[193] The Portuguese criminal law respects both the Directive and the Warsaw Convention on Trafficking of Human Beings, making the notion of 'exploitation' the central concept for considering the practice of trafficking. National Plans for protection of victims are also approved every four years.[194]

---

190. Provedor de Justiça – *Alternative Report of the Portuguese Ombudsman on the Implementation of the Convention on the Rights of the Child in the Process of Review of the Fifth and Sixth Periodic Report of Portugal*, available at http://www.provedor-jus.pt/site/public/archive/doc/Rel_Alternativo_CRC.pdf.
191. Provedor de Justiça, Contribution of the Portuguese Ombudsman on the Implementation of the Convention against Torture and Other Cruel, Inhuman or Degrading Treatment or Punishment in the Process of Review of the Seventh Periodic Report submitted by Portugal under Art. 19 of the Convention pursuant to the optional reporting procedure, page 28.
192. Law on Protection and Promotion of Children and Youngsters in Danger, Law n. 147/99, of 1 September, as last amended by Law n. 26/2018, of 5 July.
193. Directive 2011/36/EU of the European Parliament and of the Council of 5 Apr. 2011 on preventing and combating trafficking in human beings and protecting its victims.
194. The IV Plan on Fighting against the Trafficking on Human Beings was approved by a Resolution of the Council of Ministries dated 19/06/2018, n. 80/2018. It encompasses the period from 2018 to 2021.

341. The IL, on its turn, foresees special residence permits for persons who were victims of trafficking in human beings. Conditions for receiving this special permit are more favourable than what the Directive requires. They are applicable both to victims of trafficking and to victims of smuggling of migrants.

342. According to Article 109 IL, a residence permit may be awarded to these victims even if they have entered the country irregularly or do not fulfil the conditions for a residence permit. Public authorities or associations working with victims must inform them of the right to acquire a residence permit. Article 111 sets forth, according to the Council Directive 2004/81/EC,[195] that victims have a waiting period, aimed at allowing them to recover and escape from traffickers' or smugglers' control. This period has a minimum duration of thirty days and a maximum duration of sixty days. During this period, the victim cannot be expelled and has the right to receive adequate treatment – such as health and medical support, means of subsistence, psychological care when needed (especially as regards particularly vulnerable victims), protection and security and also translation services and legal aid (Article 112).

343. The residence permit is granted after the expiry of the reflection period provided for in Article 111, if the following situations occur: (a) the victim's presence in the national territory is deemed important for the investigation and judicial proceedings; (b) the victim is willing to cooperate with the authorities in the investigation; and (c) the victim has broken the relationship that he or she had with the alleged authors of the infractions. The residence permit may be granted before the expiry of the reflection period if the victim has broken the relationship with the alleged authors of the infractions (Article 109 IL).

344. The IL in this part must be read together with Decree-Law n. 368/2007. This Decree sets forth that the first and second conditions (criterion a) and b)) do not need to be fulfilled when 'personal circumstances of the victim' justify the granting of a residence permit. Such circumstances may be related to the victim's safety or health, or that of their family members or persons who have close relationships with them, with their family situation, or other situations of vulnerability. Therefore, if one of these situations happens, a residence permit can be granted even if the victim does not cooperate with the authorities. In any case, it is always required that any connection with the agents of the crime has ended. In the case of children, their best interests must always be considered, which will, of course, include special protection in view of their inherent vulnerability. As we can see, in Portugal, the victim may acquire the residence permit aimed at her protection irrespective of her willingness to cooperate with the authorities. The law considered that the victim's security would prevail above the legality of the residence or criminal prosecution interests. The State is interested in protecting the victim per se, irrespective of its interest in prosecuting those who have committed the crimes considered.

195. Council Directive 2004/81 of 29 Apr. 2004 on the residence permit issued to third-country nationals who are victims of trafficking in human beings or who have been the subject of an action to facilitate illegal immigration, who cooperate with the competent authorities.

345. The residence permit granted under this regime is valid for a period of one year and is renewable for equal periods if the conditions continue to be fulfilled or if the need to protect the identified person remains (Article 109(5) IL).

346. In cases where the victim is a minor, Article 114 IL requires that his or her best interest is taken into account in all situations. The proceedings must be adequate to their age and maturity. The State must also provide access to schooling and designate a legal representative. Moreover, every effort must be made to establish the child's identity and nationality, as well as to locate his or her family as soon as possible.

§4. OTHERS

347. Article 122 IL is another provision that sets forth, together with Article 123, cases of 'special residence permits'. It foresees a list of situations where, due to specific fundamental and human rights or to other fitting reasons, third-country nationals shall acquire the right to reside in Portugal irrespective of holding a visa or having legally entered into the territory. Therefore, if persons fall upon one of these cases, they may have their status 'regularized'.

348. The variety of cases that fall under Article 122 IL can be divided into different grounds. First, we can point out those cases that are justified by the objective of protecting the migrants' private and family life – for example, by awarding residence to those who are deeply integrated into the territory. That is the case of adult children of holders of a residence permit, who have normally stayed in the national territory since they were 10 years old (Article 122 (1)(c)). This hypothesis concern persons *who were not born* in the national territory, although having parents therein, and have never regularized their legal status through family reunification. That also is the case of adults *who were born* in the national territory and who have not left the country or have lived in Portugal since the age of 10 years old (Article 122 (1)(d)). (i) IL, the case of those who have lost the Portuguese nationality and have remained in the national territory for the last fifteen years (Article 122(1)(i) IL) and those who have not been absent from national territory and whose right of residence has expired (Article 122(1)(j) IL).

349. Respect for private life also foresees the protection of several foreigners who have entered and lived in Portugal under specific regimes and are willing to remain therein. That is the case of foreigners who have ceased to benefit from the right of asylum in Portugal due to having ended the reasons that justified their protection (Article 122(1)(f)), those who have benefitted from the residence permit for students and researchers and are willing to seek employment in Portugal (Article 122(1)(o), (p) and (q)).

350. Second, several cases aim at protecting the best interests of the child. That is the case of foreign children who are mandatorily subjected to tutorship under the Civil Code (Article 122(1)(e)). Children who were born in the national territory and who have stayed there and are attending pre-school education or primary school, secondary or professional education may also be regularized (Article 122(1)(b)).[196] In this latter case, they may acquire a residence permit even if their parents are irregularly staying in the country. In order to guarantee the right to family life, their parents may, then, acquire themselves a residence permit, provided that they effectively exercise their parental responsibilities. These resident permits may be asked at the same time (Article 122(4)). Moreover, those foreigners who cannot be expelled due to the confirmed protection of family life must also be awarded a residence permit (e.g., parents of minor children holding Portuguese citizenship). Both these latter cases are protected by Article 122(1)(k).

351. Besides these situations, there are also other circumstances aimed at protecting foreign citizens' fundamental rights. That is the case of the protection of victims of labour exploitation or victims of trafficking and human smuggling after the end of their residence permit (Article 122(1)(m) and (n)).[197] That is also the case of foreigners who suffer from a disease that requires prolonged medical assistance that prevents them from returning to the country, in order to avoid risk to their own health (Article 122(1)(g)). In this latter situation, the foreigners' right to health requires their presence in the Portuguese territory. In the most severe cases, this presence could be required to respect the prohibition of ill-treatment.[198] The 2022 legal amendments expanded the right to benefit from this residence permit to foreign citizens who accompany the applicant as a companion or informal caregiver.

352. Finally, a special mention must be made to an exceptional regularization scheme adopted in Portugal during the Covid-19 pandemic. On 18 March 2020, the date of the first declaration of the state of emergency in Portugal due to the pandemic crisis, the immigration services had a vast number of pending applications for regularizations, and the Ombudsman had hundreds of complaints regarding the severe delays in these procedures. The Covid-19 crisis would undoubtedly worsen this scenario, leaving more people in a precarious state. Thus, in an Order dated 27 March, the Government established that, at the date of the declaration of the state of emergency, all migrants and asylum seekers with pending residence requests would be treated as legal residents until 30 June 2020. This measure aimed to reduce the risks to public health, allowing all these migrants to be covered by the same health system as national citizens. At the same time, it allowed thousands of migrants with pending applications to have their legal situation regularized. This measure affected the lives of approximately 260,000 immigrants, who saw their legal status temporarily regularized.

---

196. However, according to Ar. 122(5) and (6), whenever the child, for no reasonable reason, stops attending his or her educational institution, the temporary residence permit granted under para. 1(b) and para. 4 is cancelled or not renewed.
197. *See* Part VI, Ch. 2, §1.
198. Following the case law of the ECtHR, which has affirmed, although in very exceptional circumstances, that expulsion of severely ill persons could amount to a violation of Art. 3 of the ECHR – *see* ruling dated 02/05/1997, *D. v. United Kingdom*, appl. n. 30240/96. The standard of protection affirmed in this case was, however, moderated in the case *Paposhvili v Belgium* (ruling dated 13/12/2016, appl. n. 41738/10).

353. On 8 November 2020, the Government enacted a new order, extending the regularization effects to all migrants who had submitted their applications between 18 March and 15 October 2020. This new order benefited more than 116,700 migrants. Overall, these two orders resulted in the temporary regularization of 356,700 immigrants.

354. The regularization measures adopted during the pandemic were to be applauded – it also was understood that *public health would be more effectively protected* if *more rights would be conferred to migrants*. The basic idea is very simple indeed: if irregularly staying migrants could benefit from the same healthcare as residents, then the disease could be more easily controlled.

355. However, these regularization measures adopted during the Covid-19 crisis were only, precisely, *public health measures*. They were not tentative recasts of the immigration system – and they were *not even extraordinary regularizations*. They only represented *temporary measures in the context of the responses to the public health crisis*.

Chapter 8. Family Reunification

356. Family reunification is grounded on the fundamental right to family unity, which is recognized by the Portuguese Constitution.[199] The Portuguese Immigration Law has traditionally recognized the importance of this mechanism and, therefore, has traditionally recognized a broad right to family reunification. This trend was maintained and even strengthened after the approval of the EU's Directive on Family Reunification with third-country nationals.[200]

357. Articles 98–108 IL foresee more favourable solutions concerning the right to family reunification than those enshrined in Directive 2003/86/EC on the right to family reunification. The right to family reunification is recognized to those who hold a residence permit granted for a one-year minimum period. Contrary to the Directive, the law does not make references to any 'perspective of obtaining a permanent residence' in the territory. It also does not set forth a waiting period for the immigrant before having his/her family members join him/her. Migrants can request family reunification immediately or, when applying for a residence permit, they may simultaneously apply for family reunification (Article 81(4)). Moreover, the reunification with family members who are already present in Portuguese territory is allowed as long as they have entered there legally (Article 98(2) IL).

358. The concept of family is also broader than it would result from EU law (Article 99 IL). It encompasses the spouse and the minor children, but also adult children lacking capacity or who are studying in an educational institution in Portugal. Children who were adopted according to a decision of the competent authority of the country of origin are also eligible. The immigrant or his/her spouse must have the custody of minor children. Moreover, the reunification of first-degree relatives in the direct ascending line of the resident or his/her spouse is also allowed, provided that they are dependent on them. The same goes for the reunification of minor siblings, provided that the resident holds their guardianship, in accordance with a decision made by the relevant authority of the country of origin, recognized by Portugal. Besides that, family reunification may be authorized with the partner with whom the foreign resident maintains, either in the national territory or abroad, a de facto union duly recognized under the law, as well as with the partner's children – including adopted children (Article 100 IL).

359. As for material conditions, Article 101, n 1. IL requires the applicant to have adequate accommodation and sufficient means of subsistence. Nonetheless, these conditions are not applicable to family reunification with refugees (Article 101(2) IL).

---

199. *See* Ana Rita Gil, 'Um Caso de Europeização do Direito Constitucional Português – A Afirmação de um Direito Fundamental ao Reagrupamento Familiar', *Revista de Direito Público*, ano I, 2009, n. 2, p. 9 e ss.
200. Directive 2003/86/EC of 22 Sep. 2003 on the right to family reunification.

360. The SEF has been developing a somehow demanding practice on what may represent 'sufficient means of subsistence'. A governmental act sets forth the monetary amounts that a migrant must gather to be allowed to be joined by each family member.[201] Contrary to the *Chakroun* CJEU case,[202] which sets forth that some flexibility is needed when analysing whether an applicant has sufficient means of subsistence, in Portugal this evaluation is still understood very literally, by merely checking if the applicant receives the precise amount enshrined in the regulation, which varies according to the number of family members that he or she wants to be reunited with.

361. Regarding the procedure, the decision on family reunification must be issued in a three-month delay after the application, which can be extended, in exceptional circumstances, for more than three months. If no decision is reached within six months, the request is considered as tacitly granted (Article 105 IL). When examining the application, the SEF may conduct interviews, namely for analysing the effectiveness of a family relationship. As regards de facto unions, and since no official certification of the relationship may exist, the SEF must take into account factors such as the existence of a common child, prior cohabitation, registration of the de facto union or any other means of proof (Article 104 IL). These requirements mirror those used by the ECtHR when analysing whether a union must be considered as 'family life' for the purpose of Article 8 ECHR.[203]

362. In order to enter the territory for the purpose of being reunited with the applicants, family members must be issued an entry visa, in cases of citizens from countries of which these visas are required (Article 64 IL). In cases where the permit was tacitly granted, the applicant must require from the SEF a certification of the tacit decision and must inform the Consular Services for the purpose of being issued with the necessary visa.

363. This regime of tacit approval raises several questions. First, it may raise doubts regarding its compatibility with EU law. In case *X*, the CJEU stated that the Directive would oppose national laws to establish that the authorities could issue a residence permit in favour of the applicant, without first analysing the fulfilment of the necessary requirements.[204] Second, it may be difficult to obtain a certification of a tacit decision. Oftentimes, decisions are not expressly taken due to SEF's work overload. It is not guaranteed that this overload will not also interfere with the *certification of the tacit decision*. Moreover, the need for a certification is, per se, contradictory to the very *nature of tacit decisions*. A pure tacit regime would consider satisfying that the applicant would prove the decision by showing the mere application.

---

201. Portaria n. 1563/2007 of 11 December.
202. Ruling dated 4 Mar. 2010, *Chakroun*, proc. n. C-578/08.
203. *See*, among others, ruling dated 27/10/1994, *Kroon and others v. The Netherlands*, app. n. 18535/91.
204. Ruling dated 20 Nov. 2019, *X*. proc. n. C-706/18.

364. There are several reasons for refusing a family reunification application. That would be the case not only when the requirements for exercising the right to family reunification are not met but also when the family member is refused to enter the national territory, and also when his/her presence represents a threat to public policy, public security or public health. In these cases, before issuing a decision, the authority must take into consideration the seriousness or type of infringement to public order or security perpetrated by the family member, or the dangers that may arise from his/her presence in the national territory. Such authority must also take into account the nature and solidity of the person's family relationships, the duration of his/her stay in Portugal and the existence of family, cultural and social ties with the country of origin. These duties are also imposed by the ECtHR case law on protection of the right to family life under Article 8 ECHR. According to this case law, the administrative authority must also consider the age and the best interest of the children involved, even if such duty is not mentioned by Article 106 IL.

365. In case of refusal, the applicant may appeal to the competent Administrative Court. Normally, the appeal does not have a suspensive effect – except in cases where the family member is already residing in the territory, and the application was rejected because the conditions for family reunification were not met (Article 106(8) IL). Naturally, as in other cases, the applicant may request for a precautionary measure requiring the suspension of the administrative decision.

366. The IL sets forth that the first residence permit awarded to family members by virtue of family reunification has the same length as the sponsor's permit (Article 107(1) IL). However, if the last one has a permanent residence permit, the duration of the family members' residence permit will be of two years, renewable for three years (Article 107(2) IL). Two years after the issuance of the first residence permit, and insofar as the family ties persist, family members are entitled to an autonomous authorization with a duration identical to that of the resident (Article 107(3) IL). The 2022 amendments to the IL enlarged the right to an autonomous residence in several ways. First, all family members who have minor children residing in Portugal shall have an immediate right to such residence. The same goes for spouses who are married to the resident for more than five years (Article 107(5) IL). Also, in exceptional cases, an autonomous residence permit may be granted before the expiry of the general period of two years: this may happen namely in cases of legal separation of persons and goods, divorce, widowhood, death of the family member, reach of the age of majority, and also accusation by the Public Prosecutor for the crime of domestic violence (Article 107(4) IL). The autonomous authorization is valid for two years, renewable for a period of three years.

Part III. Loss of Residence Rights

Chapter 1. Conditions for the Loss of Residence

367. The conditions under which the residence right is lost are naturally dependent on the type of residence permit. Indeed, in some cases, a more favourable treatment is awarded, whereas in other, additional grounds for loss are foreseen. We will begin by explaining the general rules applicable to most cases.

§1. General Rules

368. General rules are enshrined in Article 85 IL, which mentions, exhaustively, the cases under which a residence permit may be cancelled. The first ground is a decision of judicial expulsion or a coercive removal order from the national territory. The resident may be subjected to one of these decisions in the cases that will be further explained below.[205] Second, the residence permit shall also be cancelled if it was granted on the basis of false or misleading statements, false or falsified documents, or through the use of fraudulent means. Finally, the residence shall be lost if there are serious reasons to believe that its holder has committed serious criminal acts or there are real indications that he or she intends to commit acts of this nature, namely in the territory of the European Union. On the same basis, residence shall also be lost for reasons of public order or security.

369. In this first set of cases, the loss of residence right is due to a misconduct of the resident. However, the last two cases are somehow vague, which may lead to an arbitrary use from the authorities. Even in these 'general' cases of residence loss, and although Article 85 does not mention it, the authorities must respect other fundamental rights that may be at stake, such as the right to respect for family and private life.

370. Article 85(2) foresees additional grounds for the loss of the right of residence. That may happen when the person concerned, without reasonable reasons, is absent from the country during certain periods of time: (1) six consecutive months or eight interpolated months, during the total period of validity of the authorization

205. Part V, Chapter I, §4.

when the person holds a temporary residence permit; *or* (2) twenty-four consecutive months or, in a period of three years, thirty interpolated months when the person holds a permanent residence permit. An absence beyond these limits must be justified by a request submitted to SEF before the resident leaves the national territory or, in exceptional cases, after leaving the territory.

371. However, according to paragraph 4 of Article 85 IL, citizens who were absent for longer periods may not lose their residence when they prove that during their absence from the national territory, they have developed a professional or business activity or also a cultural or social activity.

372. Despite this last possibility, we must acknowledge that paragraph 2 may lead to interferences on the resident's right to respect for private life and intimacy. If these limits could be understood in cases of temporary residence, they are hardly justifiable in cases where permanent residents are concerned. This is even more unjustifiable if we take into consideration that the time limits are not applicable when absences were justifiable due to work, business, cultural and social activities. This leaves out family reasons, for example, in the country of origin. Therefore, a resident may lose his or her residency for having travelled to his or her country of origin due to pressing but lingering family reasons.

§2. EU Citizens

373. EU citizens receive a more favourable treatment. Both the FMD and the FML provide special protection against loss of residence and expulsion. As we saw above, restrictions on the right to residence in this realm can only take place on the grounds of public order or public security. But even these limited reasons must be restricted interpreted, according to the numerous case law of the CJEU – which was then implemented by the FMD.

374. Thus, there are several limits for the loss of residence of EU citizens. First, reasons of public order, public security and public health cannot be invoked for economic purposes (Article 22). Measures taken for reasons of public policy or public security must comply with the principle of proportionality, as required by the CJEU's case law, and must be based exclusively on the behaviour of the person, which must constitute a real, current and sufficiently serious threat that affects a fundamental interest of the society. As a consequence, justifications that are not related to the individual case or based on general prevention reasons cannot be used. Also, previous criminal convictions cannot, by themselves, serve as a basis for the measures referred to in the previous paragraph. Moreover, in order to determine whether the person concerned constitutes a danger to public order or public security when issuing the registration certificate or when issuing the residence card, the State may, whenever considered indispensable, request to other Member States information on the criminal record of the person concerned. However, this consultation cannot take place regularly (Article 22, paragraph 6).

375. According to Article 23 FML, before adopting a decision to return on reasons of public order or public security, several factors must be taken into account, such as the duration of the 'citizens' residence in the national territory, their age and health status, their family and economic situation, their social and cultural integration in the country and the importance of the ties with their country of origin.

§3. Family Reunification

376. Pursuant to Article 108 IL, the residence permit issued under the right to family reunification is cancelled when the marriage, registered partnership or adoption had as only purpose allowing the entry of the interested party into Portuguese territory. In order to respect the right to family life, the authorities must take into consideration the nature and strength of the person's family ties, their time in Portugal and the existence of family, cultural and social ties with the family in the country of origin before the decision. This is clearly a consecration of the ECtHR's case law concerning the respect of family life enshrined in Article 8 ECHR.

§4. Long-Term Residents

377. Article 131 IL sets forth that long-term residents lose their resident status in the following cases: (i) fraudulent acquiring of such status; (ii) adoption of an expulsion measure; (iii) absence from the EU territory for a period of twelve successive months; (iv) acquisition of the long-term resident status in another Member State; (v) absence from the national territory for a period of six years. Absences from the territory of the *European Union* for a period of more than twelve successive months that are justified by specific or exceptional reasons do not imply the loss of the status, particularly when the long-term resident stayed in the country of origin with the purpose of pursuing a professional or entrepreneurial activity, or of a cultural or social nature. The same can be said regarding absences from the national territory for a period of more than six successive years justified by specific or exceptional reasons, particularly when the long-term resident stayed in the country of origin for purposes of carrying out a professional or entrepreneurial activity, or of a cultural or social nature (Article 131(2) and (3) IL).

378. Although Article 131 foresees that absences from the territories of the European Union or from the national territory may lead to the loss of the long-term residence permit, it nonetheless softens this sanction, by allowing the title's reacquisition (paragraph 4). Moreover, in cases where the loss of the long-term residence is only based on absence from the territory, and not on one of the general rules (namely one of the cases that lead to the removal of the citizen from the territory, as it will be seen below on Part V, Chapter 1., §4), he or she shall be granted a residence permit with visa exemption (paragraph 11).

379. Article 120, on its turn, foresees the cases whereby those holding a long-term resident status in another Member State of the European Union may lose their residence permit in Portugal. That may happen for reasons of public order or public security, taking into account the seriousness or the type of offence against public order or public security committed, or the dangers that may arise from the person's stay in the national territory, as well as the duration of residence and existence of connections to the country. That may also take place when the conditions for acquiring the residence right cease to be met: the third-country national no longer exercises a subordinate professional activity, an independent professional activity, or a study programme or professional training action, nor presents a reasonable reason for taking up residence in the national territory; or he/she has lost their means of subsistence or accommodation.[206]

§5. Residence Permit for Children in Schools

380. As already explained above, Article 122 IL sets forth a number of cases of regularization of migrants' status.[207] Some of these cases were grounded on the protection of the best interests of the child, namely on their right to education. Nonetheless, however controversial it may seem, those children who have acquired a right to reside in the Portuguese territory for having been born there, and being enrolled in a Portuguese school, may lose their residence in case they cease to attend their school for no reasonable reason.

§6. Victims of Trafficking of Human Beings

381. As seen above, victims of trafficking of human beings can benefit from a special residence permit if some conditions are met.[208] One of these conditions is to have ceased any contact with the perpetrators of the crime. Under the terms of Article 115 IL, in addition to general public order cases, victims can lose their residence permit if they actively and voluntarily resume, on their own initiative, contact with the alleged perpetrators of the crime if the authorities consider that their cooperation is fraudulent or that the victim's complaint is unfounded or if they fail to cooperate. Naturally, the latter case does not apply to situations in which a residence permit was granted regardless of the victim's cooperation, under the terms of Decree-Law 368/2007.

206. According to para. 5, resources must be assessed by reference to their nature and regularity, considering the level of minimum wages and pensions.
207. Chapter 6., §4.
208. *See* Ch. 6., §3.

Chapter 2. Legal and Administrative Procedures

382. The IL sets forth some basic rules that apply to all loss of residence cases. The member of the Government responsible for the area of internal administration is competent for cancellation, with the power of delegation to the SEF's National Director. The loss of residence entails the seizure of the corresponding permit. It must be notified to the interested person and must also be electronically communicated to the HCM, with an indication of the grounds for the decision. The notification to the interested person must indicate the grounds for cancellation, along with information regarding the right to appeal and respective time limits.

383. Although the IL does not foresee it expressly in all cases, the general Administrative Procedures Code shall be applicable.[209] Its rules on preliminary hearings, in particular, shall be observed. This means that, before taking a decision on cancelling a residence permit, the SEF must always give the migrant an opportunity to be heard.

384. Also, although this is only mentioned in some cases, we must point out that all decisions can only be made after taking into consideration the migrant's ties with the host country, his or her private and family life therein, his or her ties with the country of origin and, being the case, the seriousness of the threat that he/she represents to the host society.[210] Indeed, this balance is required by the ECHR, according to the ECtHR in all cases, and the IL must be interpreted in conformity.

385. Some particular rules apply to specific residence permits. That is the case of the loss of a family reunification permit, where enquiries and specific checks may be performed in cases where there are well-founded reasons to suspect of fraud, or of a marriage, partnership or adoption of convenience (Article 198 IL). These enquiries must obviously be proportionate, in order to respect the right to intimacy and private life.

209. As approved by Decree-Law n. 4/2015 of 7 January, last amended by Law n. 72/2020, of 16 November.

210. That is the case, first and foremost, of EU citizens, to whom both the FMD and the FML provide special protection against loss of residence. As seen above, restrictions on the right to residence in this realm can only take place on the grounds of public order or public security.

Part IV. Sanctions

Chapter 1. Sanctions Foreseen in the Immigration Law

386. There are several illegal activities foreseen in the IL that may give rise to sanctions. These sanctions can be of an administrative nature or of a criminal/penal nature.

§1. Administrative Sanctions

387. Administrative sanctions are mainly aimed at punishing foreigners who did not fully respect their duties under the IL or employers who have wrongfully used the work of foreigners who are irregularly staying in the territory.

I. Failure to Comply with Duties Regarding the Entry and Stay in the Territory

388. The stay of a foreign citizen in the Portuguese territory for a longer period than that was authorized is an offence punishable through the payment of a fine. The fine depends on the number of days that exceeded the authorized stay: it can be from 80 European Dollar (EUR) (in cases where the alien remained irregularly less than 30 days) to EUR 700 (in cases where the alien has remained irregularly for more than 180 days) (Article 192 IL). Article 201, by the same token, concerns the non-timely renewal of residence permit. The request for renewal of a temporary residence permit submitted after the period provided for in Article 78 constitutes an administrative offence punishable by a fine of EUR 75 to EUR 300.

389. Foreign citizens who have not entered into the Portuguese territory by border posts during opening hours (as requested by Article 6 IL) incur an infraction punishable by a fine of 200 to 400 Euros. The embarkation and disembarkation of foreign citizens outside the border posts qualified for this purpose constitutes an offence punishable by a fine of 50,000 to 100,000 Euros. The transport company and its representatives in Portuguese territory are jointly liable for the payment (Article 202 IL). Moreover, foreign citizens who did not declare their entry into the territory, within three working days from the date of entry into the country through a border not subject to control, when coming from another Member State (as required by Article 14 IL), may be punished with a fine of EUR 60 to EUR 160, according to Article 197. On its turn, lack of presentation of travel documents issued by foreigner authorities constitutes an offence punishable by a fine of EUR 60 to EUR 120, according to Article 199.

390. Article 193 IL on its turn sets forth the fines that shall be applicable to unauthorized access to the international port areas (from EUR 300 to EUR 900) and unauthorized access on board vessels (from EUR 500 to EUR 1,000).

391. The transportation to Portuguese territory, of a foreign citizen who does not have valid travel document or visa, by carrier or by any person in the exercise of a professional activity, also constitutes a punishable offence, for each foreign citizen transported, with a fine of EUR 4,000 to EUR 6,000, in the case of legal persons, and from EUR 3,000 to EUR 5,000, in the case of natural persons. These administrative sanctions are enshrined in Article 194, aimed at transposing the Directive on carriers' sanctions.[211]

392. Other sanctions are foreseen for violations of rules regarding stays in the Portuguese territory. First, foreign residents must keep the SEF informed on any change of their address or marital status, as required by Article 86 IL. Failing to respect this requirement may lead to a punishment of EUR 45 to EUR 90 (Article 202). Also, failure to register foreign citizens in electronic form, in accordance with paragraph 4 of Article 15, or failure to submit the accommodation bulletin, pursuant to paragraph 1 or 2 of Article 16, constitutes an infraction punishable under Article 203 – which can be from EUR 100 to EUR 2,000.

393. Foreigners who exercise an independent professional activity without holding the proper residence permit commit an offence punishable by a fine of EUR 300 to EUR 1,200 (Article 198 IL).

394. Parents to foreign children who are born in the Portuguese territory and who fail to ask for a residence permit for them within six months after they were born also commit an administrative offence, punishable by a penalty from EUR 60 to EUR 120 (Article 200 IL).

395. Article 204 IL sets forth some general rules for all administrative sanctions. In these cases, negligence is always punishable, but the minimum and maximum fine's amounts are reduced to half of the amounts.

II. Use of the Activity of an Irregularly Staying Foreigner

396. The use of the activity of an irregularly staying foreign national may give rise to the imposition of an administrative penalty to the offender, that is, a fine

211. Council Directive 2001/51/EC of 28 Jun. 2001 supplementing the provisions of Art. 26 of the Convention implementing the Schengen Agreement of 14 Jun. 1985.

which depends on the number of irregularly staying third-country nationals who are hired (Article 198 – A, paragraph 1, als. a) to d)).[212]

397. Recognizing the special vulnerability of those who work irregularly, the IL also provides for special measures to protect their interests. Thus, it establishes the joint liability of the employer, the user and the general contractor: (i) for the payment of wage credits arising from an employment contract, its violation or termination;[213] (ii) for penalties arising from failure to comply with labour legislation; (iii) for penalties arising from failure to declare income subject to deductions for the tax administration and social security, in respect of work done by a foreign worker whose activity has been used irregularly; (iv) for the payment of the expenses necessary for the stay and removal of the foreign nationals, and the payment of any expenses arising from the transfer of money resulting from labour credits to the country to which the foreign citizen has returned voluntarily or coercively (Article 198 – A, paragraph 5, als. a) to e), IL).

§2. PENAL SANCTIONS

398. Chapter IX IL foresees several types of crimes: (i) 'Aid to illegal immigration' or 'Human smuggling' as known in English (Article 183 IL); (ii) 'Association of aid to illegal immigration' (Article 184 IL); (iii) 'Attracting illegal labour' (Article 185 IL); 'Use of the activity of a foreign national in an illegal situation' (Article 185 – A IL). All these criminal offences, despite their distinctive features, have in common the fact that they require the victim's participation. Otherwise, if the crimes are committed against the victim's will, we will be before other legal types of crimes (e.g., kidnapping or human trafficking), which are punished under the Portuguese Penal Code.[214]

399. To give a concrete idea of how this reality is present in the Portuguese territory, in 2019, the SEF recorded 126 crimes of aid to illegal immigration, 13 of association of aid to illegal immigration and 5 of attracting illegal labour.[215]

212. Cf. Art. 198 – A, para. 1 IL: ' 1 – Whoever uses the activity of a foreign citizen not qualified with a residence permit or visa authorizing the exercise of a subordinated professional activity, shall be subject to the imposition of one of the following fines: (a) from (euro) 2000 to (euro) 10 000, if in case of using the activity of 1 to 4 citizens; (b) from (euro) 4000 to (euro) 15 000, in case of 5 to 10 citizens; (c) from (euro) 6000 to (euro) 30 000, in case of 11 to 50 citizens; (d) from (euro) 10 000 to (euro) 90 000, in case of more than 50 citizens.'

213. For the purpose of accounting for wage credits, the IL establishes the presumption, not only that the level of remuneration corresponds to the minimum monthly remuneration guaranteed by law, in collective agreements or in accordance with practices established in the sectors of activity concerned, but also that the employment relationship has minimum duration of three months, unless the employer, the user of the activity or the worker proves otherwise (Art. 198 – A, para. 8 IL).

214. Albano Pinto, AAVV, *Commentary on Extravagant Criminal Laws*, Paulo Pinto de Albuquerque and José Branco (Org.), Universidade Católica Editora, 2010, vol. I, p. 123.

215. SEF, *Relatório de Imigração, Fronteiras e Asilo 2019*, Serviço de Estrangeiros e Fronteiras, Lisboa, 2020. Available in https://sefstat.sef.pt/Docs/Rifa2019.pdf.

I. Aid to Irregular Immigration

400. According to Article 183(1) IL, whoever favours or facilitates, in any way, the entry or irregular transit of a foreign citizen into the national territory shall be punished with imprisonment of up to three years. In paragraph 2 of Article 183 IL, the applicable penal framework is increased – becoming one to five years in prison – if the agent acts with intention of making a profit or, according to paragraph 3, the action is characterized by the transportation or maintenance of the foreign citizen in inhuman or degrading conditions, or by endangering his/her life, or by causing them a serious offence to their physical integrity or death. In the latter case, because aiding irregular immigration represents a genuine attack on the dignity of the human person, the agent is more severely punished, with imprisonment from two to eight years.

401. The attempt to commit the crime is also punishable (Article 160(4)).[216]

402. The crime definition is almost equivalent to the one foreseen in Article 1, (a) and (b), of the Council Directive 2002/90/EC of 28 November 2002.[217] However, the Portuguese Law does not provide – in accordance with Article 2 of the above-mentioned Directive – for exemption from punishment for situations in which the agent acts for a humanitarian purpose, i.e., when the purpose of aiding irregular immigration is to provide assistance or relief to someone seeking asylum or other humanitarian protection on Portuguese territory.

403. It should be noted that, given the vulnerability, dependence and fragility of the victim of this type of crime, the Portuguese Law allows that the foreigners – pursuant that some conditions are met[218] – may benefit from a temporary residence permit in Portugal, even if they have entered the country irregularly or do not fulfil the conditions for benefiting from a residence permit (cf. Article 109, paragraph 1 IL). In short, by granting this temporary residence permit, the law aims, on the one hand, to protect victims against this type of situation and, on the other, make it possible for victims to cooperate with the ongoing judicial investigations and proceedings.

216. It means that the agent who commits acts of execution of the crime is still punished, even if it not consummated (Art. 22 of the CC).

217. Council Directive 2002/90/EC of 28 Nov. 2002, defining the facilitation of unauthorized entry, transit and residence.

218. According to Art. 109, n. 2 IL, the residence permit referred to in the preceding paragraph shall be granted after the expiry of the reflection period provided for in Art. 111, provided that: (a) it is necessary to extend the stay of the person concerned in the national territory, taking into account the interest that his presence represents for investigations and judicial proceedings; (b) the person concerned shows a clear will to cooperate with the authorities in the investigation and persecution of trafficking in persons or the facilitation of illegal immigration; (c) the person concerned has cut the links he/she had with the alleged perpetrators of the offences referred to in the preceding paragraph.

II. Association of Aid to Irregular Immigration

404. Article 184 IL foresees as crime the foundation, organization or association of a group with the purpose of committing the crime of 'Aiding to illegal immigration'.[219] What is punishable in this provision is the very *creation of the group* for the purpose of committing this particular type of crime, regardless, therefore, whether or not the criminal activity was indeed executed. The founder and members may be sentenced to between one to six years of imprisonment (Article 184(1) IL), while the head of the group, organization or association is punishable by a penalty ranging from two to eight years of imprisonment (Article 184(3) IL).

III. Attracting Illegal Labour

405. Article 185, paragraph 1 IL sets forth the crime of attracting illegal labour. Under the terms of this provision, whoever, with profitable intent for himself or for a third party, attracts or gathers foreign citizens who do not hold a residence permit or a visa entitling them to exercise a professional activity in the country, with the aim of introducing them in the labour market, is punished by an imprisonment penalty from one to five years. The applicable penal framework is aggravated by two to six years of imprisonment if the conduct is exercised repeatedly, i.e., if it consists of a habitual practice of attracting illegal labour and not an isolated act (Article 185(2) IL).

IV. Use of the Activity of a Foreign Citizen in an Illegal Situation

406. The use of illegal labour – i.e., of foreign workers who do not hold a residence permit or visa entitling them to stay legally in Portugal – constitutes a criminal offence provided for in Article 185 – A IL when one of the following circumstances occurs: (i) it occurs in a habitual manner; (ii) it involves the employment of a minor, in an illegal situation, even if admitted to work under the Labour Code (LC); (iii) it involves the employment of a victim of criminal offences linked to trafficking in human beings with the knowledge of the employer.

407. The situation envisaged in (i) is punished by a prison sentence of up to 1 year or a fine of up to 240 days (Article 185 – A, paragraph 1 IL). This penal framework is aggravated by a prison sentence of up to two years or a fine of up to 480 days when the usual hiring of illegal work is done through the use of a significant number of foreigners in an irregular administrative situation (Article 185 – A, paragraph 2 IL).

---

219. Cf. Art. 184, para. 1 IL: 'Who promotes or founds a group, organization or association whose purpose or activity is directed to the practice of the crimes foreseen in the previous Art. shall be punished by imprisonment from one to six years.'.

408. In the case of the employment of a minor in an irregular administrative situation, as referred to in (ii), the applicable penalty is imprisonment of up to two years or a fine of up to 480 days.

409. The IL also foresees an aggravation of the penal framework if the conduct described in (i) and (ii) above is accompanied by particularly abusive or degrading working conditions, with the perpetrator for these cases being sentenced to between one and five years of imprisonment, if a more serious penalty is not imposed by virtue of another legal provision.

410. Finally, when the hypothesis described in (iii) occurs, the offending agent is punished with imprisonment from two to six years, if a more serious penalty does not fall under another legal provision (Article 185 – A (5) IL).

411. A final point that should be noted about Article 185 – A is the fact that it results from the transposition of the above-mentioned Directive 2009/52/EC, which aims to strengthen the fight against illegal immigration, one of the areas of the European Union's common immigration policy (cf. Article 79(1) and paragraph 2 (c) of the Treaty on the Functioning of the European Union (TFEU).[220] The adoption of the Directive resulted from the recognition that the possibility to work irregularly in the Members States' territory was still a 'push factor' that attracted third-country nationals to enter irregularly in the EU. Its core objectives were then to end that 'push factor' through: (i) penalizing employers for employing irregular labour by deterring them from this practice through effective, proportionate and dissuasive sanctions;[221] (ii) establishing communication networks between employers and national authorities responsible for border control; (iii) enabling third-country nationals who found themselves in an irregular situation to return to their countries of origin; (iv) facilitating the payment of sums due to workers in an irregular administrative situation for work actually done, as well as contributions and taxes due to the State.

---

220. *See* Art. 79(1) TFEU: 'The Union shall develop a common immigration policy aimed at ensuring, at all stages, effective management of migration flows, fair treatment of third country nationals residing legally in the Member States, as well as preventing illegal immigration and trafficking in human beings and stepping up the fight against these phenomena.'

221. In accordance with recital 3 of Directive 2009/52/EC a genuine 'prohibition on the employment of third country nationals not authorized to reside in the EU' is introduced.

Chapter 2. Sanctions Foreseen in the Criminal Code

412. The Portuguese Criminal Code (CC) also foresees sanctions in the realm of migration activities, as regards fighting against the trafficking of human beings.

413. The prevention and fight against trafficking of human beings is part of a global action that takes into account the highly organized and transnational nature of the phenomenon. In this regard, account should be taken of the large number of international instruments aimed at pursuing this aim, among which we highlight: (i) the 2000 United Nations Protocol on the Prevention, Repression and Punishment of Human Trafficking, in particular women and children, in addition to the Convention against Transnational Organized Crime; (ii) the 2005 Council of Europe Convention on Combating Trafficking in Human Beings; (iii) Directive 2011/36/EU of the European Parliament and the Council of 05 April 2011 on the prevention and fight against trafficking in human beings and the protection of victims, replacing Council Framework Decision 2002/629/JAI.

414. Under the Portuguese Law, we must distinguish the crime of migrants' smuggling, set out in Articles 183 and 184 IL, from the crime of human trafficking, provided for and punishable by Article 160 CC. The crime of migrants' smuggling is foreseen, as seen, in the Immigration Law, under the designation of 'aid to illegal immigration'.

415. There are some significant differences between these two crimes, especially as to: (i) the legal interest protected by each type of crime (considering that in human trafficking the legal interests protected are the victim's dignity and personal freedom); (ii) the presence or lack of consent (in the crime of migrants' smuggling, the migrant agrees with the action, which is not preceded by misleading or violence); (iii) the freedom of the victim (in most cases of migrants' smuggling, the immigrant is not placed in a hierarchical relationship with the smuggler); (iv) the payment made (usually, in cases of migrants' smuggling, immigrants pay for the transport and reception service in the country of origin); (v) the purpose of recruitment (in human trafficking, victims are used in criminal activities).[222]

416. Pursuant to Article 160(1) CC, the crime of trafficking has three elements: (1) an action, (2) made with certain purposes and (3) with certain means. As for the action, it can be one of the following: to offer, deliver, recruit, entice, accept, transport, house or welcome a person. These actions are meant for the purposes, among others, of 'exploitation, including sexual exploitation, exploitation of work, begging, slavery, organ extraction or exploitation of other criminal activities'. These actions must be taken through one of the expressly mentioned means: violence, abduction or serious threat, through ruse or fraudulent manoeuvre; with abuse of

222. In this sense, Paulo Pinto de Albuquerque, *Comentário do Código de Processo Penal à luz da Constituição da República e da Convenção Europeia dos Direitos do Homem*, Universidade Católica Editora, 2010, p. 492, Paulo Sousa Mendes, 'Tráfico de Pessoas', *Jornadas sobre a Revisão do Código Penal,* Centro de de Estudos Judiciários, 2007, p. 8.

authority, a hierarchical, economic, work or family dependency relationship; taking advantage of psychic disability or a situation of special vulnerability of the victim; or by obtaining the consent of the person who has control over the victim. The crime is punished with a prison sentence of three to ten years.

417. According to Article 160(2) CC, whoever practices these facts against minors also commits this crime. However, in this case, the use of any of the specific mentioned means is irrelevant. Moreover, if the agent acts using any of the above-mentioned means, professionally or with a profit-making intention, the applicable penal framework is aggravated to its maximum limit, and the agent may be punished with a prison sentence of three to twelve years (cf. Article 160(3) CC). According to Article 160(5), CC whoever offers, delivers, solicits, or accepts a minor, or obtain or gives consent in its use, upon payment or other consideration, shall be punished with imprisonment from one to five years.

418. The penalties provided for in paragraphs 1 and 3 of Article 160 shall be aggravated by one-third, within their minimum and maximum limits, if the conduct referred to: (i) endangers the life of the victim; (ii) has been committed with particular violence or has caused the victim particularly serious harm; (iii) has been committed by an official in the performance of his duties; (iv) has been committed in the context of a criminal association; (v) or has resulted in the victim's suicide (Article 160(4)(a)–(e) CC, respectively).

419. The Criminal Code also punishes the user of the services provided by victims of trafficking. Article 160(6) provides for the punishment of those who are aware of the practice of a human trafficking's crime, use the services or organs of the victim. In this case, the agent is punished with imprisonment from one to five years if more serious penalty is not applicable by another legal provision.

420. Article 160 also provides for the penalization of whoever retains, hides, damages, or destroys identification or travel documents of a victim. In this case, the agent shall be punished with imprisonment of up to three years if a more serious penalty is not applicable by another legal provision (Article 160(7) CC).

421. It should be noted that in any of the above cases, the victim's consent to the crimes does not in any way exclude the illegality of the act (Article 160(8) CC).

Chapter 3. Detention

422. Under the Portuguese Law, having an illegal status or trying to enter irregularly in the country is not, as such, a criminal offence. However, the Portuguese Constitution expressly allows the application of a detention measure in the context of the IL's enforcement. The detention of immigrants is foreseen in Article 27(3)(f) of the Constitution as an exception to the right to personal freedom. The Constitution allows detention of irregularly staying migrants in cases where they have entered or stayed irregularly in the national territory, or with a view to removal for extradition or expulsion purposes.

423. Article 27 of the Constitution also sets forth some guarantees that must be applicable to every detention procedure. Namely, it sets forth the duty to immediately inform the reasons of the detention (Article 27(4)), and to submit the deprivation of liberty to judicial control within forty-eight hours. The judge must hear the detained person and provide him/her all the defence guarantees. Moreover, the detained immigrant may benefit from the constitutional guarantee of *habeas corpus*, foreseen in Article 31 of the Constitution. According to this provision, the migrant may ask the Supreme Court of Justice his/her immediate release and to declare the detention null and void, even if such detention has already been controlled judicially when the detention is manifestly ill-founded or disrespects the law (e.g., the maximum delay of detention has already expired).

424. The IL regulates detention in these two cases: in case of illegal entry and in case of expulsion following an illegal stay. Article 40 IL sets forth guarantees in case of detention of migrants whose entry into the national territory was refused. Whenever their removal is not possible within forty-eight hours, the immigrant must be presented to a judge. The judge shall hear the foreigner and decide his/her detention or other measures. During their stay in a detention facility or in the international zone of an airport or seaport, migrants may communicate with the diplomatic or consular representation of their country, or with any person of their choice. They may also receive the assistance of interpreters, as well as healthcare, including medical visits, when necessary, and all material support to meet their basic needs. The right to legal assistance is also foreseen, which may include, upon request, access to legal protection.

425. Articles 146 et seq. IL regulate detention in the context of removal proceedings of irregularly staying immigrants. According to Article 146, the foreign citizen who is found irregularly staying in the national territory shall be detained by a police authority and, when possible, handed over to the SEF. He or she shall then be presented to a judge within forty-eight hours, for validation of the detention or for deciding other measures. Although the reading of this Article points towards an almost 'automatic' application of the detention measure, this provision must be read in the light of the Return Directive,[223] which sets forth that detention must be applicable only as a 'last resort measure'. It must only be applicable when strictly necessary – when there is a risk of absconding. This risk is assessed by taking into account the personal, family, social, economic or professional situation of the foreign citizen. Article 142(3) IL sets forth some facts that shall be negatively considered in this context: unknown personal or professional domicile in the national territory, absence of any family ties in the country, doubts about the migrant's identity or preparatory acts of escape. A final decision on the measure that shall be applicable to the foreign citizen until the removal from the territory is taken by the judge, who is the responsible authority for deciding on coercion measures. The judge may opt for other measures besides detention, such as periodic presentation before the authorities or home detention with electronic surveillance (Article 142 IL).

426. In all cases where detention is applied, it cannot exceed more than the necessary period to allow the execution of the removal decision – and cannot last for more than sixty days (paragraph 3 of Article 146 IL). The maximum detention period is, thus, shorter than that allowed by the EU Return Directive.[224]

427. The law also provides, in Article 146-A, several guarantees for foreign citizens who are detained. This provision was enacted in order to fully respect the Return Directive. First, the detainee has the right, upon request, to contact his/her legal adviser, family members and the consular authorities. They must also be guaranteed the right to communicate in private with their lawyers or legal counsellors. Besides these rights, detained immigrants must also have access to emergency healthcare and basic treatments.

428. Article 146-A, in line with the Return Directive, has created the category of 'vulnerable persons'. However, the obligations towards these persons are somehow vague. The provision sets forth that 'special attention shall be paid to vulnerable persons, particularly minors, unaccompanied minors, disabled people, elderly people, pregnant women, single parents with minor children and persons who have been subjected to torture, rape or other serious forms of psychological, physical or sexual violence'. However, the law does not foresee which specific guarantees shall be granted to these persons. The only exception concerns detained accompanied minors, who shall have the possibility to engage in leisure activities, including play and recreational activities appropriate to their age, and depending on the length of their stay, and also access to education. There are no other references to vulnerable persons. The only other reference to special persons concerns detained families, to whom a separated accommodation shall be provided.

223. Directive 2008/115/EC on common standards and procedures in Member States for returning illegally staying third-country nationals.
224. According to the Directive's Art. 15(5) the detention may last up to six months, which can be extended for no more than one year.

429. The National Prevention Mechanism against torture has been developing comprehensive reports on detention conditions in so-called temporary accommodation centres, where migrants are detained in both cases of entry refusals and removal procedures. Despite their name, these centres are real detention centres where the freedom of movement of migrants is severely curtailed. According to the NPM's reports, some of these detention centres do not offer minimum conditions to accommodate migrants during the two-month accommodation periods. Migrants who were detained under Article 40 IL usually remain in a detention centre located in the airport's international area.[225] After 2017, asylum seekers who would request asylum at the border posts, and who would be subject to a fast border procedure would also be detained in these centres.[226] These centres were, then, divided in two wings – one for migrants whose entry into the territory was denied, and other for asylum seekers who have applied for asylum at the border. Both wings were very narrow, having only one common room and two dormitory rooms with bunk beds, where children were accommodated with their parents. Although Article 146-A IL mentions that protocols would be negotiated with organizations for providing support to migrants, no such agreements were finalized until 2022, exception made to the Law Bar Association. Access to leisure activities, to healthcare, to social and psychological support were very limited or non-existent. Both migrants and asylum seekers had almost no contact with the outside world, having a very limited access to phone calls. Taking into account that migrants could live under these circumstances for two months, the NPM highlighted several times that these centres encompassed several risks of ill-treatment.[227]

225. There are three detention centres in airports, named 'EECIT' (temporary accommodation centres' equivalents): in Lisbon, Oporto and Faro.

226. Article 35-A (3) (a) AL.

227. After a tragic death of a Ukrainian citizen in 2020 at the hands of SEF in the Lisbon's airports centre, these centres began to be reformed.

Chapter 4. Expulsion and Removal

430. The Portuguese Constitution sets forth, in Article 33, the main principles as regards expulsion or removal from the national territory. According to paragraph 2, the expulsion of anyone who has entered or remains regularly in the national territory, who has obtained a residence permit, or who has submitted an application for asylum that has not been refused can only be determined by a judicial authority. *A contrario*, it has been understood that removal of foreigners who were irregularly staying in the territory could be decided by the administrative authority, that is to say, by SEF.

§1. Administrative or Judicial Removal

I. Grounds

431. Article 134 IL sets forth the grounds for coercive expulsion (or administrative removal) and for judicial expulsion from the Portuguese territory: (a) illegal entry or stay in the Portuguese territory; (b) violation of national security or public order; (c) threat to the interests or dignity of the Portuguese State or its nationals; (d) interference, in an abusive way, in the exercise of political participation rights reserved to national citizens; (e) practice of acts that, had they been known by the Portuguese authorities, would have prevented the entry into the country; (f) serious reasons to believe that the foreigner has committed serious criminal acts or that he intends to commit such acts, namely in the territory of the European Union; (g) holding of a valid residence permit, or another title that grants them the right to remain in another Member State and does not comply with the obligation to go, immediately, to that Member State; and, finally (h) circumvention or attempt to circumvent the rules applicable to entry and stay, in the national territory or in the Member States of the European Union or States where the Implementing Convention is in force, namely through the use or use of identity documents or false or falsified travel documents, residence permits, visas or documents proving compliance with the conditions of entry.

432. As we can see, several of these cases use extremely vague terms that must be carefully materialized by the courts' case law.

II. Limits

433. Article 134 IL expressly foresees that refugees benefit from a more favourable regime resulting from international law or conventions to which the Portuguese State is bound. We should also add those who hold the status of subsidiary protection according to the European Union Law. Pursuant to Article 143 IL, forced administrative removal and judicial expulsion cannot be made to a State where the foreign citizen may be subject to persecution for the reasons that substantiate the granting of the right to asylum, or where the foreign citizen may suffer torture, inhuman or degrading treatment in the meaning of Article 3 of the ECHR. These persons may receive a residence right in cases where they fulfil the conditions mentioned in the IL, although no specific case of regularization is foreseen for their cases. They may also benefit from a special residence permit discretionarily issued under Article 123 (Humanitarian grounds).

434. Other provisions foresee more limits to expulsion or removal decisions. Article 135 IL foresees some limits that must be observed in all circumstances. They are aimed at protecting fundamental rights, which must prevail over reasons that may justify expulsion. First, in order to protect their right to private life, foreign citizens who were born in Portuguese territory and reside therein, or who have resided in Portugal since the age of 10 cannot be expelled. Moreover, in order to respect the right to family life, foreigners who are parents of Portuguese children, to whom they take charge of, cannot be returned either to their country of origin. This provision was enacted in order to respect the Portuguese Constitutional Court case law, which has declared unconstitutional the possibility of expelling foreigner parents who have Portuguese children living in the territory, and to whom such parents would afford alimony and education.[228] The Constitutional Court considered that such an expulsion would be tantamount to a violation of the right to family life (enshrined in Article 36 of the Constitution), or to a violation of the prohibition of expulsion of national citizens from the national territory (enshrined in Article 33 of the Constitution). In addition, foreign citizens cannot be removed or expelled from the national territory if they have custody of minor children of foreign nationality residing in Portugal and effectively exercise parental responsibilities upon them. This last rule is also clearly a recognition of the principle of the best interests of the foreigner children, which can also reclaim that he/she remains in the host country.

435. In the original reading of Article 135 IL, these limits were absolute – that is to say, in these cases, these migrants could not be expelled under any circumstances. However, due to the increase of security concerns in the EU – especially after the Charlie Hebdo terrorist attacks, these limits ceased to be applicable in the event of a well-founded suspicion of the involvement on crimes of terrorism, sabotage, or attack on national security or of condemnation for such crimes (Article 135(2) IL).

436. Some categories of migrants have a stronger protection against expulsion. That is the case of long-term residents. According to Article 136 IL, the decision to judicially expel a long-term resident can only be based on the fact that it represents a real and sufficiently serious threat to public order or public security and should not be based on economic reasons. The law also foresees expressly that, before a decision is made to expel a long-term resident, the judicial authority must consider: (a) the duration of residence in the territory; (b) the migrant's age; (c) the consequences of the expulsion to the migrant and to their family members; (d) the links with the country of residence or the absence of links with the country of origin.

228. Ruling n. 232/2004, of 25/03/2004.

437. A special regime is also foreseen for those who have a right to permanent residence. They cannot be expelled from the Portuguese territory, except for serious reasons of public order or public security (Article 151(3) IL).

438. One must highlight that, although the IL only foresees the need to balance the foreigners' fundamental rights with the seriousness of the offences in the case of expulsion of long-term residents (and, partially, in the case of permanent residents), we must consider migrants' human rights in *all expulsion or removal cases*, according to the ECtHR's case law.[229] Thus, their rights to private and family life, the best interests of the children involved, the prohibition of ill-treatment, etc., must always be balanced against the reasons that justify the measure of expulsion or removal.

III. Procedure

439. Removal under the grounds mentioned in Article 134 IL may take place under an administrative procedure – where the migrant is irregularly staying in the territory – or through a judicial expulsion – when the foreigner is a legal resident. In the latter case, the expulsion is made through a special procedure, where an 'autonomous measure of judicial expulsion' is decided.

440. The competent authority for administrative removal is the SEF's National Director, personally or by delegation of powers (Article 141 IL). The foreign citizens concerned are removed from another country that accepts them.

441. The foreign citizen against whom a decision on forced removal or expulsion has been issued is granted a period to leave the national territory between 10 to twenty days (Article 138 IL). That time period may be longer. On the course of it, the special needs of vulnerable persons shall be taken into account, more specifically the needs of minors, disabled people, elderly people, pregnant women, single parents with minor children and persons who have been subject to torture, rape or other serious forms of psychological, physical or sexual violence (Article 160 IL). The foreign citizen who does not leave the national territory within the time limit fixed shall be detained and escorted to the border post with a view to be removed from the national territory. When he/she is to be removed by air, the possibilities for taking a direct flight to the country of destination shall be taken into account (Article 173 IL). If he/she does not hold a travel document, a document for that purpose will be issued, valid for one single journey (Article 27 IL).

442. A removal decision taken by the competent administrative authority of an EU Member State against a third-country national who is in the Portuguese territory and recognized according to Directive 2001/40 of 28 May, on the mutual recognition of such decisions, shall only be executed after a preliminary examination of the situation of the person concerned in order to ensure that neither the Constitution,

229. *See*, for example, the recent cases *Men v. Russia*, decision of 08/06/2021, application n. 11338/15 and *Avici v. Denmark*, decision of 30/11/2021, application n. 40240/19.

the relevant international conventions, nor the law prevents its execution. The execution of the forced removal or expulsion decision must be communicated, through diplomatic channels, to the competent authorities of the State of destination. If it is not possible to execute those decisions within forty-eight hours after the detention, the fact shall be reported to the competent judge, with a view to put the foreign citizen in a detention centre (Articles 169 and 171 IL).

§2. Ancillary Criminal Penalty of Expulsion

443. A judicial decision of expulsion can also be taken following a criminal proceeding, when the foreigner is considered guilty of having committed a crime. The Portuguese Criminal Code (CC) foresees the ancillary penalty of expulsion, which can be applied by the criminal judge to foreigners who have committed crimes in some cases.

444. According to Article 151 IL, this penalty may be applied to foreign citizens who are not resident in the country, who have been convicted of a felony in a sentence exceeding six months of actual imprisonment or in a fine as an alternative to a prison sentence of more than six months. The same penalty may be imposed on a foreign citizen residing in the country who was convicted of a felony in a sentence of more than one year in prison.

445. However, the ancillary penalty of expulsion cannot be applied automatically, even if the legal requirements are fulfilled. The Portuguese Constitutional Court has, indeed, highlighted in several occasions that the automatic application of the ancillary penalty of expulsion – with no consideration of the particular circumstances of the case and of the interests involved – would be contrary to Article 30(4) of the Constitution[230] – that sets forth that no sentence shall automatically involve the loss of any civil, professional or political right. Moreover, while deciding the application of such punishment, account must be taken of the seriousness of the facts committed, possible relapse on committing other crimes, the migrant's insertion in Portuguese social life, his personality and length of residence in Portugal. As we can see, the IL consecrates expressly the case law of the ECtHR as regards balancing the private and family life of foreigners. No mention is made, however, of the application of the ancillary penalty to irregularly staying migrants. However, an interpretation in conformity with the international obligations to which Portugal is bound demands the judge to balance the application of such penalty with the offender's fundamental rights, as affirmed by the Strasbourg Court.

446. As for the execution of the penalty, Article 151 IL sets forth that the competent judge shall order its execution as soon as the following periods of time are

230. Ruling n. 359/93, of 25/05/1993, ruling n. 434/93, of 13/07/1993, ruling n. 442/93, of 14/06/1993, ruling n. 288/94, of 23/03/1994, ruling n. 41/95, of 01/02/1995.

completed: half of the sentence, in the case of a sentence equal to or less than five years in prison, or two thirds of the sentence, in cases of a sentence of more than five years in prison.

447. However, in the cases of sentences of five years or less in prison, the judge may, upon a proposal by the director of the prison establishment, and without opposition from the sentenced person, decide to bring forward the execution of the expulsion penalty as soon as one-third of the sentence has been served, and provided that the remainder of the sentence is ensured in the country of destination (Article 151(5) IL).

Part V. Legal Remedies and Procedural Safeguards

Chapter 1. Legal Remedies in Case of Refusal

§1. Procedural Safeguards

448. All procedures concerning decisions on entry, stay or loss of residence or removal, being administrative procedures, must respect all constitutional guarantees foreseen for all administrative procedures, which are enshrined in Article 268. This constitutional provision sets forth that all administrative procedures shall guarantee the right to information (the right of individuals, whoever they are and acting in any administrative procedure, to be informed, whenever they require it, of the progress of the procedures that concern them), the right to access administrative files and records, as well as the right to know the final decisions – which implies the right to notify the administrative acts and the respective grounds. This right to notification encompasses the duty to duly ground the final decision (paragraph 3 of Article 268). Finally, the individual's rights to participation in the administrative procedure are also recognized in the Constitution. This right encompasses, *inter alia*, the right to be heard by the competent authority before a final decision is made.

449. Despite all these constitutional guarantees, the Immigration Law only foresees expressly some of them in certain procedures. For example, the right to a prior hearing is expressly referred to in Article 38, regarding decisions on entry refusals, or in Article 108, regarding the decision to cancel the residence permit issued under the right to family reunification. The same right is granted during the coercive administrative removal procedure in Article 148 IL. In other cases, although the law does not refer expressly to the need of a prior hearing, the constitutional guarantees must obviously apply. In addition, with regard to all decisions, the rules of the Code of Administrative Procedure, which imposes the duty of information, as well as prior hearing, which is currently provided for in Article 12 and in Articles 121 et seq. shall apply, as ancillary legislation. Moreover, as seen previously, in several removal cases, the administration must consider several factors before taking the decision, such as his/her family life or insertion in the country.[231] It will only be able to carry out these considerations after hearing the interested foreigner for this purpose.

---

231. Part IV, Ch. 4.

450. Finally, the Immigration Law also provides for the notification of decisions to interested parties in several provisions, together with the factual and legal grounds.[232] In particular, decisions to refuse entry must always be notified, in a language that the foreigner can understand, under the terms of Article 38, mentioning its grounds of fact and law. Also Article 149(2) mentions that the decision of forced expulsion is notified to the expelled person with mention of the factual and legal grounds. Although, in other cases, the law does not refer to the need for the appointment of a translator or interpreter, as does the Code of Administrative Procedure with regard to procedures involving foreigners who do not speak the Portuguese language, it is to be understood that the duty to information and notification suggests that it should be done in a language that can be understood by the notified party.

§2. Judicial Review

451. The guarantee of an effective judicial remedy in the context of IL measures is guaranteed, first, in the Portuguese Constitution. In this realm, it stems from two provisions: from Article 20, which guarantees the fundamental right to access to courts, and from Article 268(4), which sets forth the right to an effective judicial review of administrative decisions.

452. Article 20 guarantees the right to a fair trial, with effective guarantee of the principle of adversarial procedure and of access to legal aid. One should highlight that the Constitutional Court has affirmed, several times, that foreigners enjoy the right to legal aid to the same extent as national citizens.[233] As for Article 268(4), it sets forth the possibility for the foreigner to judicially challenge any negative decision that may affect him/her. However, in cases where the refusal to issue a residence permit is at stake, the Constitution also provides that effective judicial protection may take the form of a judicial order to issue the due act. The constitutional protection also encompasses the possibility of imposing 'appropriate' precautionary measures. The Constitution does not specify which types of precautionary measures must be guaranteed, and it is up to the legislator to implement them. Such measures may be proactive or may result in the suspension of the contested decision. Thus, it is understood that the constitutional guarantee does not require that a

232. That is the case of Art. 82, n. 4, regarding decisions to refuse a permanent residence permit, of Art. 85, n. 5, regarding the decisions to cancel these residence permits, Art. 96, regarding decisions to refuse a residence permit for studies, unpaid or voluntary professional internship, Art. 105, which establishes a period of three months for the written notification of the decision regarding the request for family reunification, Art. 106(6), regarding the rejection of the request for family reunification and the need to justify it, Art. 108, regarding the decision to cancel the residence permit for the purposes of family reunification, Art. 121, on the rejection of the application for a residence permit for holders of long-term resident status in another EU Member State, Art. 121-D, paras 4 and 5, regarding decisions to refuse to grant or renew or cancel the 'EU Blue Card' and Arts 129, para. 4, and 132, relating to requests for the acquisition of long-term status.

233. Ruling n. 365/2000, dated 05/07/2000, and n. 433/2003, dated 29/09/2003.

fundamental right to suspend administrative decisions shall be recognized in all circumstances. As the ECtHR, the Constitutional Court affirms that effective judicial protection demands, however, that the effectiveness of the decision shall be safeguarded, and a serious or hardly repairable damage shall be prevented.[234]

453. The guarantees of effective remedy provided for in the Constitution and in the general law relating to administrative litigation apply to any administrative decision made in the matter of immigration. Even so, the IL expressly provides, in some cases, for the right to judicial review of administrative measures taken in this matter. Thus, among others, with regard to the decision to refuse a residence permit, in general, the law states that it is notified to the interested party with an indication of the grounds, as well as the right of judicial challenge and the respective term (Article 82(4)). Naturally, the express mention of the possibility of appeal in these cases does not mean that, in the other cases, such guarantees do not apply – since the general rules will operate.

454. The IL expressly foresees a right of appeal without suspensive effect for the third-country nationals before the administrative courts against the following decisions: (i) refusal of entry into Portuguese territory (Article 39); cancellation of a residence permit (Article 85(7)); rejection of an application for family reunification (Article 106(7)); rejection of an application for a residence permit, non-renewal or cancellation of a residence permit under the provisions on the long-term resident status (Article 121); forced removal rendered by the SEF's National Director (Article 150(1)); enforcement of a removal decided by another Member State and recognized by the SEF in accordance to Directive 2001/40 (Article 171(3)); return decision (Article 166).

455. A right of appeal with suspensive effect before the same courts is expressly foreseen against the following decisions: (1) cancellation of the permit issued under the right to family reunification on grounds that the marriage, registered partnership or adoption had as only purpose allowing the entry of the interested party in Portugal (Article 108(7)); (2) rejection of the application for a long-term resident status and loss of that status (Article 132(3)); (3) judicial expulsion of a long-term resident; (Article 136(3)).

456. The right to appeal to a superior court is also foreseen for the application of autonomous measures of judicial expulsion, which also do not entail suspensive effects (Art 158 IL). The same applies in the context of the application of the ancillary expulsion penalty, according to the general rules of the Criminal Code.

457. Finally, it should also be noted that the law provides certain guarantees for the course of the judicial process to challenge immigration decisions. In particular, it provides for the provision of translation and interpretation services at the request of the interested party. Although this mention is made in Article 150 IL, in the context of the judicial challenge of the administrative decisions of coercive removal, it

---

234. *See*, in particular, ruling n. 276/06, dated 02/05/2006.

must apply to all judicial remedies. Article 92 of the Criminal Procedures Code, applicable to autonomous measures of judicial expulsion, as well as, of course, to the application of an accessory penalty of expulsion, prescribes the appointment, without charge, of a suitable interpreter, even if the competent entity knows the language used by the defendant. The same must also be applicable in administrative courts, in procedures aimed at challenging administrative decisions.

Chapter 2. Legal Remedies in Case of Detention

458. As mentioned in Chapter 3 of Part IV, the Portuguese Constitution allows detention of irregularly staying migrants in cases where they have entered or stayed irregularly in the national territory, or with a view to removal for extradition or expulsion purposes. In both cases, detention must always be controlled judicially.

459. Whereas for judicial remedies regarding administrative decisions on immigration and asylum, administrative courts are the competent courts, on detention matters, criminal courts are competent.

460. The first opportunity to ask for a legal remedy happens when the competent judge validates the decision. In all detention cases, detention must be validated by a judge within forty-eight hours (Articles 38 and 146 IL and Article 35-A AL). The judge must verify whether there are enough grounds for detention, and the migrants can present their defence against the deprivation of liberty. Second, when a detention is confirmed by the Court, the foreigner has the right to appeal to the Appeals Court. The Criminal Procedures Code is applicable to these appeals. Appeals do not have suspensive effects, which means that the foreigner remains in detention while its reasons are being analysed by the Appeals Court.

Part VI. Access to the Labour Market and to Other Social Rights

Chapter 1. Overview of Applicable Legislation

461. Applicable legislation as regards migrants' access to labour market and other social rights encompasses several legal acts: first and foremost, the Portuguese Constitution and its general principles. Second, the IL and the AL, the Portuguese LC and all legislation regarding other social rights, which set forth their subjective scope of application.

462. As already seen, Article 15(1) of the Portuguese Constitution guarantees the general principle of equivalence of foreigners to national citizens regarding all constitutional rights. This shall encompass, in principle, every constitutional right, both the so-called rights, freedoms and guarantees as well as the economic, social and cultural rights – such as the right to work, the right to access to health, social security, and education.

463. The IL and AL also foresee that migrants who benefit from a certain legal status are entitled to a certain set of social rights. These clauses may seem redundant, as their solutions would already stem from the constitutional principle of equivalence . Thus, these clauses may give the impression that migrants with *another status* would not enjoy the same rights. That is the case of those who hold a permanent residence permit, to whom the IL guarantees equal treatment with Portuguese citizens as regards: (i) education and teaching; (ii) employment; (iii) self-employment; (iv) professional guidance, training, further training and retraining; (v) healthcare; (vi) access to the law and courts; (vii) social security; (viii) tax benefits; (ix) trade union memberships; and (x) recognition of diplomas, certificates and other professional credentials or documents granting them access to goods and services made available to the public (Article 83). That is also the case of Article 133 IL, which transposes into the domestic law Directive 2003/109/EC of 25 November 2003, on the status of third-country nationals who are long-term residents. The Directive is the result of a consensus established between the Member States at the extraordinary meeting in Tampere on 15 and 16 October 1999, based on which the European Council proclaimed that the legal status of third-country nationals, legally resident in an EU Member State, should be equal (or at least very close) to the status of EU citizens. This means that a person legally residing in a Member State during a certain period (to be determined by each Member State) should benefit in this

State from a set of uniform rights as close as possible to those enjoyed by citizens of the European Union. Thus, Article 133 IL ('Equal Treatment') provides for several rights for third-country nationals, which correspond essentially to the various paragraphs of Article 11(1) of Directive 2003/109/EC, under the same heading: (a) access to an employed or self-employed activity, provided that such activity does not entail even occasional involvement in the exercise of public authority, without prejudice to the application of the special scheme granted to citizens from Portuguese-speaking countries; (b) access to conditions of employment and working conditions, including conditions regarding dismissal and remuneration; (c) education and vocational training including study grants and allowances according to the applicable legislation; (d) recognition of professional diplomas, certificates and other qualifications in accordance to law and national procedures; (e) social security, social assistance and social protection; (f) tax benefits; (g) healthcare; (h) access to goods and services and the supply of goods and services made available to the public, as well as to procedures for obtaining accommodation; (i) freedom of association and affiliation and membership of an organization representing workers or employers, or any organization whose members are engaged in a specific occupation, including the benefits conferred by such type of organizations, without prejudice to the national provisions on public policy and public security; j) free access to the entire national territory. Considering the legal and constitutional framework mentioned above, any categorization of the economic and social rights that beneficiaries of the long-term residence status may enjoy runs the risk of being restrictive, from the very beginning, in the light of the Portuguese Constitution. For this reason, a broad reading and interpretation of long-term resident status should be promoted. In this sense, some authors claim that although long-term residents have a special status (cf. Article 133), the rights given to them are essentially identical to those provided for holders of a permanent residence permit (cf. Article 83).[235] In any way, we must recall that, despite these clauses, the principle of equivalence is applicable to other migrants that are resident in Portugal – if any of the exceptions to that principle is not applicable.[236]

464. The Portuguese Immigration Law, in its last amendment, facilitated the regularization of immigrant workers, allowing their access to social rights. Conditions for such regularization were already studied above[237] and opened up the possibility for many immigrants in an irregular administrative situation, to regularize their administrative status, and thus to have access to a range of social rights, as well as to basic goods and services that are only accessible and available to immigrants with legal residence (cf. Article 83 IL). A major part of these migrants worked in

235. José de Melo Alexandrino, 'A nova lei de entrada, permanência, saída e afastamento de estrangeiros', in *Revista da Faculdade de Direito da Universidade de Lisboa*, vol. XLIX, ns. 1 e 2, 2008, p. 20.
236. As to those exceptions, *see*, above, General Introduction, §2., 1.
237. *See* Ch. 5, §1.

the so-called informal economy, mainly in sectors of activities which were unattractive to the rest of the population (e.g., construction, domestic services, catering, cleaning, etc.) and where compliance with labour standards is insufficiently supervised by the competent authorities.

§1. Access to Labour Market

465. The Portuguese Constitution recognizes the right to work of every person (Article 58 and Article 15).[238] This recognition is particularly important, as work is essential in the life of an individual and his family.

466. As a matter of fact, work is not important just as a source of survival to the family but also to provide them a decent life and allow the individuals to flourish. In this regard, Gomes Canotilho and Vital Moreira, two important Portuguese constitutional scholars, affirm that the right to work is, for economic, social, and cultural rights, 'in the same position as the right to life within the framework of civil and political rights'.[239] For this reason, the right to work must be read and understood in conjunction with three important constitutional principles: the principle of universality (Article 12-C), the principle of equal treatment (Articles 13 and 15) and the principle of the dignity of the human person (Article 1). In other words: (i) the right to work must be recognized to all persons; (ii) without any distinction; (iii) in order to ensure and promote a dignified existence.

467. The right to work is, like all social rights, a 'positive right'; that is, it is a right dependent on active State intervention, especially through administrative and legislative measures (e.g., job creation through 'full employment policies', cf. Article 58(2) (a) of the Constitution). Nevertheless, it has also a 'negative or guarantee dimension', including the freedom to seek work and not to be arbitrarily prevented from it.[240]

468. The Portuguese Constitution emphasizes the fundamental principle of equal treatment (Article 59(1)), regarding workers' rights, expressly prohibiting discrimination on grounds of nationality, like other suspect criteria of differentiation. This provision not only forbids that some professions might be limited only to national citizens but also forbids the priority of placement based on the same criterion.[241]

469. It is in the light of the axiological-normative parameters given by the Portuguese fundamental law, in conjunction with the references resulting from the rules

238. Gomes Canotilho and Vital Moreira refer that the use by the constitutional provision of the expression 'all' does not place any doubt that it was intended to cover all people, without any restriction (cf. J.J. Gomes Canotilho & Vital Moreira, *Constituição da República Portuguesa Anotada*, Vol. I. 4.ª Ed. Coimbra Editora, 2007, p. 766).
239. *Ibid.*, p. 762.
240. *See*, for example, Art. 12(2) of the International Convention on Civil and Political Rights (ICCPR): 'All persons are free to leave any country, including their own.'
241. J.J. Gomes Canotilho & Vital Moreira, *supra* p. 771.

and principles of international law, that the relevant provisions of the Portuguese Law must be read and analysed, in particular with regard to the conditions of access to the labour market, to which all third-country nationals who wish to work (whether as subordinated or independent workers) in the national territory are subject.

470. Access to the labour market is regulated in the Immigration Law and Asylum Law which set forth which types of residence permits allow their holders to work in Portugal, and also in the Portuguese LC.[242]

§2. Access to Social Security

471. The right to social security is enshrined in Article 63 of the Portuguese Constitution, which states that *everyone* is entitled to social security in case of illness, age, disability, widowhood and orphanhood, as well as unemployment and in all other situations where there is a lack or decrease of economical means or work ability. Law n. 4/2007 of 16 January sets forth the general basis for the system of social security.[243] It reaffirms the principle of universality (Articles 2 and 5).

472. The Portuguese system of social security encompasses the contributory social security scheme and the complementary system. The contributory system is called 'providential system' and is based on the payment of contributions and aimed at replacing the income, on the one hand, and the social protection system, which encompasses the solidarity system and the family support system (this system is mainly aimed at fighting against poverty and at guaranteeing a minimum income for a life compatible with the human dignity).

473. Every citizen who works in Portugal, irrespective of their nationality, is protected by the providential system, pursuant to their registry in the social security services and payment of the contributions. Irregularly staying immigrants may be registered and may pay their contributions to the social security. That is because in practice the social security services only demand, for registration purposes, an identification document.[244] The same applies when the employer registers their employees in the social security. However, immigrants will only be effectively protected by the social security if they have a valid residence permit title. This means that irregularly staying immigrants may pay their contributions to the social security and not benefit from its protection. The payment of such contributions has been used as an argument for the advocacy of regularization of irregularly staying immigrants.[245] And, in fact, throughout the history of the Portuguese immigration legislation, the

242. Law n. 7/2009, of 12 February, as last amended by Law n. 93/2019, of 9 September.
243. As last amended by Law n. 83-A/2013, of 30 December.
244. João Peixoto, Carolina Marçalo & Nancy Tolentino, *Imigrantes e Segurança Social em Portugal*, Observatório da Imigração, 2011, p. 48.
245. *Ibid.*, 78.

payment of contributions to the social security has been one of the conditions for regularization of irregularly staying immigrants.[246]

474. Once migrants acquire a legal status, they can benefit from all the protection afforded by the Portuguese social security system. Their family members are also protected since social protection is a right guaranteed by the family reunification system (Article 98 IR).

475. The providential system encompasses protection of workers in case of illness, contribution for family charges, maternity and paternity protection (which also encompasses protection during adoption procedures), assistance to family members with disabilities, assistance to family members during illness, protection in case of unemployment, professional diseases, disability, retirement and death.

476. Irregularly staying immigrants cannot access the non-contributory protection system either. Only Portuguese citizens, citizens of the European Union, immigrants holding a valid residence permit, refugees and stateless persons may benefit from this protection system. Another thorny question concerns the enjoyment of social security benefits. As we have seen, the registration in the Portuguese social security is not dependent on the acquisition of a valid residence permit. However, irregularly staying immigrants do not have access to social benefits, even where they regularly pay the social security contributions. This situation may lead to the disrespect of the principle of non-discrimination on the grounds of legal status.

477. By contrast, immigrants who hold a valid residence permit benefit exactly from the very same social protection that is afforded to Portuguese citizens. They have the same obligations and the same rights as the Portuguese citizens, as a special regime for social protection of immigrants has never existed.[247]

478. Some types of support (granted by the so-called providential system) are granted irrespective of where the immigrant is residing. That is the case for pensions. In these cases, the migrant can be residing in his/her country of origin and receive those allowances. Other allowances, however, are only granted if the migrant is residing in Portugal. That is the case of the unemployment or illness benefits. Also, in order to benefit from the protection afforded by the 'solidarity system', the migrant has to reside geographically in Portugal. There are some

246. *See*, for example, Art. 71 of Regulamentary Decree n. 6/2004 of 24 April and Art. 88, n. 2 and 89, n. 2 of the current immigration law (Law n. 23/2007). *See* Ch. 4., §1.

247. In 2015, the Portuguese Constitutional Court issued a ruling where it declared that the statute that demanded third-country nationals to have resided for three years in the national territory before being entitled to a 'national minimum guaranteed income' was unconstitutional. The Court considered that the three years delay disrespected the principle of proportionality. The income concerned is afforded to everyone who is deemed to live below the minimum of the human dignity. Therefore, it is afforded to those who are not employed and do not benefit from an unemployment pension. The Court considered that every person, living in the Portuguese territory – citizens and foreigners alike – should be entitled to an income allowing them to live according to Human Dignity Standards (ruling n. 296/2015, dated 25 May. 2015).

exceptions, where Portugal signed international agreements. The governmental National Plans for the integration of immigrants have been pointing out as a priority the development of such agreements, especially with the countries of origin of the major part of the population of the immigrants. There are several bilateral agreements in force in this realm, as, for example, with Andorra, Argentina, Australia, Brazil, Cabo-Verde, Canada, Chile, United States, Morocco, Moldavia, Tunisia, Uruguay, and Venezuela. Other agreements were signed, but are not yet in force. That is the case of the agreements with Angola, Guinea-Bissau, Sao Tome and Principe and Ukraine. After the signature of these agreements, the nationals of these countries may benefit from the protection afforded by the solidarity system while residing in their country of origin.

479. The National Plans for the integration of immigrants have been also advocating the support of immigrants living under conditions of extreme poverty, regardless of their legal status in Portugal. However, so far, only legally staying immigrants have benefited from the protection derived from the non-contributory scheme. This scheme encompasses, for example, the social income, which is a minimum income aimed at guaranteeing a minimum standard of living.

480. Article 20 of the FML is dedicated to the guarantee of equal treatment of EU citizens and national citizens. However, according to its paragraph 3, Union citizens or their families are not entitled to benefits from the solidarity subsystem during the first three months of residence or for a longer period if the Union citizen entered the national territory to seek employment under the terms of paragraph b) of paragraph 4 of Article 9.

§3. Access to Schooling and Healthcare

481. The Portuguese Constitution sets forth that *everybody* has the right to health protection (Article 64). It also guarantees adequate support for children of immigrants and sets forth, as a State task, the implementation of their right to education (Article 74, n. 2, *j)*).

482. Any foreigner who is in the country and needs any kind of healthcare has the right to be assisted at a health centre or a hospital. Health services cannot refuse to provide medical care on any grounds of nationality, lack of economic resources, and legal status.

483. Legally staying immigrants have the same rights as Portuguese citizens to benefit from the National Health Care System. Foreigners without residence permit, residence or work visa – have to ask for a certificate of residence in their parish councils, proving that they have lived in Portugal for more than ninety days in order to benefit from the healthcare system.[248] They may, nonetheless, benefit from the National Health Care System, provided that they pay contributions to the social

248. Decision of the Ministry of Justice n. 360/2001.

security. These rights are enshrined in a decision of the Ministry of Health dated 2001. This decision refers to the International Covenant for Social, Economic and Cultural Rights, the Conventions of the International Labour Organisation and the European Social Charter.

484. Immigrants that pay contributions to the social security benefit from the National Health Care System under the same conditions as national citizens. Despite the Law on Healthcare mentioning that healthcare tends to be free, taking into account the personal economic and social conditions, in reality the user must pay a healthcare fee according to the rates in force for each type of care. Children up to 12 years of age and pregnant women are exempted from paying fees. Family planning or sexual and reproductive healthcare, treatment of diseases that endanger public health, and vaccines included in the National Vaccination Programme are also free of charge.

485. By contrast, migrants that do not pay contributions to the social security may be charged with expenses incurred by the healthcare services.

486. Article 83 IL guarantees the right to schooling, professional and vocational training to all legal residents, including access to scholarships.

487. Decree-Law n. 67/2004 of 25 March has created a national registry of children who are irregularly residing in Portugal. It is aimed at guaranteeing the access of those children to healthcare and to schooling, irrespective of their legal status. It encompasses a clause that guarantees that information gathered by the public services cannot be used against these children's family members for the purpose of enforcement of IL. As mentioned previously, the High Commissioner for Migrations is the governmental body responsible for integration of immigrants. It provides support for ensuring an effective access to schooling and health to immigrants.[249]

488. Portugal has also developed a support programme for patients coming from several countries that provides housing, medical support, and entry visas for the purpose of medical treatment, for both the patients and their accompanying family members. The largest part of these agreements was celebrated with African Portuguese-speaking countries.

489. Last but not least, another reality important to mention is that of immigrant workers in an irregular administrative situation, especially those who, while gathering all the conditions that the IL determines for their regularization (as subordinate or independent workers, on the grounds of Articles 88 and 89 IL, respectively), face difficulties in acquiring a residence permit by this means (e.g., due to lack of information about their rights and duties; lengthy bureaucratic regularization processes; difficulty in obtaining the necessary documentation; etc.). Until they obtain

249. Decree-Law n. 31/2014 of 27 February.

their regularization, these migrants do not have any legal status, and for these reasons face several difficulties in accessing the most basic and fundamental social rights (such as education, healthcare, and social security) and basic services and goods as well. Indeed, they feel like (and are seen as) 'without rights', using here the very expressive words of José de Melo Alexandrino.[250]

§4. Labour Rights

490. The Portuguese Constitution provides, in its Article 59,[251] a range of labour guarantees that, in line with the universalistic provision that precedes it (Article 58), should apply to 'all workers', regardless of age, sex, race, citizenship, territory of origin, religion, political or ideological convictions. Thus, all workers are entitled to: (i) retribution for work (paragraph 1/a); (ii) organization of work under socially dignified conditions, in order to provide personal development and to enable the reconciliation of work and family life (paragraph 1/b); (iii) right to work in hygienic, safe, and health conditions (paragraph 1/c); rest and leisure, a maximum limit of working hours, weekly rest and paid periodic leave (paragraph 1/d); (iv) material assistance, in case of non-voluntary unemployment (paragraph 1/e); (v) assistance and fair reparation when victims of an accident at work or occupational disease (paragraph 1/f).

491. The Portuguese LC provides, in Article 4 and within the scope of private subordinated labour relations, the 'principle of equal treatment of foreign or stateless workers'. The principle of equal treatment is further affirmed by Article 24 of the LC, which provides that 'the worker or jobseeker is entitled to equal opportunities and treatment with regard to access to employment, vocational training and promotion or career and working conditions, and may not be privileged, benefited, impaired, deprived of any right or exempt from any duty due to, namely, ancestry, age, sex, sexual orientation, gender identity, marital status, family situation, economic situation, education, origin or social condition, genetic heritage, reduced working capacity, disability, chronic illness, nationality, ethnic origin or race, territory of origin, language, religion, political or ideological convictions and trade union membership'. Additionally, it adds that the State shall promote equal access to such rights. Accordingly, Article 25(1) of the LC prohibits the employer from

250. José de Melo Alexandrino, *supra* p. 20.
251. The universality of workers' rights, provided for in this provision, was inspired by the most relevant and binding international norms of the Portuguese State, in terms of human rights in particular: the Universal Declaration of Human Rights (UDHR) (Arts 24 and 25); the ICCPR (Art. 8); the International Covenant on Economic, Social and Cultural Rights (ICESCR) (Arts 2, 3, 7, 10 and 12); ILO Convention n. 95 (Protection of Wages Convention); ILO Convention n. 122 (Employment Policy Convention); ILO Convention n. 131 (Minimum Wage Fixing Convention); ILO Convention n. 138 (Minimum Age Convention); ILO Convention n. 159 (Vocational Rehabilitation and Employment (Disabled Persons) Convention); ILO Convention n. 161 (Occupational Health Services Convention).

engaging in any direct or indirect discrimination, based on one of the prohibited factors of discrimination referred to above, which do not constitute a closed or exhaustive list.

492. The third-country national worker enjoys all the rights and guarantees that the LC provides to all workers: (i) personality rights (Articles 14–22) and other essential guarantees (Article 129); (ii) prohibition of discrimination (Articles 23–28), protection against harassment (Article 29) and against discrimination on grounds of sex (Articles 30–32); and right to vocational training (Articles 130–134). Migrant workers also benefit from: (i) protection of parenthood (Articles 33–65); (ii) prohibition of child labour (Articles 66–83); (iii) protection in case of reduced working capacity (Article 84); (iv) disabilities or chronic illness (Articles 85–88); (v) student worker (Articles 89–96 – A). However, foreign workers are subjected to the same labour duties as national workers are (cf. Articles 126 and 128 of the LC). Moreover, all international instruments that guarantee labour rights, to which Portugal is party, must also be applicable to foreign workers.

493. An important question to be addressed concerns the labour rights of foreigners or stateless persons working in an irregular administrative situation. Must they benefit from labour rights enshrined in the labour legislation? Pedro Romano Martinez states that the Labour Portuguese Code does not apply to foreigners who are in such a situation, except as regards certain basic rules of protection, like the reparation of accidents at work (cf. Article 281) and the payment of wages (cf. Article 258 and ss.).[252] At this point, we are led to disagree with the author, positioning ourselves alongside Jorge Miranda and Rui Medeiros, who affirm that the principle of equal treatment enshrined in the CRP establishes two equivalences: (i) the first between nationals and foreigners; (ii) the second among foreigners allowed to reside in our territory and those who are only present in the Portuguese territory (i.e.,, who do not hold a valid residence title), at least regarding a certain number of fundamental rights. Thus, the reading of the LC provision, which provides for equal treatment between foreign and national workers (cf. Article 4 of the LC), shall be implemented in the light of the constitutional provisions (Article 15(1) and Article

252. Pedro Romano Martinez, *Direito do Trabalho* Almedina, 7.ª Ed., Coimbra, 2015, p. 399. This doctrine – despite being not very representative among the authors – has had some acceptance by the jurisprudence of the higher Portuguese courts. In a case where a foreign citizen, working in Portugal without a work visa, challenged his/her dismissal for deeming it unlawful, the Court of Appeal of Coimbra stated that: (i) it follows from labour law that the foreign citizen who is working in Portugal without authorization does not enjoy the rights and is not subject to the duties provided for Portuguese workers; (ii) the constitutional principle enshrined in Art. 15 of the CRP supposes that foreign citizens have legalized their situation in the national territory; (iii) thus, 'in relation to a foreign citizen who is not authorized to pursue a professional activity in Portugal, there is no need analyse an employment contract, much less an unlawful dismissal and its consequences' (cf. Judgment of the Court of Appeal of Coimbra, of 17-03-2009, case n. 773/06.7TTAVR. C1, reported by Lord Judge Felizardo Paiva). However, recognizing the existence of a subordinate working relationship between fourteen undocumented foreign citizens and the owner of a brothel, *see* Judgment of the Court of Appeal of Lisbon, of 12-07-2004, case n. 8933/2004 8933/2004 5, reported by Mrs. Filomena Lima.

58(1)):[253] in their broadest terms. In other words: following the designation usually adopted by some Portuguese legal scholars, an 'interpretation according to the Constitution' should be made, and the lawyer is constitutionally bound to seek, among the various possible meanings of a given legal norm, the one that most closely approximates the axiological-normative meaning prescribed by the Fundamental Law.[254]

494. José de Melo Alexandrino affirms the existence, in Part I of the Constitution, of a set of hermeneutic canons that may be of great use when the interpreter/applicator of the law has doubts about the attribution/ownership of a certain fundamental right to a foreign citizen. Thus, the interpreter must assume that the right is constitutionally granted/recognized to all persons (principle of universality, cf. Article 12(1) of the CRP), namely to all foreigners and stateless persons who are or reside in Portugal (principle of equal treatment, cf. Article 15(1) of the CRP). Finally, and in accordance with Article 16(2) of the Constitution, the methodological outcome obtained must be in accordance with the Universal Declaration of Human Rights, to the extent that the CRP raises it to the parameter of interpretation and integration of constitutional and legal norms that enshrine fundamental rights. The recognition of the existence and relevance of these methodological principles leads the author to state that 'foreigners benefit from all fundamental rights (and all human rights provided for in the Universal Declaration of Human Rights and the European Convention on Human Rights) that have not been expressly excluded by the legislator'.[255]

253. Article 58(1) of the CRP clearly sets forth the universality of the right to work by simply stating that 'everyone has the right to work'.
254. José de Melo Alexandrino, op. cit, p. 28.
255. *Ibid.*, p. 20.

Chapter 2. Conditions to Work

§1. Migrants Who Are Entitled to Work in Portugal

495. The pursuit of a better quality of life is one of the main reasons that motivates people to leave their country of origin. Seeking labour opportunities not only embodies the possibility of finding or reacquiring a decent existence but also represents a fundamental element for the integration of the individual in the society where he/she provides his professional activity.

496. Nevertheless, people migrate for many reasons, which surpass the mere desire to work in Portugal. The myriad of residence permits is also very diverse. It is important to map which residence permits, besides labour residence permits – allow their holders to work in the Portuguese territory.

I. Exercise of Professional Activity by the Holder of a Residence Permit for Research, Studies, Professional Traineeship and Volunteers

497. Before 2022, access to work by holders of residence permits for the purpose of studies, research, traineeship, and volunteers was limited. However, as seen before, the 2022 amendments to the IL opened the Portuguese labour market to foreigners through a set of different measures, such as the creation of a visa for job search. In line with this philosophy, access to job markets for all foreigner residents has been facilitated. Thus, currently, Article 97 sets forth that holders of a residence permit for research purposes, higher or secondary education studies – including under EU mobility schemes – trainees, and also volunteers may carry out a professional, subordinate or independent activity, in addition to the activity that gave rise to the visa. This represents a big commitment of the Portuguese Government towards a full integration of migrants in the society. In fact, keeping limits to accessing the labour market for foreigners residing in Portugal for another purpose would be incoherent with the attribution of visas for job search. The free access to work for those who are already legally residing in Portugal is, indeed, the only solution that is compatible with the general opening of the job markets to foreigners who are still residing abroad.

II. Exercise of a Professional Activity by the Holders of a Temporary Stay Permit for 'Special Reasons'

A. *General Aspects*

498. The Portuguese IL sets forth, as we have seen before, 'special residence permits' that cover a set of diverse situations, which have in common the protection of certain fundamental/human rights.[256] In these special cases, the potential holder of a residence permit does not need to demonstrate to SEF the legal entry into the national territory (i.e., a valid visa). In these cases, apart from the possible residence's temporary nature, and other aspects related to the specific purposes of the temporary residence permit, its holders have the same rights as the holders of a permanent residence permit, as foreseen in Article 83 IL, including the right to exercise professional activity (independent or subordinated).[257]

III. Exercise of Professional Activity by Victims of Crimes of Human Trafficking or Action to Aid Illegal Immigration

499. As mentioned previously, the IL grants a temporary residence permit to the victims of crimes of human trafficking or of action to aid illegal immigration for two main reasons: (i) to enable the victims to help in the prosecution and punishment of the author(s) of such crimes, namely, contributing with relevant information and/or documentation to support the ongoing investigations and judicial proceedings within the national territory; (ii) and also, to assure the necessary protection of the victims (cf. Article 109 IL).

500. However, this type of residence permit does not allow its holder to carry out any kind of professional activity (subordinated or independent) since it necessarily has a temporary nature, that is, the period necessary to the pursuit of the investigations and judicial proceedings and to the assurance of the victim's safety.

501. Accordingly, with Article 122(n) IL, the third-country national who has been the holder of a residence permit for such reasons does not need a visa to acquire a temporary residence permit, having thereafter the same rights of a permanent residence permit holder, among which is included the right to exercise professional activity (subordinated or independent).

502. The application for the residence permit provided herein must be accompanied by a declaration issued by the judicial authority which certificates the cessation of the need for cooperation in the investigations and proceedings, or by certificate of the judicial sentence.[258]

IV. Exercise of Professional Activity by Victims of Abusive Labour Conditions

503. Labour exploitation is another 'special reason' for granting a temporary residence permit under the Portuguese Immigration Law. According to Article 122

256. *See* Ch. 6., §4.
257. Cf. Art. 83 IL (b) (c). *See* A. C. Júlio Pereira & José de Cândido Pinho, *Direito de Estrangeiros: Entrada, permanência, saída e afastamento*, Coimbra Editora, Coimbra, 2008, p. 264-265.
258. Cf. Art. 61(16) IR.

IL, paragraph 2 (m), those who have been victims of a criminal offence or serious/very serious administrative offence related to a labour relationship, of where there is evidence certified by the inspection service in the labour area, can hold a special residence permit, provided that the victim has denounced the infraction to the competent authorities and wishes to collaborate with them. The concept of 'abusive labour conditions' present here is clarified in Article 122 IL, paragraph 2 (m) as being the conditions under which there is 'no social protection'; or there is 'no adequate work time'; or there are 'abusive wages'; or still, 'child labour in an illegal situation' was used.

504. As we have seen in the case of victims of human trafficking or aid illegal immigration, the holders of this residence title are automatically and equally holders of the rights set out in Article 83 IL for the permanent residence holders. Thus, they may carry out any type of professional activity (subordinated or independent).

(g) Exercise of Professional Activity by Holders of a Resident Permit by Family Reunification

505. According to the Family Reunification Directive, family members are entitled to work in the same way as the sponsor (Article 14). Thus, for example, researchers have the right to family reunification (Article 91-B(10) IL), as well as researchers under mobility programmes (Article 91-C, paragraph 3) – but their family members may only work where the researcher is also entitled to do so. This was a limitation before the 2022 amendments, where researchers did not have a free access to the labour market.

506. However, it is our view that family members, from the moment they have an autonomous and valid residence permit, can enjoy all the rights recognized to those who have a permanent resident status (cf. Article 83 IL), which includes the exercise of a professional activity (subordinated or independent) within Portuguese territory.

(h) Exercise of Professional Activity by Holders of a Humanitarian Residence Permit

507. As we have seen, the IL foresees an exceptional regime where, under certain circumstances, the Government may grant a residence permit, for 'humanitarian reasons', to individuals who do not fall in any of the expressly legally foreseen cases.[259]

508. From the moment that these persons hold a right of residence, they must have access to all rights that the IL recognizes to residents (cf. Article 83 IL), among which is the possibility of engaging in an independent or subordinated professional activity.

259. *See* Ch. 6, §4.

(i) Residence Permit for Persons who Had Benefitted from International Protection in Portugal

509. The IL foresees the possibility to award a temporary residence permit to those who no longer hold the refugee or subsidiary protection status due to the cessation of the reasons which grounded the concession of the international protection (cf. Article 122(f) IL).

510. In this case, like other cases foreseen in Article 122, holders shall be entitled to carry out a professional activity (either subordinated or independent). According to the Portuguese Asylum Law, the access to the national labour market is allowed to the asylum seeker since the moment they have a 'provisory resident permit'.[260]

511. The application for a residence permit submitted by a foreign national who has been beneficiary of refugee status is accompanied by a proof of accommodation, a proof of means of subsistence, and a declaration authorizing the consultation of its Portuguese criminal record by the SEF.[261]

§2. Form and Content of a Work Contract Celebrated with Foreign Workers

512. The Portuguese LC, after providing in Article 4, for the 'principle of equal treatment of a foreign worker or stateless persons', establishes a deviation from the general rule of freedom of form (cf. Article 110 LC)[262], determining the written form in the case of an employment contract concluded with a foreign citizen or stateless persons (cf. Article 5(1) LC). In addition, certain particular mentions must appear in this work contract agreement, namely: (i) the identification, signatures and domicile or registered office of the parties (cf. Article 5(1), al. a); (ii LC)) reference to the work visa or the worker's residence permit in the Portuguese territory[263] (cf. Article 5(1), al. b) LC); (iii) the employer's activity (cf. Article 5(1), al. c) LC); (iv) the contracted activity and remuneration of the worker (cf. Article 5(1), al. d) LC); (v) the place and normal working period (cf. Article 5(1), al. e) LC); the value, periodicity and method of payment of the due remuneration (cf. Article 5(1), al. f) LC); the dates of the work contract's conclusion and of the activity's beginning (cf. Article 5(1), al. g) LC).

260. Cf. Art. 27(1) AL.
261. Cf. Art. 61(8) IR.
262. According to Art. 110 of the LC 'the employment contract does not depend on compliance in a special form, except when the law determines otherwise'.
263. However, while a decision regarding the application for a residence permit is pending, for reasons that are not attributable to the applicant, he/she may carry out a professional activity in accordance with the law.

513. The employer is further obliged to notify to the service with inspective competence on Labour Conditions[264] of the Ministry responsible for the labour area the celebration of a work contract with a foreigner worker, before the beginning of its execution (Article 5(5) LC).[265]

264. In Portugal, this competence belongs to the Authority for Working Conditions (ACT).
265. Except for the need to observe the written form and the obligation to communicate its celebration to the ACT (cf. Art. 5(1) and 5, respectively), the employment contract celebrated with a foreign national shall not obey to any particular requirement in relation to contracts celebrated with national citizens.

Chapter 3. Sanctions Against Illegal Employment

§1. Sanctions Against Employers

514. The prohibition and punishment of the use of the activity of a foreign citizen in an irregular situation (cf. Article 185 – A IL) were introduced in the Portuguese Immigration Law in order to transpose Directive n. 2009/52/EC of the European Parliament and the Council of 18 June, which lays down minimum standards on sanctions and measures against employers of irregular third-country nationals. Taking into consideration that an important 'pull factor' for illegal immigration to the EU was the job market where migrants could work without the required legal status, the Union adopted a general prohibition of the employment of third-country nationals who do not have the right to reside in the EU. In order to make this command dissuasive and effective, the Directive sets forth a number of minimum sanctions (administrative and criminal)[266] to those who employ irregularly staying migrants.

515. In accordance with the Directive, the IL provides, in Article 185 – A (1), the prohibition and punishment of the use of foreign citizen activity in an illegal situation. According to this provision, whoever uses the work of foreign citizens who do not hold a residence permit or visa that enables them to remain legally in Portugal, shall be punished with imprisonment of up to one year or with a penalty of fine of up to 240 days. If the employer is a legal person, the applicable penalties are doubled, and the activity may also be banned for a period of three months to five years (cf. Article 185 – A (7) IL).

516. For the most serious situations, such as the simultaneous use of the activity of a significant number of illegal foreign nationals or if the employer uses the illegal labour force of minors (even if empowered to provide work under the LC), the offender is more severely punished, with a prison sentence of up to two years or a fine of up to 480 days (cf. Article 185 – A (2)(3) IL).

517. If any of the behaviours described above is accompanied by particularly abusive or degrading working conditions, the perpetrator shall be punished with imprisonment from one to five years, if a more serious penalty is not applicable under another legal provision (cf. Article 185 – A (4) IL). Furthermore, when the employer or other beneficiary of the work uses undocumented immigrants with the knowledge that they are victims of the crime of human trafficking,[267] he or she shall be punished with imprisonment from two to six years if a more serious penalty is not foreseen in another legal provision (cf. Article 185 – A (5) of IL).

266. Criminal penalties are provided for the most serious situations, such as: (i) the employment of minors; (ii) exploitation of persons by subjecting them to inhuman and/or degrading employment conditions; or association with certain crimes (e.g., trafficking in persons; aid for illegal immigration).

267. Provided for in Art. 160 CC.

518. In addition to criminal measures, the IL also provides for the application of effective, proportionate, and dissuasive administrative sanctions against the employer of undocumented third-country nationals. According to Article 198 – A (1) IL, whoever uses the activity of a foreign citizen not qualified with a residence permit or visa authorizing the exercise of a subordinated professional activity, shall be subject to the application of one of the following fines: (a) from (EUR) 2,000 to (EUR) 10,000, in case of one to four workers; (b) from (EUR) 4,000 to (EUR) 15,000, in case of five to ten workers; (c) from (EUR) 6,000 to (EUR) 30,000, in case of eleven to fifty workers; (d) From (EUR) 10,000 to (EUR) 90,000, in case of more than fifty workers. Additionally, the penalties may be applied provided for in Articles 21 and following of the General Regime of Administrative Offences (RGCO), as well as the obligation to reimburse some or all public benefits, aid or subventions, including EU fundings, granted to the employer up to twelve months before the offence, whenever it was committed in the exercise of the activity for which the funding was allocated (cf. Article 7, (1) al. (a) of Directive 2009/52/EC and Article 198 – A paragraph 2 (a) to (c) IL).

519. Recognizing the prevalence of subcontracting in certain affected sectors, the Portuguese Law sought to ensure that at least the contractor, for whom the employer is directly subcontracted, can be held liable for the payment of financial penalties jointly with or subrogating to the employer. Accordingly, the employer, the 'user' IL legal labour by way of a service agreement contract or an occasional employment contract/cession and the general contractor shall be jointly and severally liable for: (a) the payment of the fines and the wage claims arising from the employment contract, its infringement or its termination; (b) the penalties arising from non-compliance with labour law; (c) the penalties arising from non-declaration of income subject to discounts for the tax administration and social security in relation to the work carried out by the foreign worker whose activity was used illegally; (d) the payment of the expenses necessary for the stay and removal of the foreign nationals involved; (e) the payment of any expenses that result from the sending of sums arising from labour credits to the country to which the foreign citizen has returned voluntarily or coercively (cf. Article 198 – A (5) IL). The construction owner who does not obtain a declaration of compliance with the obligations arising from the law in relation to foreign workers hired from the other Contracting Party responds jointly and in the terms just mentioned (cf. Article 198 – A (6) IL). Finally, if the construction owner is the Public Administration, a disciplinary procedure may be opened against the respective responsible (cf. Article 198 – A (7) IL).

520. For the purpose of accounting for wage credits and income subject to discounts for the tax administration and social security, it is presumed that, without prejudice to the provisions of labour and tax legislation, the level of remuneration corresponds, at least, to the minimum monthly remuneration guaranteed by law, in collective agreements or in accordance with practices established in the sectors of activity concerned, and that the working relationship is at least three months long, unless the employer, the user of illegal labour or the worker proves otherwise (cf. Article 198 – A (8) IL).

521. Finally, in the event of non-payment of the unpaid amounts relating to wage claims, as well as the payment of the expenses necessary for the stay and removal of the foreign citizens, the notice of settlement made in the respective proceedings constitutes an enforcement order. The rules of the judicial common enforcement procedure for payment of a certain amount shall be applied (cf. Article 198 – A (10) IL).

§2. Sanctions Against Workers

522. A foreign worker who is irregularly staying in the Portuguese territory is not subject to sanctions for his/her illegal *work* per se but rather for his/her illegal *entry and/or stay* in the national territory.[268] He or she may also be subject to a decision of coercive removal or expulsion in accordance with Article 134 (1), al. a) IL.[269]

523. That is not the case, as we will see, as regards the unauthorized exercise of an independent professional activity by a foreign citizen who is not legally qualified for that purpose.[270] The Portuguese IL chose unequivocally to differentiate the sanctions against illegal exercise of self-employment work from the sanctions applied to the use of the labour of a foreign citizen in an illegal situation, which, as we have seen above, fall on the employer or user of this activity.

268. *See* Part V, Ch. 1.
269. *See* Part V, Ch. 4.
270. *See* Part VII, Ch. 3.

Chapter 4. Legal Remedies and Procedural Safeguards

524. As we have seen above, third-country nationals who are allowed to develop a subordinate professional activity enjoy the rights and are subject to the same duties as workers with Portuguese nationality (principle of equal treatment)[271]. The same is applicable when conflicts arise in the context of an employment relationship with a third-country national. The basic principles in this context are enshrined in Article 20 of the Constitution, which sets forth the fundamental right of access to law and effective judicial protection. As Gomes Canotilho and Vital Moreira state, Article 20 enshrines a series of rights that are part of a 'general right to legal protection': (i) right of access to courts (n. 1); (ii) right to legal information and consultation (n. 2); (iii) right to legal representation[272] (n. 2); (iv) right to lawyer's assistance (n. 2).

525. The right to legal aid is especially important in the context of the protection of third-country national workers, for it is aimed at promoting equality for all regarding access to courts, preventing its denial due to insufficient economic means. The Law on Legal Aid sets forth that citizens of the European Union, as well as foreigners and stateless persons with a valid residence permit in a Member State of the European Union, who demonstrate that they are in a situation of economic insufficiency, are entitled to legal aid.[273]

526. The IL also mentions, among the rights of the holder of a residence permit, the right of access to the law and courts (Article 83, paragraph (f)). Thus, the judicial Portuguese courts are competent to decide any case arising from a labour relationship between a Portuguese employer and a third-country national.

527. As regards access to courts for third-country nationals who do not have their administrative status regularized, answers may seem more difficult. If one considers the constitutional provisions mentioned above, the answer would be positive. However, if we only keep in mind the relevant provisions of IL, namely its Article 83 ('Rights of the holder of residence permit'), we may have some doubts. Nevertheless, we must take into account the provisions of Article 198 – A and 198 – B IL. The Portuguese IL, in line with the EU's outlook on this matter, provides for some procedures (judicial and non-judicial) that can be triggered by workers working in an irregular situation when their labour rights and guarantees are disrespected. For example, it establishes a simplified complaint regime in which the unions or associations of immigrants with recognized representativeness have the legitimacy to lodge a complaint with the proper inspection service of the Ministry responsible for employment against the employer (or the user of illegal labour), in particular in the

271. Cf. Art. 4 of the LC.
272. The right to legal representation is intended to promote equality for all in access to law and courts, to prevent it from being ensured by insufficient economic means. The Law on Legal Aid foresees that 'nationals and nationals of the European Union are entitled under this Law, as well as foreigners and stateless persons with a valid residence permit in a Member State of the European Union, who demonstrate that they are in a situation of economic insufficiency'.
273. *See*, among many others, the Constitutional Court's ruling ns 305/2000 and 208/2004.

following cases: (a) failure to pay wage credits; (b) social unprotection, wage or hourly exploitation or particularly abusive working conditions; (c) illegal use of child activity (cf. Article 198 – A (a) to (c) IL). Additionally, certain organizations, which purpose is the defence or promotion of the rights and interests of immigrants, have legitimacy to intervene in some cases involving migrant workers, as, for example, those that involve illegal labour, child labour, discrimination, etc. They may intervene in these cases on behalf or in representation of the person concerned, provided that the following conditions are met: (a) the defence of the interests in question must be expressly included in their duties or in their statutory objectives; (b) the person concerned has given express authorization for the intervention (cf. Article 198, paragraph 2 (a) (b) IL).

Part VII. Access to Self-Employed Activities

Chapter 1. Overview of Applicable Legislation

528. The constitutional principle of assimilation, enshrined in Article 15, encompasses the fundamental freedom to pursue a private economic activity. Migrants whose residence title enables them to exercise a self-employed activity shall be entitled to the same rights and duties as Portuguese citizens. These rights and duties are foreseen in the Social Security Law,[274] which sets forth the contributions to be paid by these professionals, as well as their social benefits, and the Tax Code, which foresees the legal tax regimes to which these workers are subjected to.[275]

274. Law n. 4/2007, of 16 January, as last amended by Law n. 83-A/2013, of 30 December.
275. Portuguese Tax Code, approved by Decree-Law n. 442-A/88, of 30/11, as last amended in 2021.

Chapter 2. Conditions Self-Employment

529. According to Article 83 IL, the holder of a residence permit, whatever its type (residence permit for the exercise of professional activity, residence permit for investment activity, residence permit for research, study, professional internship, or volunteering, among others), is entitled, *inter alia*, to the exercise of an independent professional activity. He or she is also entitled to professional guidance, training, and professional improvement.

530. The legal resident must register his or her activity with the Tax Authority and the Social Security, and pay the necessary contributions, as it is the case for every Portuguese citizen.

Chapter 3. Sanctions for Illegal Self-Employment

531. The exercise of independent professional activity by a third-country national without a proper residence permit, when required, shall constitute an administrative offence punishable with a fine of EUR 300 to EUR 1,200.[276] An ancillary penalty may be applicable, depending on the severity of the offence and the degree of the offender's guilt, under terms foreseen in Articles 21 et seq. of the General Administrative Offence Code (GAOC)[277] (e.g., prohibition of developing professions or activities that depend on a public title, an authorization or an approval of a public authority, cf. Article 21(b) (Gemini Adaptive Optics System) GAOS).

532. Thus, the exercise of an independent professional activity by a foreign citizen who does not have the appropriate residence permit, when required, constitutes an administrative infraction punishable by a fine of EUR 300 to EUR 1,200 (Article 198, paragraph 1 IL), and the ancillary fines provided for in Articles 21 and following of the GAOS may also be applied to the offender (Article 198, paragraphs 1 and 2 IL).

276. Cf. Art. 198(1) of IL.
277. Decree-Law 83/432 of October 27.

Chapter 4. Legal Remedies and Procedural Safeguards

533. As we have seen regarding the subordinate workers, also independent workers are submitted to the same rights and duties as the Portuguese self-employed workers. In practice, this means that, in case of a litigation situation, independent foreign workers have full access to all the legal and judicial means at the disposition of the Portuguese citizen, including legal aid. Depending on the nature of the relationship (public or private) which is underlying the conflict, the competent judicial organs will be the administrative courts or the judicial courts. For example, in the specific context of the independent workers, if they have a litigation with the SEF, regarding the concession or the renovation of their residence permit, they must submit the question to the competent Administrative Court in order to have an effective and binding solution. The same can be said regarding their social security or tax rights and duties. When the litigation concerns civil law – for example, a service contract that enabled them to work in the territory – they may apply to the judicial courts in order to enforce the service contract.

Selected Bibliography

AA.VV., *The relevance of migration for the 2030 Agenda for Sustainable Development: The Global Compact for Safe, Orderly and Regular Migration*, Constança Urbano de Sousa (org.), 2019.

Albuquerque, Paulo Pinto, *Comentário do Código Penal à Luz da Constituição da República e da Convenção Europeia dos Direitos do Homem*, 2.ª Ed, Universidade Católica Editora, Lisboa, 2010.

Alexandrino, José de Melo, 'A nova lei de entrada, permanência, saída e afastamento de estrangeiros', *Revista da Faculdade de Direito da Universidade de Lisboa*, vol. XLIX, ns.º 1 e 2, 2008.

Almeida, Carlota Pizarro de, 'Exclusões Formais, Exclusões Materiais – o Lugar do Outro ; Discriminação contra Imigrantes', Revista da Faculdade de Direito da Universidade de Lisboa, vol.XLV, ns.º 1 e 2, 2004, p. 37 e ss.

Canotilho, J. J. Gomes; Moreira, Vital, *Constituição da República Portuguesa Anotada*, Vol. I., 4.ª Ed., Coimbra Editora, Coimbra, 2007.

Gil, Ana Rita, 'Um Caso de Europeização do Direito Constitucional Português – A Afirmação de um Direito Fundamental ao Reagrupamento Familiar', *Revista de Direito Público*, ano I, 2009, n. 2, pp. 9–62.

Gil, Ana Rita, 'Princípios de Direito da Nacionalidade – sua consagração no ordenamento jurídico Português', *O Direito*, 142.º, 2010, IV, pp. 723–760.

Gil, Ana Rita, *Study on children's involvement in judicial proceedings – contextual overview for civil justice – Portugal*, European Commission, Directorate-General for Justice and Consumers, 2014.

Gil, Ana Rita *Imigração e Direitos Humanos,* Petrony, 2017.

Gil, Ana Rita. 'Breve Nótula sobre as recentes alterações à Lei dos Estrangeiros, aprovadas pelas Leis n. 59/2017, de 31 de julho, e n. 102/2017, de 28 de agosto', *in* AA.VV., *O contencioso de direito administrativo relativo a cidadãos estrangeiros e ao regime da entrada, permanência, saída e afastamento do território português, bem como do estatuto de residente de longa duração,* Sofia David (coord.), Centro de Estudos Judiciários, 2017, pp. 47–54. Available in: http://www.cej.mj.pt/cej/recursos/ebooks/Administrativo_fiscal/eb_estrangeiros_2ed.pdf.

Gil, Ana Rita, 'O Papel do Advogado na defesa dos direitos das pessoas carecidas de proteção internacional', *Themis*, Ano XIX, n. 34, 2018, pp. 7–42.

Gil, Ana Rita, 'O papel dos Tribunais Judiciais na proteção das crianças migrantes – exigências decorrentes do Direito Internacional e Europeu', *Julgar*, n. 37, 2019, pp. 109–142.

Gil, Ana Rita, 'Regularizações do estatuto do estrangeiro – de alteração em alteração, um direito em expansão', Vida Judiciária, novembro de 2019.

Gil, Ana Rita & Lino Ribeiro, *Prestações Sociais e Cidadania,* Relatório do Tribunal Constitucional Português apresentado à XVII Conferência Trilateral dos Tribunais Constitucionais de Espanha, Itália e Portugal, 2016.

Gil, Ana Rita & Piçarra, Nuno, *Study on the legal requirements specific to minors travelling alone or accompanied, legally entering or leaving the Member States, focusing on EU/AC minors and with a separate section on third-country minors*, Ramboll, 2012.

Gomes, Carla Amado & Leão, Anabela Costa, *A Condição de Imigrante – Uma análise de Direito Constitucional e de Direito Administrativo*, Almedina, Coimbra, 2010.

Gomes, Charles P., 'Les Limites de la Souveraineté – les Changements Juridiques dans les cas d'Immigration en France et aux États Unis', in *Revue Française de Science Politique*, vol. 50, n. 3, Juin 2000, pp. 413–438.

Grewe, Constance, 'Le Juge Constitutionnel et l'interprétation Européenne', AA.VV., L'interprétation de la Convention Européenne des Droits de l'Homme, Fréderic Sudre (dir.) Bruylant, 1998.

Howard, Marc M. (2009), *The Politics of Citizenship in Europe*, New York: Cambridge University Press.

Leão, Anabela Costa, 'Ac. TC n. 232/04 (expulsão de estrangeiros com filhos menores a cargo)', Jurisprudência Constitucional, n. 3, 2004, p. 38.

Leitão, José, & Luís Nunes de Almeida, 'Les Droits et Libertés des Étrangers en Situation Irrégulière Portugal', *Annuaire International de Justice Constitutionnelle*, Presses Universitaires d'Aix-Marseille, Economica, 1998.

Martinez, Pedro Romano, *Direito do Trabalho*, Almedina, Coimbra, 7.ª Ed. 2015.

Matias, Gonçalo Saraiva, *Migrações e Cidadania, Fundação Francisco Manuel dos Santos,* 2014.

Mendes, Paulo Sousa. 'Tráfico de pessoas' in 'Jornadas sobre a revisão do Código Penal', Centro de Estudos Judiciários, Lisboa, 2007.

Mendes, Duarte Miranda 'Estrangeiro', AA.VV., *Enciclopédia da Constituição Portuguesa*, Jorge Bacelar Gouveia & Francisco Pereira Coutinho (coord.), Quid Juris, 2013.

Mendes, Paulo Sousa, 'Tráfico de Pessoas', *Jornadas sobre a Revisão do Código Penal,* Centro de de Estudos Judiciários, 2007.

Oliveira, Andreia Sofia Pinto, *O Direito de Asilo na Constituição Portuguesa – Âmbito de protecção de um direito fundamental*, Coimbra Editora, 2009.

Oliveira, Carlos Pamplona de, *A Jurisprudência Constitucional sobre Cidadãos Estrangeiros*, Relatório apresentado no encontro trianual dos Tribunais Constitucionais de Portugal, Espanha e Itália, em Madrid, 26 e 27 de setembro de 2008.

Peixoto, João, Marçalo, Carolina &Tolentino, Nancy C. *Imigrantes e Segurança Social em Portugal*, Observatório da Imigração, 2011.

Pereira, A. C. Júlio & Pinho, José de Cândido, *Direito de Estrangeiros: Entrada, permanência, saída e afastamento*, Coimbra Editora, Coimbra, 2008.

Piçarra, Nuno & Gil, Ana Rita, *Report on Citizenship Law*, EUDO Citizenship Observatory, European University Institute, Florence, November 2012.

Piçarra, Nuno & Gil, Ana Rita, *Study on the Requirements Specific to Minors Travelling Alone or Accompanied, Legally Entering or Leaving the Member States/ Associated Countries*, Ramboll, EurAsyllum, 2012.

Piçarra, Nuno & Borges, Francisco 'Portugal – Exceptional grant of residence permits to irregular migrants' in *Policies on irregular migrants, Volume III – France, Portugal and Poland*, Council of Europe Publishing, 2010.

Pinto, Albano, AAVV, *Commentary on Extravagant Criminal Laws*, Paulo Pinto de Albuquerque and José Branco (Org.), Universidade Católica Editora, 2010, vol. I, p. 123.

Pinto, Ana Luísa, *A pena acessória de expulsão de estrangeiros do território nacional*, Coimbra, Coimbra Editora, 2005.

Pinto, Albano, in Paulo Pinto de Albuquerque and José Branco, *Comentário das Leis Penais Extravagantes*, vol. I, Universidade Católica Editora, Lisboa, 2007.

Pires, Rui Pena, *Migrações e Integração. Teoria e aplicações à sociedade portuguesa*, Celta Editora, 2003.

Santos, Vanda, *O Discurso Oficial do Estado sobre a Emigração dos anos 60 a 80 e Imigração dos Anos 90 à Actualidade*, Observatório da Imigração, 2004.

Silva, Jorge Pereira da, *Direitos de Cidadania e Direito à Cidadania*, Alto Comissariado para a Imigração e Minorias Étnicas, Lisboa, 2004.

Silva, Jorge Pereira da, 'Artigo 15.º – Princípio da Equiparação', in Jorge Miranda, & Rui Medeiros, *Constituição da República Portuguesa Anotada*, Tomo I, 2ª Edição, Coimbra Editora, 2010.

Szymczak, David, *La Convention Européenne des Droits de l'Homme et le Juge Constitutionnel National,* Bruylant, 2007.

Thirion, W. v. The cost of non-Europe in the area of legal migration. Bruxelas: European Added Value Unit, 2019. Accessible in: EPRS_STU (2019)631736_EN.pdf.

Torres, Mário, 'Os Direitos dos Imigrantes na Legislação Portuguesa', in AA.VV., *A Política Europeia de Imigração*, Actas do Seminário de Lisboa de 9 de Outubro de 2001, Serviço das Publicações Oficiais das Comunidades Europeias, Luxemburgo, 2002, pp. 57–65.

Documents

ACIDI, *More Diversity Better Humanity*, p. 10, available at http://www.acidi.gov.pt/institucional_book.pdf.

Alto Comissariado para as Migações, *Plano Estratégico para as Migrações 2015–2020.*

Committee, European Economic and Social Committee, *The costs of non-immigration and non-integration*, 2018.

Provedor de Justiça – *Relatório à Assembleia da República – 2018*, available in htt p://www.provedor-jus.pt/site/public/archive/doc/Relat2019_web.pdf.

Provedor de Justiça – *Relatório à Assembleia da República – 2019*, available in htt p://www.provedor-jus.pt/site/public/archive/doc/Relat2019_web.pdf.

Provedor de Justiça, *Relatório à Assembleia da República 2018 – Mecanismo Nacional de Prevenção,* available at http://www.provedor-jus.pt/?idc=107.

Provedor de Justiça, *Relatório à Assembleia da República 2019– Mecanismo Nacional de Prevenção,* available at http://www.provedor-jus.pt/?idc=107.

Selected Bibliography

Provedor de Justiça – *Alternative Report Of The Portuguese Ombudsman on the Implementation of the Convention on the Rights of the Child in the Process of Review of the Fifth and Sixth Periodic Report of Portugal*, available at http://www.provedor-jus.pt/site/public/archive/doc/Rel_Alternativo_CRC.pdf.

SEF, *Relatório de Imigração, Fronteiras e Asilo 2012*, Serviço de Estrangeiros e Fronteiras, Lisboa, 2013.

SEF, *Relatório de Imigração, Fronteiras e Asilo 2013* Serviço de Estrangeiros e Fronteiras, Lisboa, 2014. Available in https://sefstat.sef.pt/Docs/Rifa2013.pdf.

SEF *Relatório de Imigração, Fronteiras e Asilo 2019*, Serviço de Estrangeiros e Fronteiras, Lisboa, 2020. Available in https://sefstat.sef.pt/Docs/Rifa2019.pdf.

United Nations Development Programme, *Overcoming Barriers: Human Mobility and Development*, 2009. Available at http://hdr.undp.org/sites/default/files/reports/269/hdr_2009_en_complete.pdf.

www.ingramcontent.com/pod-product-compliance
Lightning Source LLC
Chambersburg PA
CBHW071339230926
51846CB00002B/394
* 9 7 8 9 4 0 3 5 0 0 0 7 2 *